BD

Absolute
Beginner's
Guide to
Computers and
the Internet

Michael Miller

201 West 103rd Street,
Indianapolis, Indiana 46290

Absolute Beginner's Guide to Computers and the Internet

International Standard Book Number: 0-7897-8012-7

Library of Congress Catalog Card Number: 2001094302

Printed in the United States of America

First Printing: December 2001

05   04   03   02   4   3   2   1

Trademarks

Warning and Disclaimer

Associate Publisher
Dean Miller

Managing Editor
Thomas F. Hayes

Copy Editor
Megan Wade

Indexer
Chris Barrick

Proofreader
Bob LaRoche

Technical Editor
Aaron Clow

Team Coordinator
Cindy Teeters

Interior Designer
Kevin Spear

Cover Designer
Trina Wurst

Page Layout
Scan Communications Group, Inc.

Contents at a Glance

Table of Contents

About the Author

Michael Miller is a successful and prolific author with a reputation for practical advice and technical accuracy and an unerring empathy for the needs of his readers.

Mr. Miller has written more than three dozen how-to and reference books since 1989, for Que and other major publishers. His books for Que include *Special Edition Using the Internet and Web*, *The Complete Idiot's Guide to Online Search Secrets*, and, with Jim Louderback, *TechTV's Guide to Microsoft Windows XP for Home Users*. He is known for his casual, easy-to-read writing style and his practical, real-world advice—as well as his ability to explain a wide variety of complex topics to an everyday audience.

Mr. Miller is also president of The Molehill Group, a strategic consulting and authoring firm based in Carmel, Indiana. As a consultant, he specializes in providing strategic advice to and writing business plans for Internet- and technology-based businesses.

You can e-mail Mr. Miller directly at abg@molehillgroup.com. His Web site is located at www.molehillgroup.com.

Dedication

To my nephews Alec and Ben Hauser, who always make summer vacation fun.

Acknowledgments

Thanks to the usual suspects at Que, including but not limited to Dean Miller, Thomas Hayes, Aaron Clow, and Megan Wade.

Tell Us What You Think!

As the reader of this book, *you* are our most important critic and commentator. We value your opinion and want to know what we're doing right, what we could do better, what areas you'd like to see us publish in, and any other words of wisdom you're willing to pass our way.

As an Associate Publisher for Que, I welcome your comments. You can fax, e-mail, or write me directly to let me know what you did or didn't like about this book—as well as what we can do to make our books stronger.

Please note that I cannot help you with technical problems related to the topic of this book, and that due to the high volume of mail I receive, I might not be able to reply to every message.

When you write, please be sure to include this book's title and author as well as your name and phone or fax number. I will carefully review your comments and share them with the author and editors who worked on the book.

Fax: 317-581-4666

E-mail: feedback@quepublishing.com

Mail: Dean Miller
Que
201 West 103rd Street
Indianapolis, IN 46290 USA

Introduction

First things first.

Computers aren't supposed to be scary.

Intimidating, sometimes. Difficult to use, perhaps. Inherently unreliable, most definitely.

But scary? Definitely not.

Computers aren't scary because there's nothing they can do to hurt you. And there's not much you can do to hurt them. It's kind of a wary coexistence between man and machine, but the relationship has the potential to be quite beneficial.

To you, anyway.

A lot of people think that they're scared of computers because they think they're unfamiliar with them. But that isn't really true.

You see, even if you've never actually used a computer before, you've been exposed to computers and all they can do for at least the last 20 years or so. Whenever you make a deposit at your bank, you're working with computers. Whenever you make a purchase at a retail store, you're working with computers. Whenever you watch a television show, or read a newspaper article, or look at a picture in a magazine, you're working with computers.

That's because computers are used in all those applications. Somebody, somewhere, is working behind the scenes with a computer to manage your bank account; finalize your purchase; and make those TV shows, newspaper articles, and magazine pictures look good.

In fact, it's hard to imagine, here at the dawn of the twenty-first century, how we ever got by without all those keyboards, mice, and monitors. (Or, for that matter, the Internet.)

However, just because computers have been around for awhile doesn't mean that everyone knows how to use them. It's not unusual to feel a little trepidation the first time you sit down in front of that intimidating monitor and keyboard. Which keys should you press? What do they mean by "double-clicking the mouse?" And what are all those little pictures onscreen?

As foreign as all this might seem at first, computers really aren't that hard to understand—or to use. You have to learn a few basic concepts, of course (all the pressing and clicking and whatnot), and it helps to understand exactly what part of the system does what. But once you get the hang of things, computers really are fairly easy to use.

Which, of course, is where this book comes in.

Absolute Beginner's Guide to Computers and the Internet will help you figure out how to use your new computer system. You'll learn how computers work, how to connect all the pieces and parts together, and how to start using them. You'll learn about computer hardware and software, about Windows and operating systems, and about the Internet. And after you're comfortable with the basic concepts (which won't take too long, trust me), you'll learn how to actually do stuff.

You'll learn how to do useful stuff, like writing letters and balancing your checkbook and making your own personalized greeting cards. Fun stuff, like listening to music and watching movies and playing games. Online stuff, like searching for information and sending e-mail and chatting with friends via instant messages. And essential stuff, like copying files and troubleshooting problems and protecting against thieves and hackers.

All you have to do is sit yourself down in front of your computer, try not to be scared (there's nothing to be scared of, really), and work your way through the chapters and activities in this book. And remember that computers aren't hard to use, they don't break easily, and they let you do all sorts of fun and useful stuff once you get the hang of them.

Really!

How This Book Is Organized

There are two main sections of this book. The first major section is composed of 10 chapters, grouped into two "parts," and provides a general introduction to basic computing concepts. If you have no prior experience with computers, you should probably read these chapters first.

The second major section of this book contains 75 "Do It Now" activities, grouped into 16 parts. These activities anticipate the most likely things you'll want to do with your computer and present these tasks in a hands-on, step-by-step fashion. Pick the thing you want to do, read through the activity, and then sit down at your computer and do it!

What will you find in these sections and parts and chapters? Here's a brief overview:

- **Part 1, "Absolute Basics"**—These four chapters help absolute beginners get up to speed about personal computers in general, and hardware, software, Windows, the Internet, and home networking.

- **Part 2, "Getting Started"**—These six chapters present a hands-on guide to setting up and using your new computer system. You'll learn how to connect everything together, install new hardware and software, get connected to the Internet, and start surfing the Web.

■ **Part 3, "Do It Now: Communicating on Paper"**—This is the first of the parts that present step-by-step activities. The activities in this part all revolve around using Microsoft Word—to write and print letters, create fancy reports, and so on.

■ **Part 4, "Do It Now: Communicating Online"**—The activities here revolve around communicating via the Internet. You'll learn how to send and receive e-mail, read and post to newsgroups, send and receive instant messages, and chat with your friends in online chat rooms.

■ **Part 5, "Do It Now: Working with Numbers"**—These activities revolve around crunching numbers with the Microsoft Works Spreadsheet.

■ **Part 6, "Do It Now: Managing Your Finances"**—These activities show you how to use various resources to manage your personal finances. You'll learn how to use Microsoft Money to create a budget, manage your bank account, and pay your bills—online, if you want. You'll also learn how to use the Internet to find stock quotes, trade stocks and other securities, and arrange home and auto loans.

■ **Part 7, "Do It Now: Filing and Reporting"**—These activities help you use Microsoft Works Database to manage large groups of items, electronically.

■ **Part 8, "Do It Now: Reading the Latest News"**—These activities show you the best sites on the Web for up-to-the-minute news, sports, and weather information.

■ **Part 9, "Do It Now: Searching and Researching"**—These activities are all about finding things online—including people's addresses, health-related information, and answers to your kids' tough homework questions. You'll learn which search engines provide the best results (hint: try Google) and how to best use those sites.

■ **Part 10, "Do It Now: Buying and Selling Online"**—These activities help you shop smart and safe—and even sell your own stuff at eBay, the world's largest online auction site.

■ **Part 11, "Do It Now: Working with Pictures"**—These activities will help you use your digital camera, scanner, and computer system to touch up your pictures and use them to create photo albums and other fun projects.

■ **Part 12, "Do It Now: Creating Fun Projects"**—Speaking of fun projects, these activities show you how to use your computer to make things—including banners, holiday cards, and your own personal Web pages.

■ **Part 13, "Do It Now: Playing Games"**—These activities show you how to turn your computer into a world-class game machine—and how to go online to find worthy opponents.

■ **Part 14, "Do It Now: Playing and Recording Music"**—These activities tell you everything you need to know to find, download, and listen to music from the Internet—and to record your own custom music CDs.

■ **Part 15, "Do It Now: Watching TV and Movies"**—These activities show you how to use your computer system to watch the latest DVD movies, as well as live "Webcasts" on the Internet.

■ **Part 16, "Do It Now: Working with Files"**—These activities present the most common things you'll need to do with computer files, including copying, moving, deleting, and renaming files. You'll even learn how to send files via e-mail and download files from the Internet.

■ **Part 17, "Do It Now: Taking Care of Your PC"**—These activities might not be a lot of fun, but they are necessary. You'll learn what you need to do to keep your computer in tip-top shape—including changing the way Windows looks and acts, making backup copies of your most important files, and setting up your own home computer network.

■ **Part 18, "Do It Now: Dealing with Problems"**—Let's hope you never have to use this part of the book, but if you do, you'll learn how to find and fix common problems, protect your kids from all the bad stuff on the Internet, and protect your computer system from malicious hackers.

Taken together, the 10 chapters and 75 activities in this book will help you progress from absolute beginner to experienced computer user. Just read what you need, and before long you'll be using your computer like a pro!

Conventions Used in This Book

I hope that this book is easy enough to figure out on its own, without requiring its own instruction manual. As you read through the pages, however, it helps to know precisely how I've presented specific types of information.

Menu Commands

Most computer programs operate via a series of pull-down menus. You use your mouse to pull down a menu and then select an option from that menu. This sort of operation is indicated like this throughout the book:

Pull down the File menu and select New.

or

Click the Windows Start menu and select All Programs, Accessories, Notepad.

All you have to do is follow the instructions in order, using your mouse to click each item in turn. When there are submenus tacked onto the main menu (as in the All Programs, Accessories, Notepad example), just keep clicking the selections until you come to the last one—which should open the program or activate the command you wanted!

Shortcut Key Combinations

When you're using your computer keyboard, sometimes you have to press two keys at the same time. These "two-key" combinations are called *shortcut keys* and are shown as the key names joined with a plus sign (+).

For example, Ctrl+W indicates that you should press the W key while holding down the Ctrl key. It's no more complex than that.

Web Page Addresses

There are a lot of Web page addresses in this book. (That's because you'll probably be spending a lot of time on the Internet.) They're noted as such:

`www.molehillgroup.com`

Technically, a Web page address is supposed to start with `http://` (as in `http://www.molehillgroup.com`). Because Internet Explorer and other Web browsers automatically insert this piece of the address, however, you don't have to type it— and I haven't included it in any of the addresses in this book.

Special Elements

This book also includes a few special elements that provide additional information not included in the basic text. These elements are designed to supplement the text to make your learning faster, easier, and more efficient.

A *tip* is a piece of advice—a little trick, actually—that helps you use your computer more effectively or maneuver around problems or limitations

A *note* is designed to provide information that is generally useful but not specifically necessary for what you're doing at the moment. Some are like extended tips—interesting, but not essential.

A *caution* will tell you to beware of a potentially dangerous act or situation. In some cases, ignoring a caution could cause you significant problem—so pay attention to them!

Let Me Know What You Think

I always love to hear from readers. If you want to contact me, feel free to e-mail me at abg@molehillgroup.com. I can't promise that I'll answer every message, but I will promise that I'll read each one!

If you want to learn more about me and any new books I have cooking, check out my Molehill Group Web site at www.molehillgroup.com. Who knows—you might find some other books there that you'd like to read.

PART

I

ABSOLUTE BASICS

PERSONAL COMPUTER BASICS

You're reading this book because you just bought a new computer, are thinking about buying a new computer, or maybe even had someone give you her old computer. (Nothing wrong with high-tech hand-me-downs!) At this point you might not be totally sure what it is you've gotten yourself into. Just what is this mess of boxes and cables, and what can you—or *should* you—do with it?

This chapter serves as an introduction to the entire concept of personal computers—what they do, how they work, and that sort of thing. Then, after you've read this general overview, you can move on to the other three chapters in this section and learn more about the various parts of your computer system.

Of course, if you want to skip the background and get right to using your computer, that's okay, too. For step-by-step instructions on how to connect and configure your new PC, go directly to Chapter 5, "Set Up Your New Computer System."

What Your Computer Can—and *Can't*—Do

What good is a personal computer, anyway?

Everybody has one, you know. Maybe you got one just so you wouldn't feel left out. But what do you do with it?

Good for Work

A lot of people use their home PCs for work-related purposes. You can bring home work from the office and finish it on your home PC, at night or on weekends. Or, if you work at home, you can use your computer to run your business—everything from typing memos and reports to generating invoices and setting budgets.

In short, anything you can do with a normal office PC, you can probably do on your home PC.

Good for Play

All work and no play makes Jack a dull boy, so there's no reason not to have a little fun with your new PC. Not only can you use your PC to play the latest games, you can also use it to track your favorite hobby, create interesting crafts projects, print pictures from your latest family vacation, listen to your favorite songs, and watch your favorite videos. In fact, with the right software and hardware, you can even use your PC to edit movies you take with your video camcorder!

Good for Managing Your Finances

You don't have to be a professional accountant to use your PC to manage your finances. Software programs such as Microsoft Money and Quicken let you create budgets, write checks, and balance your accounts, right from your computer screen. You can even set up your system to automatically pay bills online—no checks necessary.

Good for Keeping in Touch

Want to send a letter to a friend? With your new PC (and a word processor program), it's a cinch. Even better, save a stamp and send that friend an electronic letter—called an *e-mail*—over the Internet. And if that person's online the same time you are, you can chat with him in real time via an instant messaging program. Many families use their PCs for almost all their communications!

Good for Getting Online

Speaking of e-mail, chances are one of the main reasons you purchased your PC was to get connected to the Internet. The Internet's a great tool; in addition to e-mail and instant messaging, you can browse the World Wide Web, which is chock full of interesting and informative content and services. Now you won't feel left out when people start talking about "double-you double-you double-you" this and "dot-com" that—because you'll be online, too.

Getting to Know Your Personal Computer System

Now that you know *why* you have that brand-new personal computer sitting on your desk, you might be interested in just *what* it is that you have. It's important to know what each part of your system is, what it does, and how to hook it all together.

Figure 1.1 shows the pieces and parts of a typical computer system. Note that no two computer systems are identical because you can add new components to the system— or disconnect some pieces you don't have any use for.

FIGURE 1.1

A typical personal computer system.

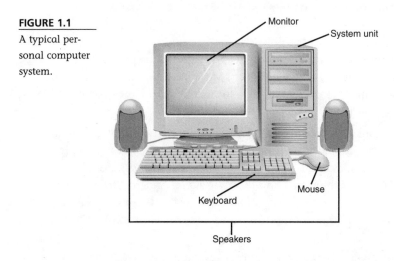

The main part of your system is called the *system unit*. This box contains the brains and the engine behind your entire system. Just about everything else in the system plugs into this box, so there are lots of connectors on the back. On the front you'll typically find a big button; this is what you use to turn your system on and off.

The part of the system you watch is called the *video display* or *monitor*. The monitor displays everything your system does, so it's a little like watching a TV show you can interact with.

Your main means for interacting with your computer are the *keyboard* and *mouse*. The keyboard is just that—a slightly flatter version of the old typewriter keyboard, with a few extra keys thrown in for specific computer functions. The mouse is that little thing that looks like a bar of soap with buttons; you use the mouse to point at things and move elements around onscreen.

The sounds and music your system generates are reproduced through a pair of *speakers*. Older PCs sometimes had only a single speaker, built in to the system unit. Most newer PCs, though, have separate right and left speakers (for stereo!) and sometimes have a third speaker—called a *subwoofer*—for better bass.

Inside your system unit, typically, is a separate item called a *modem*. You hook this modem up to your telephone lines and use it to connect your computer to the Internet.

Note

Most modems today are *internal*, which means they're located inside your PC system unit. Some modems, however—especially cable and DSL modems—are *external*, which means they're separate pieces of hardware that sit beside the rest of your system.

Almost all PC systems come with a separate *printer*. You use the printer to generate paper copies of documents you create onscreen. Many types of printers are available; some print only in black and white (fine for letters and memos), while others reproduce full-color images.

These items are the basic elements you'll find in almost all computer systems. Lots of other items can be added to your personal system, including *scanners* (to change a hardcopy document or picture to electronic format), *PC cameras* (to send live video of yourself to friends and family), *digital cameras* (to transfer your snapshots to electronic format), and *joysticks* (to play the most challenging games). You can even add the appropriate items to connect multiple PCs in a simple *network*.

You can learn more about the hardware in your system in Chapter 2, "Computer Hardware Basics." If you need help connecting all the pieces and parts, turn to Chapter 5. And if you want to add a new piece of hardware to your basic system, check out Chapter 7, "Add New Hardware."

The Right Tools for the Right Tasks— Computer Software

By themselves, all those little beige boxes really aren't that useful. You can connect them and set them in place, but they won't do anything until you have some *software* to make things work.

Computer *hardware* are those things you can touch—your system unit, monitor, and the like. Computer *software*, on the other hand, is something you *can't* touch because it's nothing more than a bunch of bits and bytes. These bits and bytes, however, combine into computer programs—sometimes called *applications*—that provide specific functionality to your system.

For example, if you want to crunch some numbers, you need a piece of software called a *spreadsheet* program. If you want to write a letter, you need a *word processing* program. If you want to make changes to some pictures you took with your digital camera, you need *graphics editing* software.

In other words, you need separate software for each task you want to do with your computer. Fortunately, most new computer systems come with a lot of this software already installed, for free. (Any additional software you need, however, you'll have to buy and install yourself—as described in Chapter 8, "Add New Software.")

Making Everything Work—with Windows

When you're not using a specific piece of application software, you interface with your computer via a special piece of software called an *operating system*. As the name implies, this program makes your system operate; it's your gateway to the hardware part of your system.

The operating system is also how your application software interfaces with your computer hardware. When you want to print a document from your word processor, that software works with the operating system to send the document to your printer.

Figure 1.2 shows how your software, operating system, and hardware work together.

Most computers today ship with an operating system called Windows. This operating system has been around for about 15 years and is published by Microsoft Corporation. Computers manufactured by Apple Computing use a different operating system, called the Mac OS. Therefore, computers running Windows and computers by Apple aren't totally compatible with each other.

FIGURE 1.2

The various layers of control in a typical PC system.

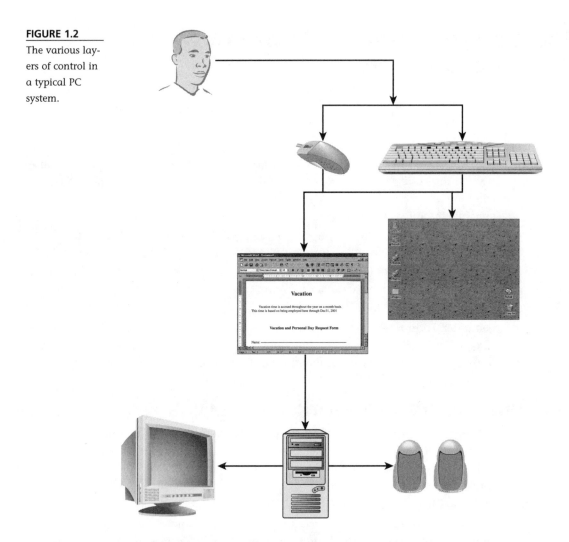

There have been several different versions of Windows over the years. The current version is called Windows XP, and if you have a new PC, this is probably the version you're using. (Older versions—which look different but work pretty much the same—include Windows 95, Windows 98, and Windows Me.) You use Windows to launch specific programs and to perform various system maintenance functions—such as copying files and turning off your computer.

You can learn more about Windows and other computer software in Chapter 3, "Windows and Software Basics."

Don't Worry, You Can't Screw It Up—Much

The next few chapters of this book tell you more about the various components of your computer system, and then Part II, "Getting Started," presents step-by-step instructions for connecting everything, installing your software, and getting your system up and running. Before you read those chapters, there's one other important thing you need to know about your computer system.

A lot of people are afraid of their computers. They think if they press the wrong key or click the wrong button that they'll break something or will have to call in an expensive repairperson to put things right.

This really isn't true.

The important thing to know is that it's really, really difficult to break your computer system. Yes, you can drop something and break it easily enough, but in terms of breaking your system through normal use, it just doesn't happen that often.

It is possible to make mistakes, of course. You can click the wrong button and accidentally delete a file you didn't want to delete or turn off your system and lose a document you forgot to save. But in terms of doing serious harm just by clicking your mouse, it's unlikely.

So don't be afraid of the thing. Your computer is a tool, just like a hammer or a blender or a camera. After you learn how to use it, it can be a very useful tool. But it's *your* tool, which means *you* tell *it* what to do—not vice versa. Remember that you're in control and that you're not going to break anything, and you'll have a lot of fun—and maybe even get some real work done!

Things to Remember

Here are the key points to remember from this chapter:

- Your computer system is composed of various pieces of hardware, almost all of which plug into that big beige box called the system unit.
- You interface with your computer hardware via a piece of software called an operating system. The operating system on your new computer is probably some version of Microsoft Windows.
- You use specific software programs to perform specific tasks, such as writing letters and editing digital photos.
- After everything is hooked up and running, you can use your computer system for work, play, communicating with others, or connecting to the Internet. All you have to do is purchase and install the appropriate software programs, and then you'll be ready to go!

2

COMPUTER HARDWARE BASICS

As you learned in Chapter 1, "Personal Computer Basics," computer hardware are those parts of your system you can actually see and touch. This includes your system unit and everything connected to it, including your monitor, keyboard, mouse, and printer.

This chapter presents all the various pieces of hardware you can have in a computer system—including those parts you can't always see because they're built in to your system unit. So, if you're curious about microprocessors and memory and modems and monitors, read on—this is the chapter for you!

Your PC's System Unit—The Mother Ship

The most important piece of hardware in your computer system is the *system unit*. This is the big, ugly box that houses your disk drives and many other components. You can find system units that lie horizontally on your desk (like the one in Figure 2.1) or ones that stand straight up (like the one in Figure 2.2). The vertical models often are called *towers* or *mini-towers*.

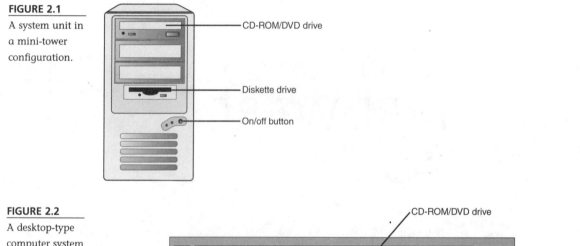

FIGURE 2.1
A system unit in a mini-tower configuration.

CD-ROM/DVD drive

Diskette drive

On/off button

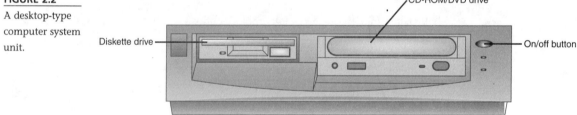

FIGURE 2.2
A desktop-type computer system unit.

CD-ROM/DVD drive

Diskette drive

On/off button

Note

Desktop computer systems are composed of all these separate components. Portable PCs, on the other hand, have all that stuff crammed into a single case. So, you don't have a separate system unit, monitor, keyboard, and mouse—they're part of one very compact unit. Learn more about personal computers in the section "Portable PCs—Lightweight All-in-One Systems," later in this chapter.

The back of the system unit typically is covered with all types of connectors. This is because all the other parts of your computer system connect to your system unit, and they all have to have a place to plug in. And, because each component has its own unique type of connector, you end up with the assortment of jacks (called *ports* in the computer world) that you see in Figure 2.3.

FIGURE 2.3

The back of a typical system unit—just look at all those different connectors!

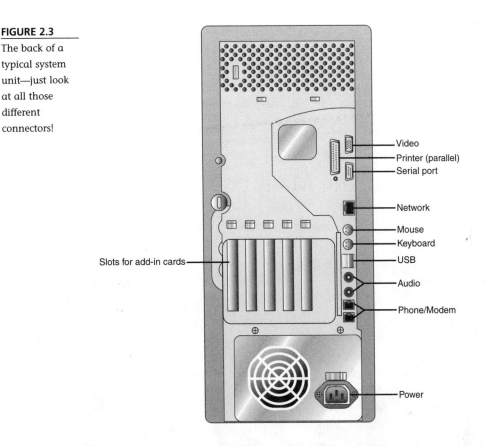

All the good stuff in your system unit is inside the case. With most system units, you can remove the case to peek and poke around inside.

To remove your system unit's case, look for some big screws or thumbscrews on either the side or back of the case. (Even better—read your PC's instruction manual for instructions specific to your unit.) With the screws loosened or removed, you should then be able to slide off the case.

Always turn off your computer before attempting to remove the system unit's case—and be careful about touching anything inside! If you have any built-up static electricity, you can seriously damage the sensitive chips and electronic components with an innocent touch.

When you open the case on your system unit, you see all sorts of computer chips and circuit boards. The really big board located at the base of the computer is called the *motherboard* because it's the "mother" for your microprocessor and memory chips, as well as for the other internal components that enable your system to function. This motherboard contains several slots, into which you can plug additional *boards* (also called *cards*) that perform specific functions.

Most PC motherboards contain six or more slots for add-on cards. For example, a video card enables your microprocessor to transmit video signals to your monitor. Other available cards enable you to add sound and modem/fax capabilities to your system.

Microprocessors: The Main Engine

We're not done looking at the system unit just yet. Buried somewhere on that big motherboard is a specific chip that controls your entire computer system. This chip is called a *microprocessor* or a *central processing unit (CPU)*.

The microprocessor is the brains inside your system. It processes all the instructions necessary for your computer to perform its duties. The more powerful the microprocessor chip, the faster and more efficiently your system runs.

Microprocessors carry out the various instructions that let your computer compute. Every input and output device hooked up to a computer—the keyboard, printer, monitor, and so on—either issues or receives instructions that the microprocessor then processes. Your software programs also issue instructions that must be implemented by the microprocessor. This chip truly is the workhorse of your system; it affects just about everything your computer does.

Different computers have different types of microprocessor chips. Many IBM-compatible computers use chips manufactured by Intel. Some use Intel-compatible chips manufactured by AMD and other firms. But all IBM-compatible computers that run the Windows operating system use Intel-compatible chips.

Note	The Apple Macintosh uses chips made by Motorola that are totally different from the Intel-compatible chips. It's because of the different processor configurations that software written for the Macintosh won't run on IBM-compatible computers—and vice versa.

In addition to having different manufacturers (and different families from the same manufacturer), you'll also run into chips that run at different speeds. CPU speed is measured in megahertz (MHz); a CPU with a speed of 1MHz can run at one million clock ticks per second! The higher the megahertz, the faster the chip runs. When you purchase a new PC, look for one with the combination of a powerful microprocessor and a high clock speed for best performance.

Today's fastest chips are actually measured in gigahertz (GHz). One GHz is equal to 1000MHZ, or one *billion* ticks per second!

If you want to know which microprocessor is installed in your system, Windows can tell you. Just follow these steps:

1. Click the Start button, and select Control Panel.
2. When the Control Panel opens, select the System icon.
3. When the System Properties dialog box appears, select the General tab.

The System section of this dialog box tells you which version of Windows you're running; the Registered To section tells you who you are (or, rather, how your version of Windows is registered); and the Computer section tells which processor you have and how much memory (RAM) you have installed.

Computer Memory: Temporary Storage

Speaking of memory, before your CPU can process any instructions you give it, your instructions must be stored somewhere, in preparation for access by the microprocessor. These instructions—along with other data processed by your system—are temporarily held in the computer's *random access memory (RAM)*. All computers have some amount of memory, which is created by a number of memory chips. The more memory that's available in a machine, the more instructions and data that can be stored at one time.

Memory is measured in terms of *bytes*. One byte is equal to approximately one character. A unit equaling approximately one thousand bytes (1,024, to be exact) is called a *kilobyte (KB)*, and a unit of approximately one thousand (1,024) kilobytes is called a *megabyte (MB)*. A thousand megabytes is a *gigabyte (GB)*.

Most computers today come with at least 128MB of memory, and some of the more expensive machines have 256MB or more. To enable your computer to run as many programs as quickly as possible, you need as much memory installed in your system as it can accept—or that you can afford. Extra memory can be added to a computer by installing a new memory module, which is as easy as plugging a "stick" directly into a slot on your system's motherboard.

If your computer doesn't possess enough memory, its CPU must constantly retrieve data from permanent storage on its hard disk. This method of data retrieval is slower than retrieving instructions and data from electronic memory. In fact, if your machine doesn't have enough memory, some programs will run very slowly (or you might experience random system crashes), and other programs won't run at all!

If your system is running Windows XP, you need a minimum of 192MB memory installed on your system—or else your system will run very sluggishly.

Hard Disk Drives: Long-Term Storage

Another important physical component inside your system unit is the *hard disk drive*. The hard disk permanently stores all your important data. Some hard disks can store more than 50 gigabytes of data. (Contrast this to your system's memory, which stores only a few dozen megabytes of data, temporarily.)

A hard disk consists of numerous metallic platters. These platters store data *magnetically*. Special read/write *heads* realign magnetic particles on the platters, much like a recording head records data onto magnetic recording tape.

Before data can be stored on any disk, including your system's hard disk, that disk must first be *formatted*. A disk that has not been formatted cannot accept any data. When you format a hard disk, your computer prepares each track and sector of the disk to accept and store data magnetically.

Of course, when you buy a new PC, your hard disk is already formatted for you. (And, in most cases, your operating system and key programs also are preinstalled.)

If you try to reformat your hard disk, you'll erase all the programs and data that have been installed—so don't do it!

Disk Drives: Portable Storage

Along with a hard disk drive, most computers have a *disk drive*. Removable disks—often called *floppy disks* or *diskettes*—work much like hard disks except that they consist of thin sheets of a magnetic-tape–like material instead of hard metallic platters. (Figure 2.4 shows a typical 3 1/2" floppy disk.)

FIGURE 2.4

Transfer files from PC to PC via disk.

Because disks are more portable than hard disks, they're typically used to store data that's transported physically from PC to PC. And disks are useful, too, for storing backup copies of the data on your PC's hard disk.

In addition to standard 3 1/2" disks, your computer system might include other types of portable storage media—most of which offer much more capacity than the 1.44MB found on a standard disk. For example, Iomega's Zip drive offers up to 250MB of portable storage on a removable disk that's slightly larger than a floppy. Sony's Superdisc can store up to 120MB on a disk that is physically compatible with—and can thus fully replace—traditional 3 1/2" drives.

CD-ROM Drives: Storage on a Disc

There's a third type of disk that is now standard on personal computer systems. This disc is called a *CD-ROM*. (The initials stand for *compact disc-read-only memory*.)

CD-ROM discs, such as the one in Figure 2.5, look just like the compact discs you play on your audio system. They're also very similar in the way they store data (audio data in the case of regular CDs and computer data in the case of CD-ROMs).

FIGURE 2.5

Store tons of data, digitally, on a shiny CD-ROM disc.

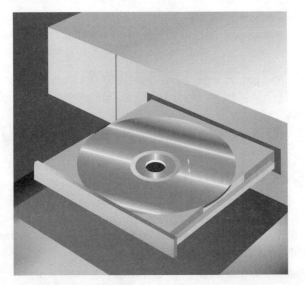

Information is encoded at a disc-manufacturing plant, using an industrial-grade laser. This information takes the form of microscopic pits (representing the 1s and 0s of computer binary language) below the disc's surface. Similar to hard and floppy disks, the information is arranged in a series of tracks and sectors, but the tracks are so close together that the disk surface is highly reflective.

Data is read from the CD-ROM disc via a drive that uses a consumer-grade laser. The laser beam follows the tracks of the disc and reads the pits, translating the data into a form your system can understand.

By the way, the *ROM* part of CD-ROM means that you can only read data from the disk; unlike normal hard disks and disks, you can't write new data to a standard CD-ROM. However, recordable (CD-R) and rewritable (CD-RW) drives are available that *do* let you write data to CD discs—although they're a bit more expensive than standard CD-ROM drives.

DVD Drives: Even More Storage on a Disc

Beyond the CD-ROM is the new *DVD* medium. DVDs can contain up to 4.7GB of data (compared to 650MB for a typical CD-ROM), and therefore are ideally suited for large applications or games that otherwise would require multiple CDs. Similar to standard CD-ROMs, DVDs are read-only, but DVD drives also can read CD-ROM discs. In addition, most DVD drives play full-length DVD movies, which turns your PC into a mini movie machine.

And, just as there are recordable CD-ROM drives, you can also find recordable DVD drives. These DVD-R drives are a little expensive ($500 or more just for the drive), but the prices are coming down—and they let you record an entire movie on a single disc.

Note   DVD really isn't an acronym for anything in particular. Some manufacturers claim that it stands for *digital versatile disc* or *digital video disc*, but it's really just a bunch of initials with no real meaning.

Keyboards: Fingertip Input

Computers receive data by reading it from disk, accepting it electronically over a modem, or receiving input directly from you, the user. You provide your input by way of what's called, in general, an *input device*; the most common input device you use to talk to your computer is the keyboard.

A computer keyboard, similar to the one in Figure 2.6, looks and functions just like a typewriter keyboard, except that computer keyboards have a few more keys. Some of these keys (such as the arrow, PgUp, PgDn, Home, and End keys) enable you to move around within a program or file. Other keys provide access to special program features. When you press a key on your keyboard, it sends an electronic signal to your system unit that tells your machine what you want it to do.

FIGURE 2.6

A standard PC keyboard.

Most PC keyboards look like the one in Figure 2.6. Some keyboards, however, have an ergonomic design that splits the keyboard into right and left parts and twists and tilts each side for maximum comfort. In addition, some manufacturers make *wireless* keyboards that connect to your system unit via radio signals—thus eliminating one cable from the back of your system.

Mice: Point-and-Click Input Devices

It's a funny name, but a necessary device.

A computer *mouse*, like the shown in Figure 2.7, is a small handheld device. Most mice consist of an oblong case with a roller underneath and two or three buttons on top. When you move the mouse along a desktop, an onscreen pointer (called a *cursor*) moves in response. When you click (press and release) a mouse button, this motion initiates an action in your program.

FIGURE 2.7

Roll the mouse back and forth to move the onscreen cursor.

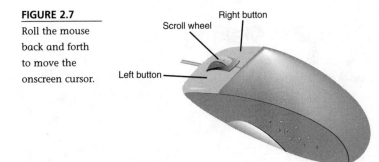

Mice come in all shapes and sizes. Some have wires, and some are wireless. Some are relatively oval in shape, and others are all curvy to better fit in the palm of your hand. Some have the typical roller ball underneath, and others use an optical sensor to determine where and how much you're rolling. Some even have extra buttons that can be programmed for specific functions or a scroll wheel you can use to scroll through long documents or Web pages.

Of course, a mouse is just *one* type of input device you can hook up to your PC. Trackballs, joysticks, game controllers, and pen pads all count as input devices, whether they work in conjunction with a mouse or replace it. You can use one of these alternative devices to replace your original mouse or (in some cases) to supplement it.

If you have a portable PC, you don't have a separate mouse, but rather a built-in pointing device of some sort—a touchpad, rollerball, or TrackPoint (the thing that looks like a little rubber eraser). Fortunately, you don't have to use the built-in pointing device on a portable PC; most portables let you attach an external mouse, which then overrides the internal device.

Modems: Getting Connected

Almost all PC systems today include a *modem*. A modem enables your computer to connect to telephone lines and transmit data to and from the Internet and commercial online services (such as America Online).

Modems come in either internal (card-based) or external (hooking up to an open port on the back of your system) models. *Internal* modems usually fit into a slot on your motherboard and connect directly to a telephone line. *External* modems are free-standing devices that connect to your system unit by cable and hook directly to a phone line.

Sound Cards and Speakers: Making Noise

Every PC comes with its own built-in speaker. In fact, some systems come with multiple-speaker audio systems, complete with subwoofers and so-called "3D" sound. (Figure 2.8 shows a typical right-left-subwoofer speaker system.)

FIGURE 2.8

A typical set of right and left external speakers, complete with subwoofer.

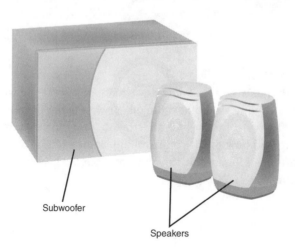

Subwoofer

Speakers

All speaker systems are driven by a sound card that is installed inside your system unit. If you upgrade your speaker system, you also might need to upgrade your sound card accordingly.

Video Cards and Monitors: Getting the Picture

Operating a computer would be difficult if you didn't constantly receive visual feedback showing you what your machine is doing. This vital function is provided by your computer's monitor.

The traditional monitor, similar to the one shown in Figure 2.9, is a lot like a little television set. Your microprocessor electronically transmits words and pictures (*text* and *graphics*, in PC lingo) to your monitor, in some approximation of how these visuals would appear on paper. You view the monitor and respond according to what you see onscreen.

FIGURE 2.9

A traditional tube-type video monitor.

Although the traditional monitor uses a picture tube (similar to the one in a normal television set) to display its picture, another type of monitor does away with the tube. A so-called *flat-screen* monitor, such as the one in Figure 2.10, uses an LCD display instead—which is not only flat, but also very thin. (These are the same types of displays used in portable PCs.)

You measure the size of a monitor by measuring from corner to corner, diagonally. The traditional desktop monitor is normally a 14" or 15" monitor; larger 17" and 19" monitors are becoming more common as they become more affordable.

FIGURE 2.10

A space-saving, flat-screen video monitor.

> The measurement is different for tube-type monitors than it is for flat-screen monitors. This is because a flat-screen monitor displays its images all the way to the edge of the screen, and traditional tube-type monitors don't. For that reason, a 15" flat-screen monitor has the same size picture as a 17" tube-type monitor.

The monitor itself does not generate the images it displays. These images are electronically crafted by a *video card* installed inside your system unit. To work correctly, both video card and monitor must be matched to display images of the same resolution.

Resolution refers to the size of the images that can be displayed onscreen and is measured in pixels. A *pixel* is a single dot on your screen; a full picture is composed of thousands of pixels. The higher the resolution, the sharper the resolution—which lets you display more (smaller) elements onscreen.

Resolution is expressed in numbers of pixels, in both the horizontal and vertical directions. The lowest-price video cards and monitors have a 640×480 or 800×600 pixel resolution; you probably want a card/monitor combination that can display at the 1024×768 resolution.

Printers: Making Hard Copies

Your monitor displays images in real time, but they're fleeting. For permanent records of your work, you must add a printer to your system. Printers create hard copy output from your software programs.

You can choose from various types of printers for your system, depending on your exact printing needs. The two main types of printer today are laser and inkjet printers.

Laser printers work much like copying machines, applying toner (powdered ink) to paper by using a small laser. *Inkjet* printers, on the other hand, shoot jets of ink to the paper's surface to create the printed image. Inkjet printers are typically a little lower priced than laser printers, although the price difference is shrinking.

You also can choose from either black-and-white or color printers. Black-and-white printers are faster than color printers and better if you're printing memos, letters, and other single-color documents. Color printers, however, are great if you have kids, and they're essential if you want to print pictures taken with a digital camera.

By the way, there's a new type of "combination" printer available that combines a printer with a scanner and a fax machine. If you need all these devices and are short on space, these are pretty good deals.

 The devices presented in this chapter are found in almost all computer systems today. However, you can add a variety of other devices to your system, either by plugging them into the back of your system unit or by inserting a new card *inside* the system unit. To learn more about optional accessories—including scanners, PC cameras, and network cards—turn to Chapter 7, "Add New Hardware."

Portable PCs—Lightweight All-in-One Systems

Before we wrap up this chapter, we need to discuss a slightly different type of computer. This type of PC combines all the various elements (except for a printer) into a single case and then adds a battery so you can use it on the go. This type of PC is called a *portable computer*—or, depending on its size, a *laptop* or *notebook* PC.

Most portable PCs, like the one in Figure 2.11, feature a flip-up LCD screen. When the screen is folded down, the PC is very portable; when the screen is flipped up, the keyboard is exposed.

All portable PCs include some sort of built-in pointing device—but typically not a standalone mouse. A portable might have a touchpad, rollerball, or Trackpoint (which looks like a miniature joystick in the middle of the keyboard). Speakers typically are built into the base of the unit, and various types of disk drives are located on the sides or underneath.

FIGURE 2.11

A typical portable PC—all those components in a single package.

The key thing about portable PCs—in addition to their small sizes and light weights—is that they can operate on battery power. Depending on the PC (and the battery), you might be able to operate a portable for up to four hours before switching batteries or plugging the unit into a wall outlet. That makes portables great for use on airplanes, in coffeshops, or anywhere plugging in a power cord is inconvenient.

The only bad thing about portable PCs is that they're more expensive than a similarly equipped desktop PC. Expect to pay almost twice as much for the same features in a portable because all the normal components have to be shrunk down to a more compact size.

Things to Remember

Here are the key things to remember about the hardware in your computer system:

- The brains and engine of your system is the system unit, which contains the microprocessor, memory, disk drives, and all the connections for your other system components.

▪ To make your system run faster, get a faster microprocessor or more memory.

▪ Data is temporarily stored in your system's memory; you store data permanently on some type of disk drive—either a hard disk, floppy disk, or CD-ROM.

▪ You can add new hardware to your system by plugging it into the back of your system unit or by inserting a new card into your system unit.

▪ Portable PCs have all the various system components combined into a single small case; they cost about twice as much as a comparable desktop PC.

WINDOWS AND SOFTWARE BASICS

3

*A*s you learned back in Chapter 1, "Personal Computer Basics," it's the software and operating system that make your hardware work. The operating system for most personal computers is Microsoft Windows, and you need to know how to use Windows to use your PC system.

This chapter gives you a brief overview of what Windows does and how it works and tells you a little bit about software programs in the bargain.

What Windows Is—and What It Does

Before you can use your computer to do *anything*, you need to know how to use Windows. This is because Windows pretty much runs your computer for you; if you don't know your way around Windows, you won't be able to do much of anything on your new PC.

Windows is a piece of software called an *operating system*. An operating system does what its name implies—it *operates* your computer *system*, working in the background every time you turn on your PC.

Equally important, Windows is what you see when you first turn on your computer, after everything turns on and boots up. The "desktop" that fills your screen is part of Windows, as is the taskbar at the bottom of the screen and the big menu that pops up when you click the Start button.

Different Versions of Windows

The version of Windows installed on your new PC is probably Windows XP. Microsoft has released different versions of Windows over the years, and XP is the latest, which is why it comes preinstalled on most new PCs.

If you've used a previous version of Windows—such as Windows 95, Windows 98, or Windows Me—on another PC, Windows XP probably looks and acts a little differently to you. Don't worry; everything that was in the old Windows is still in the new Windows—it's probably just in a slightly different place.

There are actually three different versions of Windows XP available. Home Edition (which is the version that probably came with your new PC) is the version of XP for home and small-business users. Professional Edition is designed for larger businesses and corporate users, and the 64-Bit Edition is designed for workstation-class applications. They all share the same basic functionality, so if you know how to use one of them, you know how to use all of them.

Working Your Way Around the Desktop

As you can see in Figure 3.1, the Windows XP desktop includes a number of elements. Get to know the desktop; you're going to be seeing a lot of it from now on!

FIGURE 3.1

The Windows XP
desktop—click
the Start button
to get going!

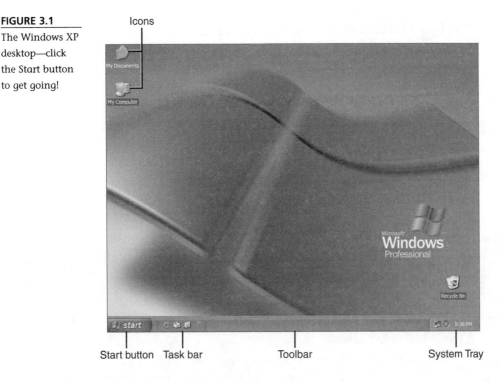

The major parts of the Windows desktop include:

- **Start button**—Opens the Start menu, which is what you use to open all your programs and documents.

- **Taskbar**—Displays buttons for your open applications and windows, as well as different toolbars for different tasks.

- **Toolbar**—A separate and optional button bar that can be attached to the main taskbar. The most popular toolbar is the Quick Launch toolbar, which includes buttons for your Web browser and e-mail programs.

- **System Tray**—The part of the taskbar that holds the clock, volume control, and icons for other utilities that run in the background of your system.

- **Shortcut icons**—These are links to software programs you can place on your desktop; a "clean" desktop includes just one icon, for the Windows Recycle Bin.

Important Windows Operations

To use Windows efficiently, you must master a few simple operations, such as pointing and clicking, dragging and dropping, and right-clicking. You perform almost all these operations with your mouse.

Pointing and Clicking

The most common mouse operation is *pointing and clicking*. Simply move the mouse so that the cursor is pointing to the object you want to select, and then click the left mouse button once. Pointing and clicking is an effective way to select menu items, directories, and files.

Double-Clicking

If you're using Windows XP's default operating mode, you'll need to *double-click* an item to activate an operation. This involves pointing at something onscreen with the cursor and then clicking the left mouse button twice in rapid succession. For example, to open program groups or launch individual programs, simply double-click a specific icon.

This classic double-click mode is activated by default on most new PCs. Windows XP also includes a new single-click mode, which makes Windows act more like a Web page. In this mode, you hover over an object to select it and single-click to activate it. To learn how to switch to single-click mode, see Activity 67, "Personalize the Way Windows Works."

Right-Clicking

When you select an item and then click the *right* mouse button, you'll often see a pop-up menu. This menu, when available, contains commands that directly relate to the selected object. Refer to your individual programs to see whether and how they use the right mouse button.

Dragging and Dropping

Dragging is a variation of clicking. To drag an object, point at it with the cursor and then press and hold down the left mouse button. Move the mouse without releasing the mouse button, and drag the object to a new location. When you're done moving the object, release the mouse button to drop it onto the new location.

You can use dragging and dropping to move files from one folder to another or to delete files by dragging them onto the Recycle Bin icon.

Hovering

When you position the cursor over an item without clicking your mouse, you're *hovering* over that item. Many operations require you to hover your cursor and then perform some other action.

Moving and Resizing Windows

Every software program you launch is displayed in a separate onscreen window. When you open more than one program, you get more than one window—and your desktop can quickly get cluttered.

There are many ways to deal with desktop clutter. One way to do this is to move a window to a new position. You do this by positioning your cursor over the window's title bar (shown in Figure 3.2) and then clicking and holding down the left button on your mouse. As long as this button is depressed, you can use your mouse to drag the window around the screen. When you release the mouse button, the window stays where you put it.

FIGURE 3.2

The various parts of a window.

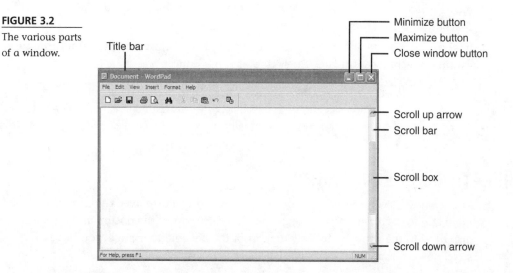

You also can change the size of most windows. You do this by positioning the cursor over the very edge of the window—any edge. If you position the cursor on either side of the window, you can resize the width. If you position the cursor on the top or bottom edge, you can resize the height. Finally, if you position the cursor on a corner, you can resize the width and height at the same time.

The cursor changes shape—to a double-ended arrow—when it's positioned over the edge of a window.

After the cursor is positioned over the window's edge, press and hold the left mouse button; then drag the window border to its new size. Release the mouse button to lock in the newly sized window.

Maximizing, Minimizing, and Closing Windows

Another way to manage a window in Windows is to make it display full-screen. You do this by maximizing the window. All you have to do is click the Maximize button at the upper-right corner of the window. (It's the button in the middle, as shown previously in Figure 3.2.)

If the window is already maximized, the Maximize button changes to a Restore Down button. When you click the Restore Down button, the window resumes its previous (pre-maximized) dimensions.

If you'd rather hide the window so it doesn't clutter your desktop, click the Minimize button. This shoves the window off the desktop, onto the Taskbar. The program in the window is still running, however—it's just not on the desktop. To restore a minimized window, all you have to do is click the window's button on the Windows Taskbar (at the bottom of the screen).

If what you really want to do is close the window (and close any program running within the window), just click the window's Close button.

If you try to close a window that contains a document you haven't saved, you'll be prompted to save the changes to the document. Because you probably don't want to lose any of your work, click Yes to save the document and then close the program.

Scrolling Through a Window

Many windows contain more information than can be displayed at once. When you have a long document or Web page, only the first part of the document or page is displayed in the window. To view the rest of the document or page, you have to scroll down through the window.

There are several ways to scroll through a window. To scroll up or down a line at a time, click the up or down arrow on the window's scrollbar. To move to a specific place in a long document, use your mouse to grab the scroll box (between the up and down arrows) and drag it to a new position.

If your mouse has a scroll wheel, you can use it to scroll through a long document. Just roll the wheel back or forward to scroll down or up through a window.

Using Menus

Most windows in Windows use a set of pull-down menus to store all the commands and operations you can perform. The menus are aligned across the top of the window, just below the title bar, in what is called a *menu bar*.

You open (or pull down) a menu by clicking the menu's name. The full menu then appears just below the menu bar. You activate a command or select a menu item by clicking it with your mouse.

Some menu items have a little black arrow to the right of the label. This indicates that additional choices are available, displayed on a submenu. Click the menu item or the arrow to display the submenu.

Other menu items have three little dots (called an *ellipsis*) to the right of the label. This indicates that additional choices are available, displayed in a dialog box. Click the menu item to display the dialog box.

If an item in a menu, toolbar, or dialog box is dimmed (or grayed), that means it isn't available for the current task.

The nice thing is, after you get the hang of this menu thing in one program, the menus should be very similar in all the other programs you use. For example, almost all programs have a File menu that lets you open, save, and close documents, as well as an Edit menu that lets you cut, copy, and paste. While each program has menus and menu items specific to its own needs, these common menus make it easy to get up and running when you install new software programs on your system.

Using Toolbars

Some Windows programs put the most frequently used operations on a *toolbar*, typically located just below the menu bar. A toolbar looks like a row of buttons, each with a small picture (called an *icon*) and maybe a bit of text. You activate the associated command or operation by clicking the button with your mouse.

If the toolbar is too long to display fully on your screen, you'll see a right arrow at the far-right side of the toolbar. Click this arrow to display the buttons that aren't currently visible.

If you're not sure which button does what, you can hover the cursor over the button to display a *tool tip*. A tool tip is a small text box that displays the button's label or other useful information.

Using Dialog Boxes, Tabs, and Buttons

When Windows or an application requires a complex set of inputs, you are often presented with a *dialog box*. A dialog box is similar to a form in which you can input various parameters and make various choices—and then register those inputs and choices when you click the OK button.

There are several different types of dialog boxes, each one customized to the task at hand. However, most dialog boxes share a set of common features, which include the following:

- **Buttons**—Most buttons either register your inputs or open an auxiliary dialog box. The most common buttons are OK (to register your inputs and close the dialog box), Cancel (to close the dialog box without registering your inputs), and Apply (to register your inputs without closing the dialog box). Click a button once to activate it.

- **Tabs**—These allow a single dialog box to display multiple "pages" of information. Think of each tab, arranged across the top of the dialog box, as a "thumbtab" to the individual page in the dialog box below it. Click the top of a tab to change to that particular page of information.

- **Text boxes**—These are empty boxes where you type in a response. Position your cursor over the empty input box, click your left mouse button, and begin typing.

- **Lists**—These are lists of available choices; lists can either scroll or drop down from what looks like an input box. Select an item from the list with your mouse; you can select multiple items in some lists by holding down the Ctrl key while clicking with your mouse.

- **Check boxes**—These are boxes that let you select (or deselect) various stand-alone options.

- **Sliders**—These are sliding bars that let you select increments between two extremes, similar to a sliding volume control on an audio system.

Using the Start Menu

All the software programs and utilities on your computer are accessed via Windows' Start menu. You display the Start menu by using your mouse to click the Start button, located in the lower-left corner of your screen.

As you can see in Figure 3.3, the Windows XP Start menu consists of two columns of icons. Your most frequently used programs are listed in the left column; basic Windows utilities and folders are listed in the right column. To open a specific program or folder, just click the icon.

FIGURE 3.3

Access all the programs on your system from the Start menu.

Frequently used programs

Windows utilities and folders

All Programs arrow

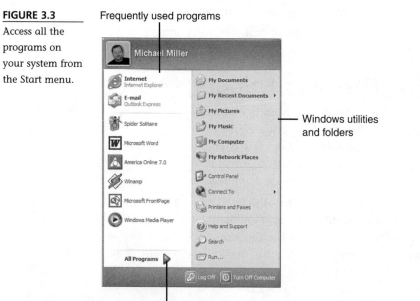

To view the rest of your programs, click the All Programs arrow. This displays a new menu called the Programs menu. From here you can access various programs, sorted by type or manufacturer. (When more programs are contained within a master folder, you'll see an arrow to the right of the title; click this arrow to display additional choices.)

Shutting Down Windows—and Your Computer

Windows starts automatically every time you turn on your computer. Although you will see lines of text flashing onscreen during the initial startup, Windows loads automatically and goes on to display the Windows desktop.

When you want to turn off your computer, you do it through Windows. In fact, you don't want to turn off your computer any other way—you *always* want to turn things off through the official Windows procedure.

 Do *not* turn off your computer without shutting down Windows. You could lose data and settings that are temporarily stored in your system's memory.

To shut down Windows and turn off your PC, follow these steps:

1. Click the Start button.
2. When the Start menu appears, click the Turn Off Computer button.
3. When the Turn Off Computer dialog box appears, click the Turn Off button.

Understanding Files and Folders

All the information on your computer is stored in *files*. A file is nothing more than a collection of data of some sort. Everything on your computer's hard drive is a separate file, with its own name, location, and properties. The contents of a file can be a document from an application (such as a Works worksheet or a Word document), or they can be the executable code for the application itself.

Every file has its own unique name. A defined structure exists for naming files, and its conventions must be followed for Windows to understand exactly what file you want when you try to access one. Each filename must consist of two parts, separated by a period—the *name* (to the left of the period) and the *extension* (to the right of the period). A filename can consist of letters, numbers, spaces, and characters and looks something like this: `this is a filename.ext`.

 By default, Windows XP hides the extensions when it displays filenames. To display extensions, use the Control Panel to open the Folder Options dialog box; then select the View tab. In the Advanced Settings list, *uncheck* the Hide Extensions for Known File Types option, and then click OK.

Windows stores files in folders. A *folder* is like a master file; each folder can contain both files and additional folders. The exact location of a file is called its *path* and contains all the folders leading to the file. For example, a file named `filename.doc` that exists in the `system` folder, that is itself contained in the `windows` folder on your `c:\` drive, has a path that looks like this: `c:\windows\system\filename.doc`.

Learning how to use files and folders is a necessary skill for all computer users. You might need to copy files from one folder to another or from your hard disk to a floppy disk. You certainly need to delete files every now and then. To do this, you use either My Computer or My Documents—both discussed later in this chapter.

Working with Software Programs

Your new computer system came with a bunch of programs preinstalled on your hard disk. These programs probably include one or more of the following:

- **Microsoft Works**—Works (or the more fully featured Works Suite) is actually a bunch of different programs bundled together. Works includes a word processor (in the form of Microsoft Word, a separate application), spreadsheet, database, calendar, and more.

- **Microsoft Office**—Office is kind of a professional version of Works, with really powerful applications—including Microsoft Word, Excel, Outlook, and PowerPoint.

- **Microsoft Word**—Typically included as part of either Works Suite or Office, Word is the world's most popular word processing program.

- **Microsoft Picture It! Publishing**—Typically included as part of Works Suite, this program is used to touch up digital photos and create fun and useful home projects.

- **Microsoft Money**—Also included as part of Works Suite, Money is used to manage your personal finances.

- **Quicken**—Quicken is the more popular competitor to Microsoft Money, a first-rate personal financial management program.

Different computer manufacturers bundle different software programs with their PCs. Chances are your new computer includes more software than what is listed here—all already installed and accessible from Windows's Start menu.

 Note

Three other programs included with most new PCs are Internet Explorer, Outlook Express, and Windows Messenger—discussed in the "Internet Utilities" section later in this chapter.

Launching a Program

To start a program, follow these steps:

1. Click the Start button.

2. If the program is displayed on the Start menu, click the program's icon.

3. If the program isn't visible on the main Start menu, click the All Programs button, find the program's icon, and then click it.

Switching Between Programs

After you've launched a few programs, it's easy to switch between one program and another. To switch to another program (and send all other open programs to the background), you can do one of the following:

- Click the application's button in the taskbar.

- Click any visible part of the application's window—including its title bar.

- Hold down the Alt key and then press the Tab key repeatedly until the application window you want is selected. (This cycles through all open windows.) When you're at the window you want, release the Alt key.

If you have multiple windows open at the same time, you can determine which is currently the active window by its title bar. The title bar for the active program is brighter, and the title bar text is bright white. An inactive title bar is more dull, with off-white text. If you have overlapping windows on your desktop, the window on top is always the active one. The active application's Taskbar button looks like it's pressed in.

Using Windows to Manage Your System

Because Windows is your interface to your computer hardware, you can use Windows to manage and configure various aspects of your system. You can even reconfigure Windows to make it look and act the way you want.

You perform all these management functions via several utilities that are built in to Windows. The most important of these utilities are My Computer, My Documents, and the Control Panel.

Managing PC Resources with My Computer

The My Computer utility lets you access each major component of your system and perform basic maintenance functions. For example, you can use My Computer to "open" the contents of your hard disk, and then copy, move, and delete individual files.

To open My Computer, follow these steps:

1. Click the Start button.

2. Select My Computer.

As you can see in Figure 3.4, the My Computer folder contains icons for each of the major components of your system—your hard disk drive, floppy disk drive, CD-ROM or DVD drive, and so on.

FIGURE 3.4

Use My Computer to manage your hard drive and other key components.

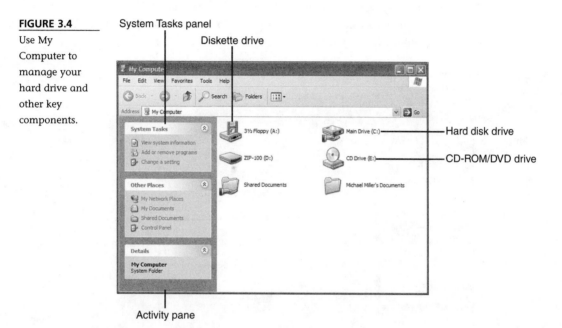

System Tasks panel

Diskette drive

Hard disk drive

CD-ROM/DVD drive

Activity pane

Each folder in Windows XP contains an *activity pane* on the left side of the window. This pane lets you view relevant information about and perform key operations on the selected item.

You can also use My Computer to view the contents of a specific drive. When you double-click the icon for that drive, you'll see a list of folders and files located on that drive. To view the contents of any folder, just double-click the icon for that folder.

Managing Files with My Documents

The documents you create with Microsoft Word and other software programs are actually separate computer files. By default, all your documents are stored somewhere in the My Documents folder.

Windows lets you access the contents of your My Documents folder with a few clicks of your mouse. Just follow these steps:

1. Click the Start button.

2. Click My Documents.

As you can see in Figure 3.5, the My Documents folder not only contains individual files, it also contains a number of other folders (sometimes called *subfolders*), such as My Pictures and My Music. Double-click a subfolder to view its contents, or use the options in the Files and Folders Tasks panel to perform specific operations—including moving, copying, and deleting.

FIGURE 3.5

Access your important document files from the My Documents folder.

Files and Folders Tasks panel

Subfolder

Document file

Activity pane

Managing Windows with the Control Panel

Most—but not all—of Windows's configuration settings are found somewhere within the Control Panel. The Control Panel is a system folder that contains a number of individual utilities that let you adjust and configure various system properties.

To open the Control Panel, follow these steps:

1. Click the Start button.

2. Click Control Panel.

When the Control Panel opens, as shown in Figure 3.6, you can select a particular category you want to configure. When the Pick a Task page appears, either click a task or click an icon to open a specific configuration utility. (When you click a task, the appropriate configuration utility is launched.)

FIGURE 3.6

The Windows XP Control Panel—configuration tasks organized by category.

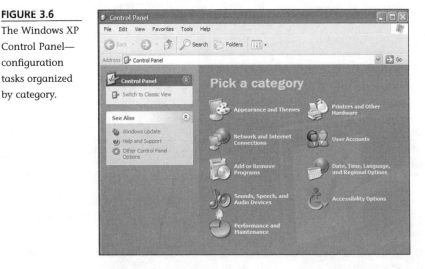

When you open a configuration utility, you'll see a dialog box for that particular item. You can then change the individual settings within that dialog box; click the OK button to register your new settings.

All the Other Things in Windows

Windows is more than just a pretty desktop and some configuration utilities. Windows also includes a large number of accessory programs and system tools you can use to perform other basic system operations.

Accessories

Windows includes a number of single-function accessory programs, all accessible from the Start menu. These programs include a calculator, some games, two basic word processors (Notepad and WordPad), a drawing program (Paint), a player for audio and video files (Windows Media Player), and a digital video editing program (Windows Movie Maker). You access most of these accessories by clicking the Start button and selecting All Programs, Accessories.

Internet Utilities

In addition to the aforementioned Windows accessories, Windows XP also gives you three important Internet utilities. These include a Web browser (Internet Explorer), an e-mail program (Outlook Express), and an instant messaging program (Windows Messenger). You access these three utilities by clicking the Start button and selecting All Programs.

System Tools

Windows XP includes a handful of technical tools you can use to keep your system running smoothly. You can access all these tools by clicking the Start button and selecting All Programs, Accessories, System Tools.

 To learn about the practical uses of these and other system tools, turn to Activity 68, "Perform Routine PC Maintenance."

Getting Help in Windows

When you can't figure out how to perform a particular task, it's time to ask for help. In Windows XP, this is done through the Help and Support Center.

To launch the Help and Support Center, follow these steps:

1. Click the Start button.
2. Click Help and Support.

The Help and Support Center lets you search for specific answers to your problems, browse the Help contents by topic, connect to another computer for remote assistance, go online for additional help, and access Windows's key system tools. Click the type of help you want, and follow the onscreen instructions from there.

Things to Remember

This chapter gave you a lot of background about Windows and the other software programs installed on your PC system. Here are the key points to remember:

- You use Windows to manage your computer system and run your software programs.
- Most functions in Windows are activated by clicking or double-clicking an icon or a button.

- All the programs and accessories on your system are accessed via the Start menu, which you display by clicking the Start button.
- Use My Computer to manage the main components of your system.
- Use My Documents to manage your document files and folders.
- Use the Control Panel to manage Windows's configuration settings.
- When you can't figure out how to do something, click the Start button and select Help and Support.

4

INTERNET AND HOME NETWORKING BASICS

ne of the main reasons you purchased your new computer was to connect to the Internet. The Internet is a giant network of computers, all connected to exchange information and messages.

You don't have to connect to the Internet to form a computer network. If you have more than one computer in your home or office, you can connect them to share files and hardware. (For example, you can have two computers share the same printer.)

Read on to learn more about networking in general and the Internet in particular.

Understanding Home Networks

A *network* is a group of two or more computers or electronic devices connected together. A *local area network (LAN)* is a network of computers that are geographically close together; a *wide area network (WAN)* is a network with computers not all in the same place. The Internet is the widest-area network today, connecting computers and computer networks from all around the world.

Why would you want to connect two computers? Maybe you want to transfer files from one computer to another. Maybe you want to share an expensive piece of hardware (such as a printer) instead of buying one for each PC. Maybe you want to connect all your computers to the same Internet connection.

When you need to share files, or printers, or an Internet connection, you need to hook all your computers together into a network—similar to the one shown in Figure 4.1.

FIGURE 4.1

Connect two computers in a network to share a printer and an Internet connection.

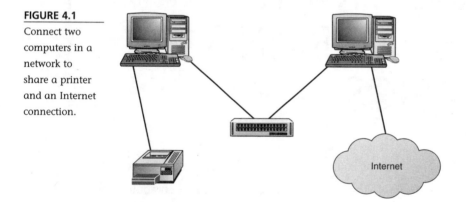

Connecting multiple computers is actually fairly simple. Each computer has to have a *network interface card (NIC)* installed and configured. If you're connecting more than two computers in your network, each network card then has to be connected to a *hub*, which is a simple device that functions like the hub of a wheel and serves as the central point in your network. Then, each computer has to be configured to function as part of the network and to share designated files, folders, and peripherals.

You can find everything you need to create your network in a preassembled networking kit. These kits typically contain all the cards, cables, and hubs you need to create your network, along with easy-to-follow instructions. (And if you don't want to open up your computer, you can even find kits that include external network "cards" that connect via USB ports!)

The configuration part of setting up a network is handled by Windows XP's Network Setup Wizard. You run the wizard on each PC that's connected to the network and tell it about anything else you have connected—such as a printer or an Internet connection you want to share.

The wizard does all the hard work, and when it's done, your network is up and running and ready to use.

To learn how to connect your computers in a network, see Activity 70, "Set Up a Home Network."

Different Ways to Connect

When it comes to physically connecting your network, you have a handful of choices. Here's a brief overview of the major types of networks to consider.

How quickly data is transferred across a network is measured in megabits per second, or Mbps. The bigger the Mbps number, the faster the network—and faster is always better than slower.

Ethernet Networks

An *Ethernet network* is a traditional wired network. You install Ethernet cards in each PC and connect the cards via Ethernet cable. Although this type of network is very easy to set up and probably the lowest-cost alternative, you must deal with all that cable—which can be a hassle if your computers are in different areas of your house. Data is transferred at either 10Mbps or 100Mbps, depending on what equipment you install.

A 100Mbps Ethernet network is called *Fast Ethernet*. Some cards and hubs are labeled 10/100 because they can handle either 10Mbps or 100Mbps data transmission, depending on the capability of the other equipment on the network.

If you're connecting your network to a DSL or cable modem connection, you'll need at least part of your network to be an Ethernet network. That's because most DSL and cable modems are designed to connect to an Ethernet card in your PC.

Wireless Networks

A *wireless network* uses radio frequency (RF) signals to connect one computer to another. The big advantage of wireless, of course, is that you don't have to run any cables—a big plus if you have a large house with computers on either end.

Windows XP supports the IEEE 802.11b wireless networking standard, which is capable of speeds up to 11Mbps. This is the same type of wireless network used in large corporations, and it's very stable and robust.

> The official marketing name for 802.11b wireless networking is *WiFi*, for *wired fidelity*. WiFi lets you connect to wireless network access points up to 150 feet away from your PC.

Another type of wireless network, also supported by Windows XP, is called HomeRF. HomeRF networks are typically a little less expensive than 802.11b wireless networks, but they're also a lot slower. For example, Diamond's HomeFree wireless system transfers data at 1Mbps, and Intel's AnyPoint Wireless HomeRF system runs at 1.6Mbps. That's not that fast, especially if you transfer large amounts of data back and forth. (It *is* fast enough for sharing a broadband Internet connection, though.)

> Intel has recently upgraded its AnyPoint line from HomeRF to the faster WiFi standard.

Phone Line Networks

When you don't want to run cables but also don't want the high cost of an 802.11b wireless network (or the low speed of a HomeRF system), consider connecting your network via your home's telephone lines.

A *phone line network* provides a similar level of convenience as a wireless network, but with higher data transfer rates and greater reliability. With telephone line networking (commonly referred to as *HomePNA*, based on the specifications developed by the Home Phone Networking Alliance), you connect each computer to an adapter that plugs into a standard phone jack. Data signals are sent from your computer through the adapter into your home phone line and received by another adapter and PC elsewhere on the network.

> Because each adapter on a HomePNA network sends its signal at a different frequency, your computer network can share the phone line with other voice and data traffic.

Many HomePNA products are available on the market, the most popular of which is Intel's AnyPoint Home Network kit. The standard AnyPoint adapter plugs into a parallel or USB port on your PC and then connects to the nearest phone line. (No hub is necessary.)

Where the earliest HomePNA networks transferred data at just 1Mbps, most current phone line networks offer 10Mbps transfer rates. So, if you need decent speed without the hassle of running lots of cable, this might be the way to go.

A Different Kind of Network—The Internet

It used to be that most people bought personal computers to do work—word processing, spreadsheets, databases, the types of programs that still make up the core of Works Suite 2000. But today, a large number of people also buy PCs to access the Internet—to send and receive e-mail, surf the Web, and chat with other users.

If you're new to the Internet, keep one thing in mind: The Internet isn't a thing. You can't touch it or see it or smell it; you can't put it in a box and buy it. The Internet is like the huge power grid that provides electricity to homes across the country—it exists between the points of usage.

So, if the Internet isn't a physical thing, what is it? It's really more simple than you might think; the Internet is nothing more than a really big computer network. In fact, it's a computer network that connects other computer networks—what some would call a "network of networks."

Just being connected to the Internet, however, really doesn't accomplish anything. It's much the same as having electricity run to your home—that wall outlet doesn't do anything until you plug something into it. The same thing is true with the Internet; the Internet itself just kind of sits there until you plug something into it that takes advantage of it.

How an Internet Connection Works

A dial-up Internet connection, such as the one shown in Figure 4.2, is actually fairly simple. It works like this:

1. Your personal computer connects to a normal phone line, using a piece of hardware called a *modem*.

2. Your modem dials into your *Internet service provider (ISP)* and logs in to your personal account. (Your ISP has a modem on its end that converts the analog signals from your modem into digital signals that its computers can understand.)

3. Your ISP plugs the signal from your computer into the Internet.

FIGURE 4.2

Your computer
connects to the
Internet via your
ISP's network.

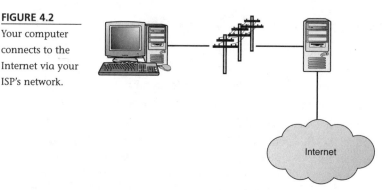

Your computer is now connected to the Internet, through your ISP. After you're connected, you can access any site or service on the Internet, as well as any mail or
news servers run by your ISP. When you disconnect from your ISP (hang up your
phone line), you're no longer connected to the Internet, and you can't access any
Internet-based sites or services—until you connect again, that is.

Note

> Some ISPs, such as America Online, are also commercial online services and provide their
> users with an easy-to-use onscreen interface and proprietary content and navigation. But
> these commercial online services also function as traditional ISPs, consolidating thousands
> of incoming telephone lines into a single gateway to the Internet for their users.

The only problem with this type of dial-up connection is that it's relatively slow.
Connection speed is measured in kilobits per second (Kbps), and a typical dial-up
connection runs at 56.6Kbps.

You can connect faster through what is called a *broadband* connection.
Broadband uses special DSL phone lines or cable lines to connect anywhere from
400Kbps to 2000Kbps. If you're interested in a broadband connection, contact
your local phone company (for DSL service) or cable company (for cable broadband) about availability.

The Most Important Parts of the Internet

When you're connected to the Internet, there are a variety of services you can use.
These include messaging services (e-mail and chat), community services (Usenet
newsgroups), and interactive/informational services (the World Wide Web). The
Internet itself doesn't actually perform any of these activities, but it does *enable* these
activities to occur. And when you connect to the Internet through your personal
computer, you have access to all these activities and more.

What follows is a little background on each of these popular services.

E-mail—The Most-Used Service on the Internet

Electronic mail *(e-mail)* is a means of communicating with other Internet users via letters, written and delivered electronically over the Internet. Although e-mail messages look a lot like traditional letters, e-mail itself is very different from the so-called "snail mail" delivered by the United States Postal Service.

When you send an electronic letter to another Internet user, that letter travels from your computer to your recipient's computer (via the Internet) almost instantly. Your messages travel at the speed of electrons over a number of phone lines and Internet connections, automatically routed to the right place just about as fast as you can click the Send button. That's a *lot* different from using the U.S. Postal Service, which can take days to deliver a similar message.

Note

To learn more about e-mail messages, see Activity 6, "Send and Receive E-mail."

The World Wide Web—Colorful, Graphic, and Interactive

The World Wide Web is the showiest part of the Internet, the place where information of all types is presented in a highly visual, often multimedia, format.

Information on the World Wide Web is presented in pages. As you can see in Figure 4.3, a *Web page* is similar to a page in a book, made up of text and pictures (also called *graphics*). A Web page differs from a book page, however, in that it can include other elements, such as audio and video, and links to other Web pages.

FIGURE 4.3

A Web page viewed with Internet Explorer.

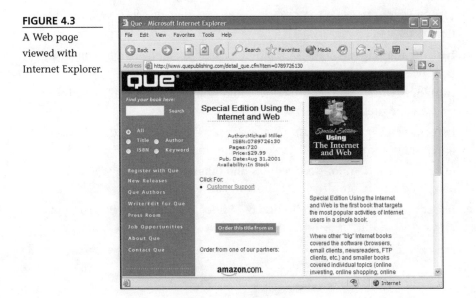

It's this linking to other Web pages that makes the Web such a dynamic way to present information. A *link* on a Web page can point to another Web page on the same site or to another site. Most links are included as part of a Web page's text and are called *hypertext links*. (If a link is part of a graphic, it's called a *graphic link*.) Links are usually in a different color from the rest of the text and often are underlined; when you click a link, you're taken directly to the linked page.

Web pages reside at a Web *site*. A Web site is nothing more than a collection of Web pages (each in its own individual computer file) residing on a host computer. The host computer is connected full-time to the Internet so you can access the site—and its Web pages—anytime you access the Internet. The main page at a Web site usually is called a *home page*, and it often serves as an opening screen that provides a brief overview and menu of everything you can find at that site. The address of a Web page is called a *URL*, which stands for uniform resource locator.

You view a Web page with a Web *browser*. The two most popular browsers today are Microsoft's Internet Explorer and Netscape Navigator. Chances are you have one or both of these browsers preinstalled on your new PC.

To learn more about the World Wide Web, see Chapter 10, "Surf the Web."

Other Parts of the Internet

E-mail and the Web are the two most popular parts of the Internet, but not the *only* parts. Here are some of the other activities you can engage in while online:

- **File Transfer Protocol (FTP)**—A method for downloading computer files from dedicated servers

- **Instant messaging (IM)**—A method for real-time, one-on-one conversations between two Internet users

- **Internet radio**—Where Web-based radio stations "broadcast" in real-time over the Internet

- **Internet Relay Chat (IRC)**—A series of servers and chat channels where groups of Internet users "talk" to each other in real-time

- **MP3**—A file format for storing songs and other audio, used by many to download and record near-CD quality music from the Internet

- **Usenet newsgroups**—A collection of online bulletin boards you can use to communicate with users interested in a particular topic

Things to Remember

Here are the key things to remember about networking and the Internet:

■ To share information or hardware between two or more computers, you have to connect them in a network.

■ There are three basic types of networks—wired, wireless (using radio frequencies), and phone line.

■ The Internet is nothing more than a giant computer network.

■ You connect to the Internet through an Internet service provider, which you reach through normal phone lines.

■ You can use a home network to share an Internet connection between multiple PCs.

■ After you're connected to the Internet, you can perform a variety of activities, including sending and receiving e-mail and surfing the World Wide Web.

PART II

GETTING STARTED

SET UP YOUR NEW COMPUTER SYSTEM

*T*he first part of this book gave you the essential background information you need to understand how your computer system works. Now it's time to put that information to work—and get your system up and running!

This chapter tells you how to connect all the various pieces and parts of your computer system. In most cases, it's as simple as plugging the right cables into the right connectors—and many manufacturers make it even easier by color-coding all the cables. In any case, as long as you can figure out which cable goes where, you'll be ready to start computing in no time.

Before You Get Started

It's important to prepare the space where you'll be putting your new PC. Obviously, the space has to be big enough to hold all the components—though you don't have to keep all the components together. You can, for example, spread out your left and right speakers, place your subwoofer on the floor, and separate the printer from the system unit. Just don't put anything so far away you can't plug it in!

You also should consider the ergonomics of your setup. You want your keyboard at or slightly below normal desktop height, and you want your monitor at or slightly below eye level. Make sure your chair is adjusted for a straight and firm sitting position with your feet flat on the floor, and then place all the pieces of your system in relation to that.

It's important, wherever you put your system, that it's in a well-ventilated location free of excess dust and smoke. (The moving parts in your computer don't like dust and dirt or any other such contaminants that can muck up the way they work.) Because your computer generates heat when it operates, you must leave enough room around the system unit for the heat to dissipate. *Never* place your computer in a confined, poorly ventilated space; your PC can overheat and shut down if it isn't sufficiently ventilated.

For extra protection to your computer, connect the power cable on your system unit to a surge suppressor rather than directly into an electrical outlet. A *surge suppressor*—which looks like a power strip with multiple outlets—protects your PC from power-line surges that could damage its delicate internal parts. When a power surge temporarily *spikes* your line voltage (causes the voltage to momentarily increase above normal levels), a surge suppressor shuts down power to your system, acting like a circuit breaker or fuse.

When you unpack your PC, be sure you keep all the manuals, CD-ROMs, disks, and cables. Put the ones you don't use in a safe place, in case you need to reinstall any software or equipment at a later date.

Connecting the Cables

Now it's time to get connected. Position your system unit so you easily can access all the connections on the back, and carefully run the cables from each of the other components so that they're hanging loose at the rear of the system unit.

Before you connect *anything* to your system unit, make sure that it's turned off.

Now start connecting the cables, in the order shown in Table 5.1.

Table 5.1   Connecting Your System Components

Order	Connection	Looks Like
1.	Connect your mouse to the mouse connector.	
2.	Connect your keyboard to the keyboard connector.	
3.	Connect your video monitor to the video connector.	
4.	Connect your printer to the parallel connector. (This connector is sometimes labeled "printer" or "LPT1.")	
5.	Connect a cable from your telephone line to the "line in" connector on your modem or modem board. Connect a cable from the "line out" connector on your modem to your telephone.	
6.	Connect the phono jack from your speaker system to the "audio out" or "sound out" connector.	
7.	Connect any other devices to the appropriate USB, parallel, or serial connector.	
8.	Plug the power cable of your video monitor into a power outlet.	
9.	If your system includes powered speakers, plug them into a power outlet.	
10.	Plug any other powered external component into a power outlet.	
11.	Plug the power cable of your system unit into a power outlet.	

Make sure that every cable is *firmly* connected—both to the system unit and the specific piece of hardware. Loose cables can cause all sorts of weird problems, so be sure they're plugged in real good.

Turning It On and Setting It Up

Now that you have everything connected, sit back and rest for a minute.

Next up is the big step—turning it all on.

It's important that you turn things on in the proper order. Follow these steps:

1. Turn on your video monitor.

2. Turn on your speaker system.

3. Turn on any other system components that are connected to your system unit—such as your printer, scanner, external modem, and so on.

4. Turn on your system unit.

Note that your system unit is the *last* thing you turn on. That's because when it powers on, it has to sense the other components of your system—which it can do only if the other components are plugged in and turned on.

Powering On for the First Time

The first time you turn on your PC is a unique experience. A brand-new, out-of-the-box system will have to perform some basic configuration operations, which include asking you to input some key information.

This first-time startup operation differs from manufacturer to manufacturer, but typically includes some or all of the following steps:

- **Windows Product Activation**—You'll be asked to input the product code found on the back of your Windows installation CD (or someplace else in the documentation that came with your new PC). Your system then phones into the Microsoft mother ship, registers your system information, and unlocks Windows for you to use. (Many manufacturers "pre-activate" Windows at the factory, so you might not have to go through this process.)

- **Windows Registration**—A slightly different process from product activation, registration requires you to input your name and other personal information, along with the Windows product code. This information then is phoned into the Microsoft mother ship to register your copy of Windows with the company, for warranty purposes.

Windows registration is optional; product activation is mandatory.

■ **Windows configuration**—During this process Windows asks a series of questions about your location, the current time and date, and other essential information. You also might be asked to create a username and password.

■ **System configuration**—This is where Windows tries to figure out all the different components that are part of your system, such as your printer, scanner, and so on. Enter the appropriate information when prompted; if asked to insert a component's installation CD, do so.

Some computer manufacturers supplement these configuration operations with setup procedures of their own. It's impossible to describe all the different options that might be presented by all the different manufacturers, so watch the screen carefully and follow all the onscreen instructions.

After you have everything configured, Windows finally starts, and then *you* can start using your system.

Some installation procedures require your computer to be restarted. In most cases, this happens automatically; then the installation process resumes where it left off.

Powering On Normally

After everything is installed and configured, starting your computer is a much simpler affair. When you turn on your computer, you'll notice a series of text messages flash across your screen. These messages are there to let you know what's going on as your computer *boots up*.

Technical types call the procedure of starting up a computer *booting* or *booting up* the system. Restarting a system (turning it off and then back on) is called *rebooting*.

After a few seconds (during which your system unit beeps and whirrs a little bit), the Windows Welcome screen appears. All registered users are listed on this screen. Click your username or picture, enter your password (if necessary), and then press the Enter key or click the green right-arrow button. After you're past the Welcome screen, you're taken directly to the Windows desktop, and your system is ready to run.

If you have only a single user on your PC and that user doesn't have a password assigned, Windows moves past the Welcome screen with no action necessary on your part.

Configuring Windows

For most users, Windows is ready to run right out of the box. You might, however, want to tweak a few of the configuration settings. The most common settings to configure are discussed in Activity 66, "Change Your Desktop Background," and Activity 67, "Personalize the Way Windows Works." Turn to those activities to figure out what—if anything—you want to tweak.

Setting Up Additional Users

If you're using your personal computer at home, chances are you're not the only person using it; it's likely that you'll be sharing your PC to some degree with your spouse and kids. Fortunately, you can configure Windows so that different people using your computer signs on with their own custom settings—and access to their own personal files.

You should assign each user in your household his own password-protected *user account*. Anyone trying to access another user's account and files without the password will then be denied access.

There are three different types of user accounts you can establish on your computer—computer administrator, limited, and guest. You'll want to set yourself up as the computer administrator because only this account can make systemwide changes to your PC, install software, and access all the files on the system. Set up other household members with limited accounts; they'll be able to use the computer and access their own files but won't be able to install software or mess up the main settings. Any guests to your household, then, can sign on via the guest account.

There can be more than one administrator account per PC, so you might want to set up your spouse with an administrator account, too.

To set up a new account on your machine, be sure you're logged on via an administrator account and then follow these steps.

Only the computer administrator can add a new user to your system. Here's how it's done:

1. Click the Start button.
2. When the Start menu appears, select Control Panel.

3. From the Control Panel, select User Accounts.

4. When the User Accounts utility opens (see Figure 5.1), select Create a New Account.

FIGURE 5.1

Use the User Accounts utility to create and change user accounts.

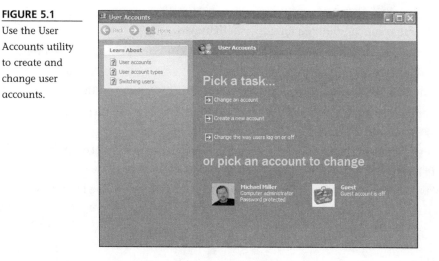

5. When the next screen appears, enter a name for the account and click Next.

6. On the next screen, check either the Computer Administrator or Limited option; then click the Create Account button.

Windows XP now creates the new account and randomly assigns a picture that will appear next to the username. You or the user can change this picture at any time by returning to the User Accounts utility, selecting the account, and then selecting the Change My Picture option.

By default, no password is assigned to the new account. If you want to assign a password, return to the User Accounts utility, select the account, and then select the Create a Password option.

If you create a password for your account, you better remember it. You won't be able to access Windows—or any of your applications and documents—if you forget the password!

Things to Remember

Here are the key points to remember when connecting and configuring your new computer:

- Most cables plug into only a specific connector—and on some new systems, they're color-coordinated for easier hookup.

- Make sure your cables are *firmly* connected; loose cables are the cause of many computer problems.

- Connect all the cables to your system unit *before* you turn on the power.

- Remember to turn on your printer and monitor before you turn on the system unit.

- If you have multiple users in your household, create a user account for each person—and assign each user his own password.

- You better remember your password—or you won't be able to log in to Windows!

TAKE YOUR SYSTEM FOR A SPIN

*n*ow that you have everything connected, configured, and powered up, it's time to take your new computer for a test drive. Just to get the feel of things, you know—open a few documents, print a few pages, that sort of thing.

That's what this chapter is about.

(If you want to take a spin around the Internet, turn to Chapter 10, "Surf the Web." This chapter is just about the computer hardware and software sitting in front of you right now.)

Playing a Game

Let's assume you followed the instructions in Chapter 5, "Set Up Your New Computer System," and that you have all the components connected and your system up and running. You should now be looking at an empty Windows desktop, similar to the one shown in Figure 6.1.

FIGURE 6.1

Start with the
Windows desktop.

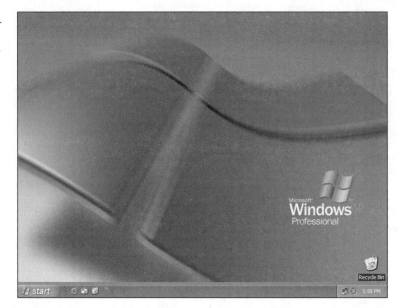

Let's start the tour of your computer system by having a little fun. Windows XP comes with a handful of computer games already installed. The game you're probably most familiar with is Solitaire, so let's launch Solitaire and play a game or two.

All you have to do is follow these steps:

1. Click the Start button, in the lower-left corner of the screen.

2. When the Start menu appears, as shown in Figure 6.2, click the All Programs button.

3. When the Programs menu appears, as shown in Figure 6.3, click the item labeled Games.

FIGURE 6.2
Click the Start
button to display
the Start menu.

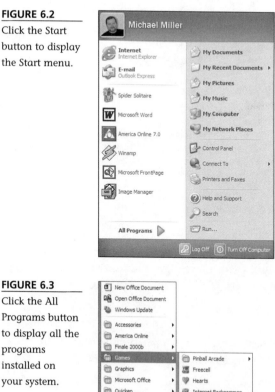

FIGURE 6.3
Click the All
Programs button
to display all the
programs
installed on
your system.

4. This displays a submenu listing all the games available in Windows. Move
   your cursor down to the one labeled Solitaire, and then click it.
5. Windows now launches the Solitaire program and displays it in a small window on your desktop, as shown in Figure 6.4.

FIGURE 6.4

Playing Solitaire
on your new
PC—window
original size.

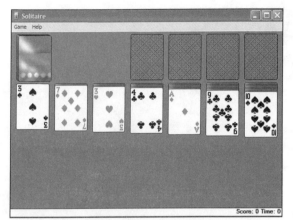

6. Before you start playing, resize the window. Move your cursor to the lower-right corner of the Solitaire window, and then drag the window border down and to the right. When the window is large enough for you, release the mouse button.

7. That was good, but maybe the game would be easier to play if it were displayed full-screen. Click the Maximize button (upper-right corner of the window, in the middle) to maximize the Solitaire window.

8. Now it's time to play. To move a card, grab it with your mouse and drag it onto another card. To turn over cards from the main deck, click the deck. To start a new game, pull down the Game menu and select Deal.

9. When you're done playing, close the Solitaire window by either clicking the window's Close button or pulling down the Game menu and selecting Exit.

Solitaire is also a good way to practice your mouse skills. You get to practice dragging and dropping (by moving cards from stack to stack) and double-clicking (to move cards to the top rows).

Launching a Program—and Printing and Saving a Document

That was fun. Now let's try something a little more productive—like creating a short note. We'll use Notepad, which is a basic word processor that's part of Microsoft Windows.

Follow these steps:

1. Click the Start button.

2. When the Start menu appears, click the All Programs button.

3. When the Programs menu appears, click the item labeled Accessories; then click the item labeled Notepad.

Note

Throughout the rest of this chapter and the book, this type of operation will be combined into a single action, as in "select All Programs, Accessories, Notepad."

4. The Notepad program now launches in its own window, as shown in Figure 6.5.

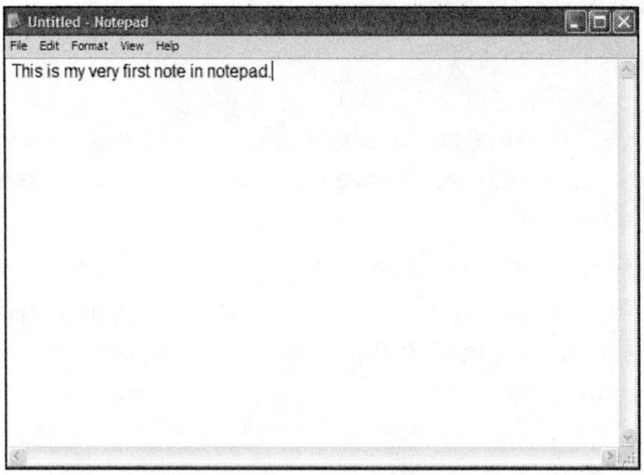

FIGURE 6.5

Writing a note with Notepad.

5. The blank white space in the middle of the screen is a new Notepad document—kind of like a blank sheet of paper. To write a note, position the cursor within the window and type the following text:

   `This is my very first note in Notepad.`

Printing Your Note

Now let's print a copy of your note. Make sure your printer is connected to your computer, and then follow these steps:

1. Pull down the File menu and select Print.

2. When the Print dialog box appears (shown in Figure 6.6), make sure the correct printer is selected in the Select Printer section; then click the Print button.

Saving Your File

Any document you create needs to be saved to your hard disk; otherwise, it won't
exist after you close the program. To save your current note as a new file, follow
these steps:

1. Pull down the File menu and select Save As.

2. When the Save As dialog box appears (shown in Figure 6.7), click the My
   Documents button on the left side of the dialog box; then type my new file
   in the File Name box.

3. Click the Save button.

What you've done here is saved your document as a file named my new file. You saved it in the My Documents folder, which is where Windows stores all new documents by default.

Closing the Program

To close Notepad, pull down the File menu and select Exit.

Viewing Your Documents

Now that you've created a document, let's take a look at it. If you remember, you saved the file in the My Documents folder, so open that folder and take a peek around.

Follow these steps:

1. Click the Start button.
2. When the Start menu appears, select My Documents.
3. When the My Documents folder opens (as shown in Figure 6.8), hover your cursor over the my new file icon.

FIGURE 6.8
Examining the contents of your My Documents folder.

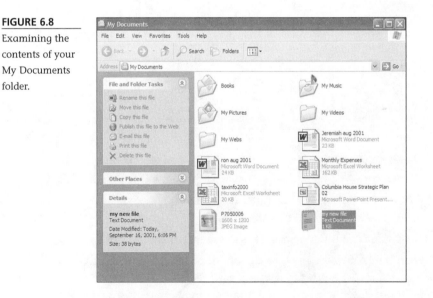

4. Information about your file is displayed in the Details panel of the activity pane, and basic tasks are displayed in the File and Folder Tasks panel.
5. To open this file for further editing, double-click the file icon. This launches Notepad with the my new file file already loaded and ready to edit.

Examining Your Hard Disk

Before we finish our quick spin around the desktop, let's examine the My Computer folder and see what's on your hard disk. Follow these steps:

1. Click the Start button.

2. When the Start menu appears, select My Computer.

3. When the My Computer folder opens (as shown in Figure 6.9), hover your cursor over your local hard disk drive—typically labeled drive C.

FIGURE 6.9

The contents of your My Computer folder.

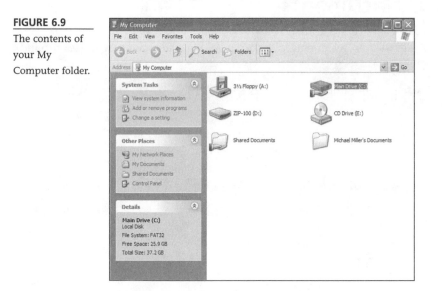

4. Information about your hard disk is displayed in the Details panel of the activity pane, and basic operations are displayed in the System Tasks panel.

5. Position your cursor over the hard disk icon, and click your *right* mouse button (in other words, *right-click* the icon).

6. This displays a pop-up menu. Select Properties from this menu.

7. When the Properties dialog box appears, select the General tab. As you can see in Figure 6.10, this tab displays a pie chart that represents how much of your hard disk is currently used and how much free space is available.

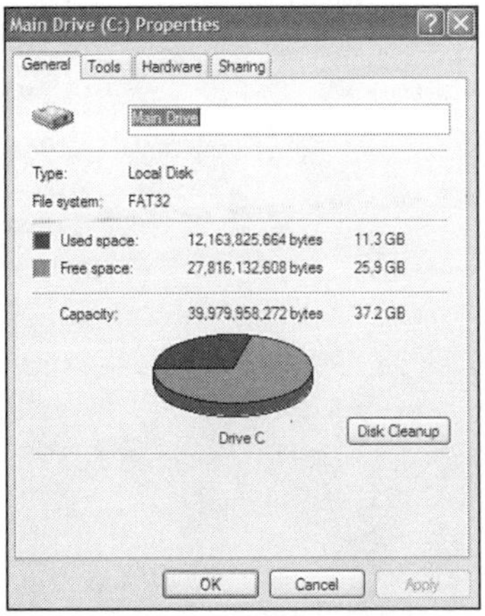

FIGURE 6.10

Viewing interesting information about your hard disk.

8. Click OK to close the dialog box.

Things to Remember

That was a fun little trip of discovery, wasn't it? Here are the key points to remember:

■ Just about everything you could want to launch or open is somewhere on the Start menu.

■ After you have a window open on your desktop, you can use your mouse to resize it—or you can maximize it to display full-screen.

■ When you want to print a file in a Windows application, pull down the File menu and select Print.

■ When you want to save a file in a Windows application, pull down the File menu and select Save As.

■ When you want to close a Windows application, pull down the File menu and select Exit—or just click the window's Close button.

ADD NEW HARDWARE

*I*f you just purchased a brand-new, right-out-of-the-box personal computer, it probably came equipped with all the components you could ever desire. However, at some point you might want to expand your system—by adding a second printer, or a scanner, or a PC camera, or something equally new and exciting.

Adding new hardware to your system is relatively easy, if you know what you're doing.

That's where this chapter comes in.

Understanding Ports

Everything that's hooked up to your PC is connected via some type of *port*. A port is simply an interface between your PC and another device—either internally (inside your PC's system unit) or externally (via a connector on the back of the system unit).

Internal ports are automatically assigned when you plug a new card into its slot inside the system unit. As for external ports, as you learned in Chapter 2, "Computer Hardware Basics," many types are available—each optimized to send and receive specific types of data. Different types of hardware connect via different types of ports.

The most common types of external ports include

- **Serial**—A *serial* port is an interface that enables communication one bit at a time, in one direction at a time. Serial ports are used to connect modems, printers, mice, and similar peripherals.

- **Parallel**—A *parallel* port is an interface that can handle communications going in two directions at once. Parallel ports typically are used to connect printers and are often referred to as *printer ports*.

- **USB**—A *Universal Serial Bus (USB)* port is a newer, faster, more intelligent type of serial port. USB devices can be added while the computer is still running, which you can't do with other types of connections. You can use USB ports to connect just about any type of device, including printers, scanners, modems, CD-ROM/DVD drives, hard drives, Zip drives, PC cameras, digital still cameras, keyboards, mice, and joysticks.

- **FireWire**—*FireWire* (also called IEEE 1394) is an interface that enables hot-pluggable, high-speed data transmission. It's typically used to connect digital video camcorders, external hard drives, and CD burners.

- **SCSI**—The *small computer system interface* (*SCSI*, pronounced "scuzzy") port is a high-speed parallel interface. You use SCSI ports to connect hard disks, CD-ROM and DVD drives, Zip drives, tape backups, and other mass storage media—as well as some scanners and printers.

- **PCMCIA**—The Personal Computer Memory Card International Association (PCMCIA) established the standard for the PC Card interface used on most of today's portable PCs. On a portable PC, the PC Card slot can be used to connect everything from modems, miniature hard disks, and additional system memory.

Most computer peripherals today connect through the USB port, although other ports are still used for specific applications.

Adding New External Hardware

Perhaps the easiest way to add new devices to your system is to add them via an external port; this way, you don't have to open your PC's case.

When attaching new devices to most ports, you should turn off your system first, connect the new device, and then restart your system. However, if you're connecting a device to a USB or FireWire port, you don't have to turn off your system to add new peripherals; the peripherals are *hot swappable*. That means you can just plug the new device into the port, and Windows will automatically recognize it in real-time.

Follow these steps to attach a new external device to your system:

1. Close Windows, and turn off your computer. (For all connections *except* USB and FireWire.)

2. Find an open port on the back of your system unit, and connect the new peripheral.

3. Restart your system. (For all connections *except* USB and FireWire.)

4. As Windows starts, it should recognize the new device and either install the proper drivers automatically or ask you to supply the device drivers (via CD-ROM or disk).

5. Windows installs the drivers and finishes the startup procedure. Your new device should now be operational.

 A *device driver* is a small software program that enables your PC to communicate with and control a specific device. Windows XP includes built-in device drivers for many popular peripherals. If Windows doesn't include a particular driver, you typically can find the driver on the peripheral's installation disk or on the peripheral manufacturer's Web site.

Adding New Internal Hardware

Adding an internal device—usually through a plug-in card—is slightly more difficult than adding an external device, primarily because you have to use a screwdriver and get "under the hood" of your system unit. Other than the extra screwing and plugging, however, the process is pretty much the same as with external devices.

Follow these steps to add a new card to your system:

1. Turn off your computer, but leave the power cable plugged in. (This protects your system against unwanted electrostatic discharge.)

2. Take the case off your system unit, per the manufacturer's instructions.

3. If the new card has switches or jumpers that need to be configured, do this before inserting the card into your system unit.

4. Find an open card slot inside the system unit, and insert the new card according to the manufacturer's instructions.

5. After the card is appropriately seated and screwed in, put the case back on the system unit and restart your system.

You probably want to see whether the new component configures properly and works fine before you close your system unit back up. For that reason, you might want to leave the case off until you're convinced everything is working okay and you don't need to do any more fiddling around inside your PC.

6. After Windows starts, it should recognize the new device and automatically install the appropriate driver.

Using the Add Hardware Wizard

In most cases, both your system and Windows will recognize the new card without any manual prompting. If, however, Windows doesn't recognize your new device, you can install it manually via the Add Hardware Wizard. To use the Add Hardware Wizard, follow these steps:

1. Click the Start button.

2. When the Start menu appears, select Control Panel.

3. When the Control Panel opens, select Printers and Other Hardware; then select the Add Hardware option from the See Also panel.

4. When the Add Hardware Wizard opens, click the Next button.

5. Windows now evaluates your system and displays a list of installed devices. To add a new device, select Add a New Hardware Device from the list, and click the Next button.

6. When the next screen appears, select Search For and Install the Hardware Automatically; then click Next.

7. Windows now looks for new plug-and-play hardware. If it can identify the new hardware, the wizard continues with the installation. If it can't find a new device, it tells you so. If this is your situation, click Next to begin a manual installation.

8. Select the type of device you want to install, and then click Next.

9. On the next screen, select the manufacturer and specific device. If you want to install the drivers that came with the device, click the Have Disk button. To use a built-in Windows driver, click the Next button.

10. When the necessary files have been loaded, follow the onscreen instructions to complete the installation.

Note, however, that in most cases new hardware is detected automatically by Windows, thus eliminating the need for this somewhat more complicated procedure.

Most Popular Peripherals

When it comes to adding stuff to your PC, what are the most popular peripherals? Here's a list of hardware you can add to or upgrade on your system:

- **Video card**—To display a higher-resolution picture on your computer monitor, provide smoother playback with visually demanding PC games, or add a second monitor for some high-end programming or development activities.

- **Monitor**—To upgrade to a larger viewing area or a flatter, more space-saving monitor.

- **Sound card**—To improve the audio capabilities of your systems; this is particularly important if you're listening to high-quality MP3 files, watching surround-sound DVD movies, playing PC games with so-called 3D sound, or mixing and recording your own digital audio.

- **Speakers**—To upgrade the quality of your computer's sound system. (Speaker systems with subwoofers are particularly popular.)

- **Keyboard**—To upgrade to a more ergonomic or wireless model.

- **Mouse**—To upgrade to a different type of controller (such as a trackball), a more fully featured unit, or a wireless model.

- **Joystick or other game controller**—To get better action with your favorite games.

- **Modem**—In case your PC doesn't have a state-of-the-art 56.6Kbps model, or if you're upgrading to broadband DSL or cable service.

- **CD-ROM drive**—In case your computer doesn't have one.

- **CD-R/RW drive**—To add recordable/rewritable capabilities to your system.

- **DVD**—To add DVD capability to your system.

Some new drives combine normal CD-ROM, CD-R/RW, and DVD capabilities into a single drive.

- **Hard drive**—To add more storage capacity to your system (can be either external or internal).
- **Removable drive (such as a Zip drive)**—To add more removable storage capacity to your system.
- **Scanner**—So you can scan photographs and documents into a digital format to store on your computer's hard drive.
- **Digital still camera**—So you can transfer images from your digital camera to your computer's hard drive.
- **PC camera**—So you can send real-time video to friends and family or create your own Webcam on the Internet.
- **Portable digital audio player**—So you can download MP3 audio files to listen to on the go.
- **Network card**—So you can connect your computer to other computers in a small home network.

Things to Remember

Here's what you need to know if you're adding new equipment to your computer system:

- If you connect a new component via the USB or FireWire ports, you don't have to turn off your PC first.
- Connecting through any other port requires you to turn off your computer, connect the new component, and then restart your system.
- When you're installing an internal card, make sure you turn off your PC before you open the system unit's case!
- In most cases, Windows automatically recognizes your new hardware and automatically installs all the necessary drivers.
- If Windows doesn't recognize the new piece of hardware, run the Add Hardware Wizard.

ADD NEW SOFTWARE

Even though most new computers come with a decent selection of software already installed, at some point in time you're going to want to add something new. Maybe you want a better spreadsheet or database program than what came with Microsoft Works. Maybe you want to add some educational software for the kids or a productivity program for yourself. Maybe you just want to play some new computer games.

Whatever type of software you're considering, installing it on your computer system is easy. In most cases software installation is so automatic you don't have to do much more than stick a disc in the CD-ROM drive and click a few onscreen buttons. Even when it isn't that automatic, Windows will walk you through the installation process step-by-step—and you'll be using your new software in no time!

Installing New Programs

Almost all software programs have their own built-in installation programs. Installing the software is as easy as running this built-in program.

Automatic Installation

If the program you're installing comes on a CD-ROM, all you have to do is insert the program's main or installation CD in your computer's CD-ROM drive. The program's installation program should then start automatically, and all you have to do is follow the onscreen instructions.

If the installation program *doesn't* start automatically, you have to launch it manually. To do this, follow these steps:

1. Click the Start button.

2. When the Start menu appears, click the Run icon.

3. When the Run dialog box appears, as shown in Figure 8.1, enter `x:\setup` in the Open box. (Replace *x* with the letter of your CD-ROM drive; if your CD-ROM is drive D, you'd enter `d:\setup`.)

4. Click OK.

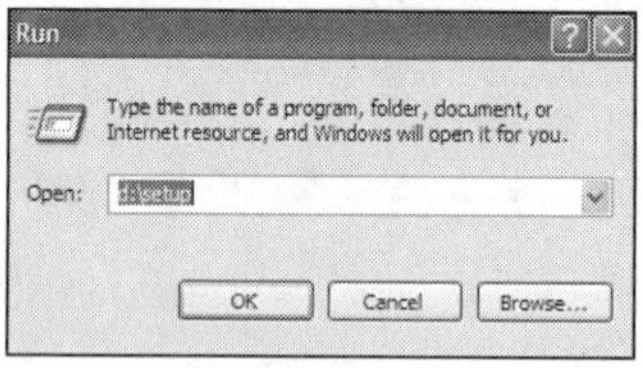

FIGURE 8.1

Enter the location and name of the installation program in the Run dialog box.

> **Run** [?] [x]
>
> Type the name of a program, folder, document, or Internet resource, and Windows will open it for you.
>
> Open: [x:\setup]
>
> [OK] [Cancel] [Browse...]

If this process doesn't work, try entering `install` instead of `setup`. (Some older programs have this different name for their installation programs.)

If the program you're installing comes on floppy disk instead of CD-ROM, you launch the setup program by inserting the first floppy disk into your PC's disk drive and then following the preceding instructions—with one small exception. Instead of entering the letter of your CD-ROM drive in the Run dialog box, just enter `a:\setup`. (The floppy disk drive is always drive A.)

Manual Installation

If the program you're installing doesn't have an automated setup program, you can install the program by using Windows's Add or Remove Programs utility.

Follow these steps:

1. Click the Start button.
2. When the Start menu appears, select Control Panel.
3. When the Control Panel opens, select Add or Remove Programs.
4. When the Add or Remove Programs dialog box appears, click the Add New Programs button.
5. When the next screen appears, as shown in Figure 8.2, click the CD or Floppy button.
6. Insert the program's installation disc or disk, and then follow the onscreen instructions to complete the installation.

FIGURE 8.2

Use the Add or Remove Programs utility to manually install a new program.

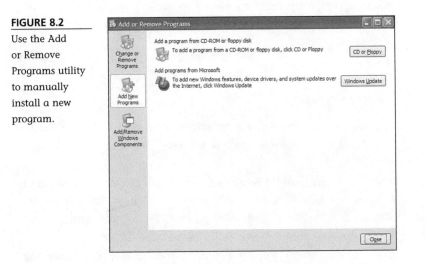

Installing Programs from the Internet

Nowadays, many software publishers make their products available via download from the Internet. Some users like this because they can get their new programs immediately. However, downloading software like this can take quite a long time, especially if you have a normal dial-up Internet connection, because the program files are so big.

Check the file size of the program before you download. If the size is larger than 2MB, you probably want to order the CD-ROM version of the program instead of trying to download it—unless you have a broadband cable or DSL Internet connection.

When you download a program from a major software publisher, the process is generally easy to follow. You probably have to read a page of do's and don'ts, agree to the publisher's licensing agreements, and then click a button to start the download. After you specify where (which folder on your hard disk) you want to save the downloaded file, the download begins.

When the download is complete, you should be notified via an onscreen dialog box. From this point, installing the program is almost identical to installing from CD or floppy disk—except that you have to enter the complete path to the installation file in the Run dialog box. (And even this is easy—just click the Browse button to find the folder where you saved the file.)

Unless you're downloading a program from a trusted download site, the downloaded file could contain a computer virus. See Activity 75, "Protect Your System from Viruses and Attacks," for more information.

Removing Old Programs

Chances are you got a *lot* of different software programs with your new PC. Chances are also that some of these are programs you'll never use—and are just taking up space on your hard disk.

For example, your new computer might have come with both Microsoft Money and Quicken installed—and you'll only use one of these. Or, there might have been multiple applications for accessing the Internet, from different ISPs. Again, you'll use only one of these, which means you can delete the ones you *don't* use.

If you're sure you won't be using a particular program, you can use Windows's Add or Remove Programs utility to remove the software from your hard disk. This frees up hard disk space for other programs you might install in the future.

To remove a software program from your PC, follow these steps:

1. Click the Start button.
2. When the Start menu appears, select Control Panel.

3. When the Control Panel opens, select Add or Remove Programs.

4. When the Add or Remove Programs dialog box appears, click the Change or Remove Programs button.

5. The next screen, shown in Figure 8.3, displays a list of all the currently installed programs on your PC. Select the program's name from the Currently Installed Programs list, and then click either the Change/Remove or Remove button.

FIGURE 8.3

Choose a program to remove from your system.

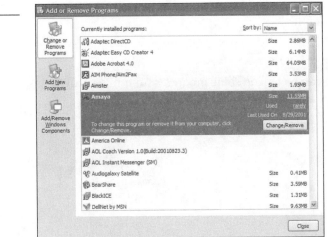

6. If prompted, confirm that you want to continue to uninstall the application. Answer any other prompts that appear onscreen; then the uninstall process will start.

Note

Some programs, such as Microsoft Word, might require you to insert the original installation disks or CD to perform the uninstall.

7. After the uninstall routine is complete, click the Close button to close the Add or Remove Programs utility.

Things to Remember

When you want to add a new software program to your computer, here's what you need to remember:

- Most programs come with their own built-in installation programs. The installation should start automatically when you insert the program's installation CD.

- If the program doesn't come with its own self-starting installation program, you can install the program by using Windows's Add or Remove Programs utility.

- The Add or Remove Programs utility can also be used to remove unused programs from your system.

- You also can download some programs from the Internet—just be careful about catching a computer virus!

GET CONNECTED TO THE INTERNET

One of the primary reasons must people buy computers is to connect to the Internet. But, before you can go online, you have to subscribe to Internet service through an Internet service provider (ISP) and then configure your computer for the new connection.

With Windows XP, setting up your computer for your particular Internet connection is fairly easy. After you have your ISP account established, all you have to do is tell Windows about your account and plug in a few cables, and then you're ready to start surfing!

Different Types of Connections

The first step in going online is establishing a connection between your computer and the Internet. Depending on what's available in your area, you can choose from two primary types of connections:

- **A dial-up connection**—This is over normal phone lines. The fastest dial-up connections transmit data at 56.6Kbps (kilobits per second). Most ISPs charge $20–$30 for normal dial-up service.

- **A broadband connection**—Has ultra-fast speeds, using DSL, digital cable, or satellite technology. With a broadband connection, data is transmitted at anywhere from 400Kbps to 2000Kbps. (Cable is typically the fastest connection, and satellite is the slowest; DSL is somewhere in between.) This means that a broadband connection is anywhere from 7 to 35 times faster than a typical dial-up connection. Most ISPs charge $40–$50 for broadband service.

Choosing an ISP

A pure ISP does nothing but connect you to the Internet and provide you with an e-mail address and mailbox—and, in some cases, storage space for your own personal Web page. You can probably find a few local ISPs operating in your city or town, or you can turn to one of a handful of national ISPs. These national ISPs offer dial-up numbers all across the U.S. (great for when you're traveling).

The two largest national ISPs are AT&T WorldNet (www.att.net) and EarthLink (www.earthlink.net). You can find a list of more than 10,000 national and local ISPs at The List (thelist.internet.com).

Commercial online services such as America Online (AOL) and the Microsoft Network (MSN) function like ISPs but also provide their own unique content and interfaces. If you sign up for AOL, for example, you use AOL's software to connect to the Internet and can also access AOL-specific content and services not available anywhere else.

Many new computer users prefer to connect to AOL because it's so easy to use. On the other hand, many experienced computer users don't like being forced to use AOL's software and prefer to go with a normal ISP.

Whichever type of service you choose, you'll pay about the same amount each month.

If you just purchased a new PC, chances are you'll find several desktop icons and menu items that link to specific online services—most likely MSN and AOL. If you don't have an ISP account yet, you can click these icons to get signed up automatically.

Before You Connect

When you sign up with an ISP, both you and the ISP have to provide certain information to each other. You provide your name, address, and credit card number, and your ISP provides a variety of semitechnical information, including

- The phone number to dial into
- Your username and password
- Your e-mail address
- The names of the ISP's incoming and outgoing mail servers
- Your e-mail account name and password
- The name of your ISP's Usenet news server

 For most ISPs, your username, e-mail account name, and the first half of your e-mail address will all be the same. It's also likely that you will be assigned a single password for both your initial login and e-mail access.

You'll need this information for when you configure Windows for your new Internet connection—which we'll discuss next.

Setting Up a Completely New Account

If you don't yet have an account with an ISP, you can use Windows XP's New Connection Wizard to find and subscribe to an ISP. All you have to do is follow these steps:

1. Click the Start button.
2. When the Start menu appears, select Connect to, Show All Connections.

 If this option doesn't appear on your Start menu, open My Computer, select Network Places, and then select View Network Connections.

3. When the Network Connections window opens, select Create a New Connection (from the Network Tasks panel).

4. When the New Connection Wizard dialog box appears, click the Next button.

5. When the Network Connection Type screen appears, as shown in Figure 9.1, check the Connect to the Internet option and then click the Next button.

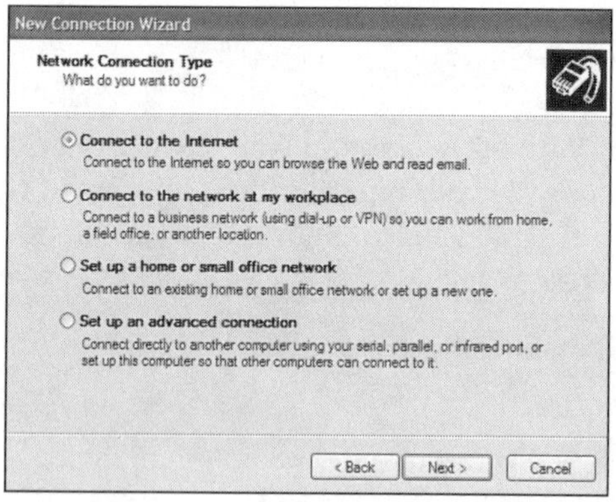

FIGURE 9.1

Setting up a new Internet connection.

6. When the Getting Ready screen appears, check the Choose from a List of Internet Providers option and then click the Next button.

7. When the next screen appears, check the Select from a List of Other ISPs option and then click the Finish button. (Alternatively, if you want to set up an account with MSN, you can click the Get Online with MSN option.)

8. Windows now opens the Online Services window. You can choose from one of the providers listed here or click the Refer Me to More Internet Service Providers icon.

9. If you choose to look for more ISPs, the wizard now dials into the Microsoft Internet Referral Service and downloads a list of available ISPs. Select an ISP from this list, and follow the onscreen instructions to sign up for a new account.

> The Microsoft Internet Referral Service isn't always accurate or complete and might not always find all the ISPs available in your area. If it can't find *any* ISPs, you'll need to obtain your own ISP subscription and then enter the information manually via the second option in the Internet Connection Wizard.

After you've selected an ISP, the wizard does everything else for you—including setting up a new connection within Windows.

Setting Up an Existing Account

If you already have an account set up with an ISP, you can create a new connection for that ISP by entering its settings manually. Just follow these steps:

1. Click the Start button.
2. When the Start menu appears, select Connect to, Show All Connections.
3. When the Network Connections window opens, select Create a New Connection (from the Network Tasks panel).
4. When the New Connection Wizard dialog box appears, click the Next button.
5. When the Network Connection Type screen appears, check the Connect to the Internet option and then click the Next button.
6. When the Getting Ready screen appears, check the Set Up My Connection Manually option; then click Next.

If your ISP provided you with an installation CD, check the Use the CD I Got from an ISP option and follow the onscreen instructions from there.

7. When the Internet Connection screen appears, select how you want to connect to the Internet. If you're connecting through a dial-up connection, check the Connect Using a Dial-Up Modem option. If you're connecting via a DSL or cable modem connection that requires manual login, check the Connect Using a Broadband Connection That Requires a Username and Password option. If you're connecting through an always-on LAN, cable modem, or DSL connection, check the Connect Using a Broadband Connection That Is Always On option. Click Next when you've made your selection.
8. Follow the onscreen instructions for your specific type of installation. You'll probably need to enter your username, password, and specific information about your ISP. The wizard now completes your connection.

Sharing an Internet Connection

If you have more than one PC in your home, you can connect them to share a single Internet connection. This is particularly useful if you have a high-speed broadband connection.

To do this, you must have your computers networked together. The main computer—the one connected to the Internet—is designated as the *host*, and all the others are called *clients*. Each of the client computers must have a network card installed, and the host must have *two* network cards installed—one to connect to your broadband modem and other to connect to your other computers.

> **Note** To learn how to connect your computers in a home network, see Activity 70, "Set Up a Home Network."

Configuring the Host PC

Assuming that you already have your computers connected in a network, setting up the network to share an Internet connection is relatively easy. Just follow these steps:

1. On the host computer, click the Start button.

2. When the Start menu appears, select Connect to, Show All Connections.

3. When the Network Connections window opens, right-click the icon for the Internet connection you want to share, and then select Properties from the pop-up menu.

4. When the Properties dialog box appears (as shown in Figure 9.2), select the Advanced tab and check the Allow Other Network Users to Connect Through This Computer's Internet Connection option.

5. Click OK.

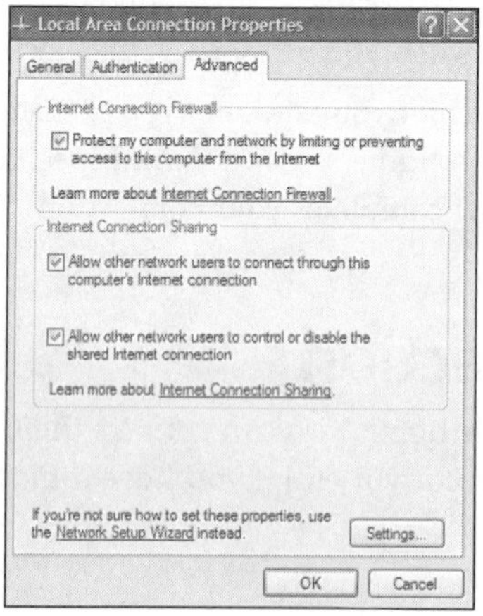

FIGURE 9.2

Sharing an Internet connection is as easy as checking a box.

When you configure Windows XP to share an Internet connection, it automatically activates the Internet Connection Firewall to protect your system from hackers and other outside attacks. To learn more about protecting your system, see Activity 75, "Protect Your System from Viruses and Attacks."

Configuring the Client PCs

Now you need to configure each of the client PCs to share this connection. If the computers are all running Windows XP, the process is fairly straightforward. Just follow these steps for each client PC:

1. Click the Start button.
2. When the Start menu appears, select Connect to, Show All Connections.
3. When the Network Connections window opens, select Create a New Connection (from the Network Tasks panel).
4. When the New Connection Wizard dialog box appears, click the Next button.
5. When the Network Connection Type screen appears, check the Connect to the Internet option and then click the Next button.
6. When the Getting Ready screen appears, check the Set Up My Connection Manually option; then click Next.
7. When the Internet Connection screen appears, check the Connect Using a Broadband Connection That Is Always On option; then click Next.
8. When the next screen appears, click the Finish button.

Configuring Non-Windows XP PCs

If any of your client computers are running older (pre-Windows XP) versions of Windows, you must run the Network Setup Wizard directly from your Windows XP installation CD.

To run the Network Setup Wizard on a pre-XP machine, follow these steps:

1. Insert the Windows XP installation CD in the PC's CD-ROM drive.
2. When the setup program launches, click the Perform Additional Tasks option.
3. When the next screen appears, select Set Up a Home or Small Office Network.
4. Follow the onscreen instructions to activate Internet Connection Sharing.

Connecting

After you've configured your PC for your ISP account, you're ready to get connected and start surfing.

How you initiate a connection differs a bit from ISP to ISP. Depending on how your ISP sets things up, you can use one or more of the following methods:

- If your ISP or online service installed its own connection software, you must launch that connection program and follow its instructions to make a connection. For example, America Online installs its own AOL software; launch this software, and then use it to connect to the Internet.

- You can probably connect to your ISP directly from Windows. Click the Start button to display the Start menu; then select Connect to and select your ISP from the list of available connections.

- If you have an always-on broadband connection, you don't need to do anything—you're already connected! Just launch Internet Explorer, Outlook Express, or any other Internet program, and you're ready to surf.

Things to Remember

When you're configuring your new PC system to connect to the Internet, remember these important points:

- You connect to the Internet through an Internet service provider; you need to set up an account with an ISP before you can connect.

- Most ISPs offer either dial-up or broadband connections. Broadband is faster but costs about twice as much per month.

- After you have an account with an ISP, you need to run the New Connection Wizard to configure Windows for your new account.

- If you have more than one computer at home, you can connect them in a network and share a single Internet connection.

SURF THE WEB

*A*fter you're signed up with an ISP and connected to the Internet, it's time to get surfing! The World Wide Web is a particular part of the Internet with all sorts of cool content and useful services, and you surf the Web with a piece of software called a *Web browser*.

The most popular Web browser today is Microsoft's Internet Explorer, and you probably have a copy of it already installed on your new PC. This chapter shows you how to use Internet Explorer and then takes you on a quick trip around the Web—just enough to get your online feet wet!

Using Internet Explorer

Internet Explorer (IE) is very easy to use. To launch IE, follow these steps:

1. Click the Start button.

2. When the Start menu appears, select Internet (at the very upper-left part of the menu).

Note Other popular Web browsers include Netscape, MSN Explorer, and the browser built in to America Online. They all look and operate very similarly to Internet Explorer.

Figure 10.1 shows the various parts of the IE program, and Table 10.1 tells you what each of the buttons on the toolbar does.

FIGURE 10.1

Microsoft's Internet Explorer Web browser.

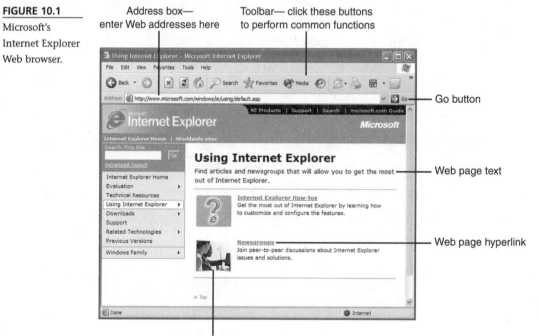

Address box—enter Web addresses here

Toolbar— click these buttons to perform common functions

Go button

Web page text

Web page hyperlink

Web page graphic

Table 10.1   Internet Explorer Toolbar Buttons

	Button	Operation
	Back	Return to the previously viewed page
	Forward	View the next page
	Stop	Stop loading the current page
	Refresh	Reload the current page
	Home	Return to your designated start page
	Search	Display the Search pane and initiate a Web search
	Favorites	Display the Favorites pane
	Media	Display the Media pane—for listening to Internet audio and watching online videos
	History	Display the History pane to see a list of recently viewed pages
	Mail	Launch your e-mail program
	Print	Print the current page
	Edit	Launch your HTML Web page editor

Basic Web Surfing

Internet Explorer enables you to quickly and easily browse the World Wide Web—just by clicking your mouse. Here's a step-by-step tour of IE's basic functions:

1. When you first launch Internet Explorer, it loads your predefined home page.

To change Internet Explorer's home page, drag a page's icon from Internet Explorer's Address box onto the Home button on the toolbar.

2. Enter a new Web address in the Address box, and press Enter (or click the Go button). Internet Explorer loads the new page.

3. Click any link on the current Web page. Internet Explorer loads the new page.

4. To return to the previous page, click the Back button (or press the Backspace key on your keyboard). If you've backed up several pages and want to return to the page you were on last, click the Forward button.

5. To return to your start page, click the Home button.

Note If you need a quick refresher course on Web pages, addresses, and hyperlinks, see Chapter 4, "Internet and Home Networking Basics."

Advanced Operations

Before we take our first cruise on the Web, let's examine a few advanced operations in Internet Explorer that can make your online life a lot easier.

Saving Your Favorite Pages

When you find a Web page you like, you can add it to a list of Favorites within Internet Explorer. This way you can easily access any of your favorite sites just by selecting them from the list.

To add a page to your Favorites list:

1. Go to the page you want to add to your Favorites list.

2. Pull down the Favorites menu, and select Add to Favorites.

3. When the Add Favorite dialog box appears, confirm the page's Name and then click the Create In button to extend the dialog box.

4. Select the folder where you want to place this link, and then click OK.

To view a page in your Favorites list:

1. Click the Favorites button. The browser window will automatically split into two panes, with your favorites displayed in the left pane (see Figure 10.2).

2. Click any folder in the Favorites pane to display the contents of that folder.

3. Click a favorite page, and that page is displayed in the right pane.

4. Click the Favorites button again to hide the Favorites pane.

FIGURE 10.2

Click the
Favorites button
to display the
Favorites pane.

Favorites
Add... Organize...
Hotmail
IBJ Home Page
Kiss.com
Molehill Group
Molehillgroup WebMail
My VZW
My-Cast
PayPal
RoadRunner Member Services
Speed Test
Web Site Source
Windows Media
ZDNNews
Vacation2000
Vacation2001
RealPlayer
Media
RealPlayer Home Page

Revisiting History

Internet Explorer has two ways of keeping track of Web pages you've visited, so you
can easily revisit them without having to reenter the Web page address.

To revisit one of the last half-dozen or so pages viewed in your current session,
click the down-arrow on the Back button. This drops down a menu containing the
last nine pages you've visited. Highlight any page on this menu to jump directly
to that page.

To revisit pages you've viewed in the past several days, you use IE's History pane.
Just follow these steps:

1. Click the History button. The browser window automatically splits into two
   panes, with your history for the past several days displayed in the left pane.

2. Your history is organized into folders for each of the past several days. Click
   any folder in the History pane to display the sites you visited that day.

3. Each site you visited on a particular day has its own subfolder. Click a subfolder to display the pages you visited within that particular site.

4. Click a specific page to display that page in the right pane.

5. Click the History button again to hide the History pane.

Tip

To sort the sites in the History pane by site, by most visited, or by most visited today, pull
down the View menu within the pane and make a new selection.

Printing

Printing a Web page is easy—just click the Print button. If you want to see a preview of the page before it prints, pull down the File menu and select Print Preview.

Let's Go Surfin'!

Okay, now you're ready to launch Internet Explorer and head out to the World Wide Web. Follow these step-by-step instructions for a quick cruise around the Web—just to see what's out there:

1. Connect to your ISP, and then launch Internet Explorer. IE launches and opens its default home page. (Typically, this is some page on Microsoft's Web site.)

2. Let's find out what's happening out in the real world by heading over to one of the most popular news sites. Enter `www.cnn.com` into the Address box, and then click the Go button. This takes you to the CNN.com site, shown in Figure 10.3. Click any headline to read the complete story.

FIGURE 10.3

Get informed at CNN.com.

3. After you've had your fill of news, it's time for a few laughs. Enter `www.comics.com` into the Address box; then click the Go button. This takes you to the Comics.com Web site, shown in Figure 10.4. Pull down one of the lists or click one of the links to view a particular comic.

FIGURE 10.4

Have some
laughs at
Comics.com.

4. Now, let's do a little searching at Google, one of the Web's premier search
   sites. Enter `www.google.com` in the Address box, and then click the Go button.
   (Figure 10.5 shows Google's home page.) Ready to search? Enter `molehill`
   `group` in the Google search box, and then click the Google Search button.

FIGURE 10.5

Search for other
Web sites at
Google.

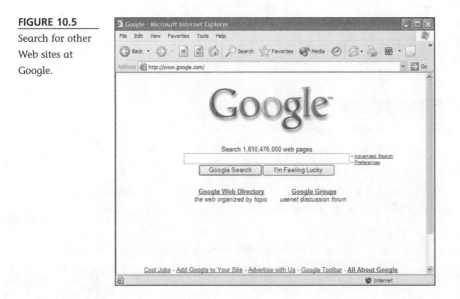

5. When the search results page appears, find the listing for The Molehill Group and click the link. You're now taken to *my* Web site, The Molehill Group (shown in Figure 10.6). Click the About button (in the left column) to learn more about me.

FIGURE 10.6

Learn more about the author at the Molehill Group Web site.

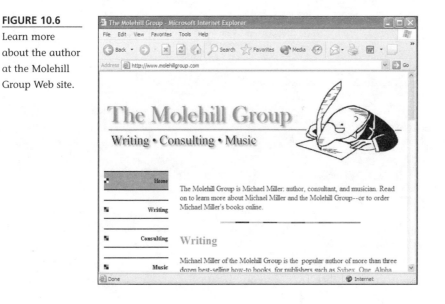

That's your quick surfing tour. You can keep surfing from here, or close Internet Explorer and disconnect from the Internet. As you can see, surfing the Web is as easy as clicking your mouse!

Things to Remember

Here are the key things to remember about surfing the Web:

- You surf the Web with a program called a Web browser; Internet Explorer is probably the browser installed on your new PC.

- You can go to a particular Web page by entering the page's address in the Address box and then clicking the Go button.

- Click a hyperlink on a Web page to jump to the linked page.

- Use IE's Favorites list to store your favorite Web pages for easy retrieval.

- Use the Back button or the History pane to revisit recently viewed Web pages.

PART III

DO IT NOW: COMMUNICATING ON PAPER

WRITE A LETTER

What You Need
- Microsoft Word
- Basic computer system

Goal
Create a new document, perform basic editing functions, and save the file.

Opening Microsoft Word

Microsoft Word is the full-featured word processing program included with both Microsoft Works Suite and Microsoft Office. You can use Word for all your writing needs—from basic letters to fancy newsletters, and everything in between.

You start Word either from the Windows Start menu or from the Works Task Launcher. When Word launches, a blank document appears in the Word workspace.

Creating a New Document

Any new Word document you create is based on what Word calls a *template*. A template combines selected styles and document settings—and, in some cases, prewritten text or calculated fields—to create the building blocks for a specific type of document. Use templates to give yourself a head start on specific types of documents.

To create a new Word document based on a specific template, pull down Word's File menu and select New. You can then select from a variety of prepared templates, as shown in Figure A1.1.

FIGURE A1.1

Select a tab to select templates of a specific type.

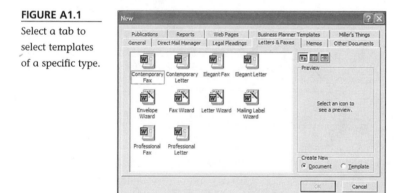

Entering Text

You enter text in a Word document at the *insertion point*, which appears onscreen as a blinking cursor. When you start typing on your keyboard, the new text is added at the insertion point.

You move the insertion point with your mouse by clicking on a new position in your text. You move the insertion point with your keyboard by using your keyboard's arrow keys.

Editing Text

After you've entered your text, it's time to edit. With Word you can delete, cut, copy, and paste text—or graphics—to and from anywhere in your document, or between documents.

Before you can edit text, though, you have to *select* the text to edit. The easiest way to select text is with your mouse: Just hold down your mouse button and drag the cursor over the text you want to select. You also can select text using your keyboard. In general, you use the Shift key—in combination with other keys—to highlight blocks of text. For example, Shift+Left Arrow selects one character to the left; Shift+End selects all text to the end of the current line.

Any text you select appears as white text against a black highlight. After you've selected a block of text, you can then edit it in a number of ways, as detailed in Table A1.1.

Table A1.1   Word Editing Operations

Operation	Key Function	Menu Function
Delete	Del	Pull down the Edit menu and select Clear.
Copy	Ctrl+Insert	Pull down the Edit menu and select Copy.
Cut	Shift+Del or Ctrl+X	Pull down the Edit menu and select Cut.
Paste	Shift+Ins	Pull entered down the Edit menu and select Paste.

Formatting Text

After your text is entered and edited, you can use Word's numerous formatting options to add some pizzazz to your document. It's easiest to edit text when you're working in Print Layout view because this displays your document as it will look when printed. To switch to this view, pull down the View menu and select Print Layout.

Formatting text is easy—and most achievable from Word's Formatting toolbar. This toolbar, located at the top of the screen, includes buttons for bold, italic, and underline, as well as font, font size, and font color. To format a block of text, highlight the text and then click the desired format button.

More text formatting options are available in the Font dialog box. To display this dialog box, pull down the Format menu and select Font. From here, you can perform both basic formatting (font, font style, font color, and so on) and advanced formatting (strikethrough, superscript, subscript, shadow, outline, emboss, engrave, character spacing, and text animation). Just select the formatting you want and click OK.

Saving the Document

Every document you make—that you want to keep—must be saved to a file.

The first time you save a file, you have to specify a filename and location. Do this by pulling down the File menu and selecting Save As.

When you make additional changes to a document, you must save those changes. Fortunately, after you've saved a file once, you don't need to go through the whole Save As routine again. To "fast save" an existing file, all you have to do is click the Save button on Word's Standard toolbar or pull down the File menu and select Save.

Activity 2

PRINT A LETTER

What You Need
- Microsoft Word
- Printer
- Basic computer system

Goal

Create a permanent hard-copy version of a word processing document.

Previewing Before You Print

When you've finished editing your document, you can instruct Word to send a copy to your printer. It's a good idea, however, to preview the printed document onscreen before you print it—so you can make any last-minute changes without wasting a lot of paper.

To view your document with Word's Print Preview, click the Print Preview button on Word's Standard toolbar (or pull down the File menu and select Print Preview).

As you can see in Figure A2.1, the to-be-printed document appears onscreen with each page of the document presented as a small thumbnail. To zoom in or out of the preview document, click the Magnifier button and then click the magnifier cursor anywhere on your document. When you're done previewing your document, click the Close button.

FIGURE A2.1

Use Print Preview to see how your document will print.

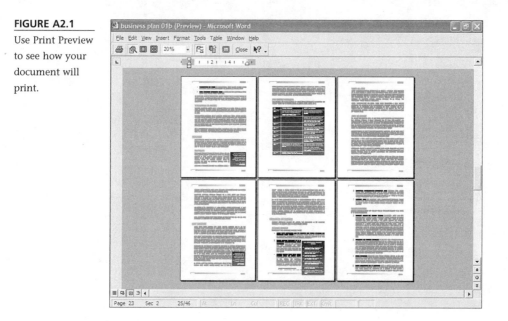

Basic Printing

The fastest way toprint a document is with Word's fast print option. You activate a fast print by clicking the Print button on Word's Standard toolbar.

When you do a fast print of your document, you send your document directly to your default printer. This bypasses the Print dialog box (discussed next) and all other configuration options.

Changing Print Options

Sometimes fast printing isn't the best way to print. For example, you might want to print multiple copies, or print to a different (nondefault) printer. For these and similar situations, you need to use Word's Print dialog box.

You open the Print dialog box, shown in Figure A2.2, by pulling down the File menu and selecting Print.

FIGURE A2.2

Print your document—with options.

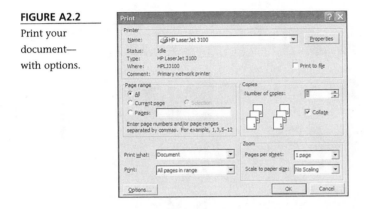

After you have the Print dialog box displayed, you can choose any one of a number of options specific to this particular print job. After you've made your choices, click the OK button to start printing.

WRITE AND PRINT A FANCY REPORT

What You Need
- Microsoft Word
- Printer
- Basic computer system

Goal
Create a complex document, complete with multiple sections and sophisticated formatting.

Formatting Paragraphs

When you're creating a complex document, you need to format more than just a few words here and there. You need to format complete paragraphs, which you do from Word's Paragraph dialog box.

You open the Paragraph dialog box by positioning your cursor within a paragraph and then pulling down the Format menu and selecting Paragraph. From here, you can precisely adjust how the entire paragraph appears, including indentation, line spacing, and widow/orphan control.

Using Word Styles

If you have you're a preferred paragraph formatting you use over and over and over, you don't have to format each paragraph individually. Instead, you can assign all your formatting to a paragraph *style* and then assign that style to specific paragraphs throughout your document. Most templates come with a selection of predesigned styles; you can modify these built-in styles or create your own custom styles.

Styles include formatting for fonts, paragraphs, tabs, borders, numbering, and more. To apply a style to a paragraph, position the insertion point anywhere in the paragraph and then pull down the Style list (in the Formatting toolbar) and select a style.

To modify a style, pull down the Format menu and select Style. When the Style dialog box appears, select the style you want to edit and click the Modify button. You can then select which style property you want to edit and then make and apply your changes.

If you click the New button in the Style dialog box, you create a new style based on the current style. Make whatever changes you want, and then save the new style under a new name.

Assigning Headings

When you're creating a long document, you probably want to separate sections of your document with headings. Headings appear as larger, bolder text, like mini-headlines.

Word includes several built-in heading styles—Heading 1, Heading 2, Heading 3, and Heading 4. Assign these styles to your document's headings, as appropriate. (And if you don't like the way they look, edit the styles to your liking—as described previously.)

Forcing Page Breaks

After you assign headings to your document, you might want to have major headings start at the top of a page (rather than fall in the middle). To force a manual page break, position the cursor at the front of the line and then press Ctrl+Enter.

An even better solution is to format the heading style to always start at the top of a page. Go to the Styles dialog box, choose to format the Paragraph element, select the Line and Page Breaks tab, and then select the Page Break Before option. This causes any text formatted with that style to always start at the top of a new page.

Using Multiple Columns

Some sophisticated documents, such as newsletters, look better when the text is displayed in multiple columns. To create multiple columns in your document, pull down the Format menu and select Columns. You can then select the number of columns to display and the size of each column.

Working with an Outline

If you have a really long document, you might find it easier to work with the various sections in the form of an outline. For this purpose, Word lets you view your document in Outline view, as shown in Figure A3.1. Just pull down the View menu and select Outline.

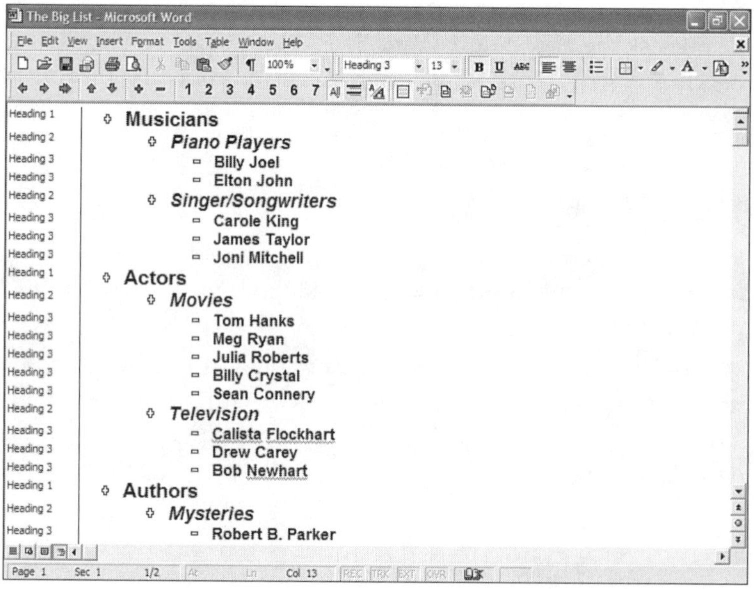

FIGURE A3.1

Use Outline view to reorganize the sections of your document.

When you're in Outline view, Word displays your headings as different outline levels. Text formatted with the Heading 1 style appears as Level 1 headings in your outline, text formatted as Heading 2 appears as Level 2 headings, and so on.

To make your outline easier to work with, you can select how many levels of headings are displayed. (Just click the appropriate number button on the Outline toolbar.) You also can choose to expand or contract various sections of the outline by clicking the plus and minus icons to the side of each Level text in your outline.

Outline view makes rearranging sections of your document extremely easy. When you're in Outline view, you can move an entire section from one place to another by selecting the Level heading and then clicking the up and down arrow buttons. (You also can drag sections from one position to another within the outline.)

Printing Your Document

After your document is properly organized, edited, and formatted, print a copy by clicking the Print button on Word's Standard toolbar.

Activity **4**

INSERT A PICTURE

WHAT YOU NEED

- Picture file
- Microsoft Word
- Basic computer system

Goal

Create a visually interesting document, complete with embedded graphics.

Inserting a Picture from the Clip Art Gallery

Although memos and letters might look fine if they contain nothing but text, other types of documents—newsletters, reports, and so on—can be jazzed up with pictures and other graphic elements. (Figure A4.1 shows a document with a graphic inserted.)

FIGURE A4.1

Jazz up your document by inserting a graphics file.

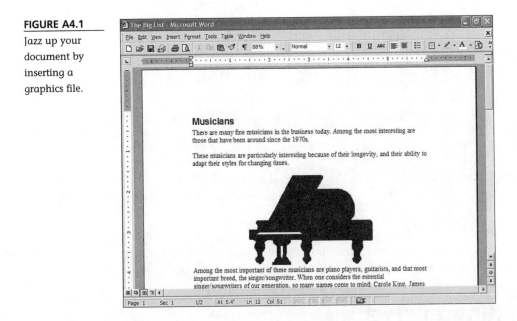

The easiest way to add a graphic to your document is to use Word's built-in Clip Art Gallery. The Clip Art Gallery is a collection of ready-to-use illustrations and photos, organized by topic, that can be pasted directly into your Word documents.

To insert a piece of clip art, position your cursor where you want the picture to appear. Then, pull down the Insert menu and select Picture, Clip Art.

This displays the Clip Art Gallery, shown in Figure A4.2. You can browse the artwork by category and then select the graphic you want for your document. When you double-click a graphic, it's automatically inserted into your document.

FIGURE A4.2

Use Word's Clip Art Gallery to add graphics to your document.

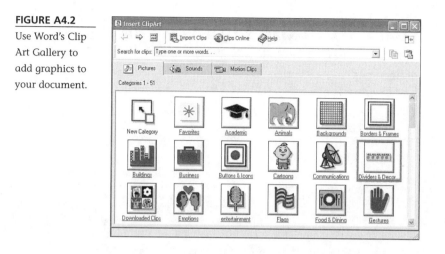

Inserting Other Types of Picture Files

You're not limited to using graphics from the Clip Art Gallery. Word lets you insert any type of graphics file into your document—including GIF, JPG, BMP, TIF, and other popular graphic formats.

To insert a graphics file, pull down the Insert menu and select Picture, From File. When the Insert Picture dialog box appears, navigate to and select the picture you want to insert. Click the Insert button to insert that picture.

Formatting the Picture

After you've inserted a picture in your document, you might need to format it for best appearance.

To format the picture itself, double-click the picture. This displays the Format Picture dialog box, which lets you format colors, line, size, layout, brightness, contrast, and other settings.

To move your picture to another position in your document, use your mouse to drag it to its new position. You also can resize the graphic by clicking the picture and then dragging a selection handle to resize that side or corner of the graphic.

To change the way text flows around the graphic, double-click the graphic to display the Format Picture dialog box and then select the Layout tab. You can choose to display the picture inline with the text, wrap around the text as a square, flow in front of the text, or display behind the text.

CREATE A TABLE

What You Need
- Microsoft Word
- Basic computer system

Goal
Insert a formatted table to display data in rows and columns.

Inserting a Basic Table

If you have a lot of rows and columns of text or numbers in your document, you might want to display this data in a table. A table is a great way to display this type of data in an easy-to-read format.

To insert a table, position the insertion point where you want the table to appear. Then, pull down the Table button and select Insert, Table. When the Insert Table dialog box appears, select the number of rows and columns you want for your table and then click OK.

 When you're planning the rows and columns of your table, remember to add a row for labels.

Your table will now appear on your desktop, like the one in Figure A5.1, ready for data input or formatting.

FIGURE A5.1

Use a table to display data in rows and columns.

	2000	2001	2002
Cows	200	250	300
Pigs	300	350	325
Chickens	400	500	600
Aardvarks	20	22	25
Geckos	1000	1250	1500
Trout	9	10	11
Lawyers	50	60	75
Lions	6	12	15
Tigers	3	3	5
Bears	2	4	6
Rabbits	2	50	1000
Lice	5000	7500	9800

Entering Data

To enter data in your table, position the cursor in the upper-left cell; then start typing. Move from cell to cell by pressing the Tab key.

Adding and Deleting Rows and Columns

To add a new row or column to your table, begin by positioning the cursor where you want the new row or column to appear. Then, pull down the Table menu, select Insert, and choose what you want to insert.

To delete a row or column, position your cursor in the row or column you want to delete. Then, pull down the Table menu, select Delete, and choose what you want to delete.

Resizing Table Columns

Sometimes you might need to resize a column to hold all the data you want to add. To resize a column, position your cursor on any column divider and drag it left or right.

You also can automatically resize a column to fit the widest piece of data in the column. Just double-click the appropriate column divider, and that column will be automatically resized.

Formatting the Table

Word's default table is a little plain. To add visual appeal to your table, reformat it with one of Word's predefined table formats. Just pull down the Table menu and select Table AutoFormat. When the Table AutoFormat dialog box appears, select from the list of formats, select elements of the style you want to apply, and then click OK.

You also can modify individual elements separately. For example, to modify the borders in your table, pull down the Format menu and select Borders and Shading. You can then select from a variety of border formats, including line thickness and color.

This same dialog box also lets you apply background shading to the cells in your table. Just select the Shading tab and then select which color you want to use for the background fill.

To configure the table's alignment, pull down the Table menu and select Table Properties. When the Table Properties dialog box appears, select the Table tab and then select the appropriate alignment and text wrapping options.

Formatting Individual Cells

To format the background of an individual cell, pull down the Format menu and select Borders and Shading. Select the Shading tab, and then pull down the Apply To list and select Cell. The fill color you select will be applied to the currently selected cell in your table.

Sorting the Table

After you've entered data into your table, you can sort that data by a variety of criteria. Just select the rows and columns you want to sort; then pull down the Table menu and select Sort. When the Sort dialog box appears, pull down the first Sort By list and select which column you want to sort by. If you want to do a subsort on a second or third column, make those selections and then click the OK button.

Merging Cells

To improve the appearance of your table, you might want to merge two or more adjacent cells, especially in the table's head.

To merge two or more cells, select the cells, pull down the Table menu, and select Merge Cells. To undo a merge, select the merged cell, pull down the Table menu, and then select Split Cells.

PART IV

DO IT NOW: COMMUNICATING ONLINE

Activity **6**

SEND AND RECEIVE E-MAIL

WHAT YOU NEED

- Outlook Express
- Internet connection
- Basic computer system

Goal

Create an e-mail message and send it to yourself.

Composing and Sending a New Message

E-mail is the modern way to communicate with friends, family, and colleagues. An e-mail message is like a regular letter, except that it's composed electronically and delivered almost immediately via the Internet.

There are several programs you can use to send and receive e-mail messages. The e-mail program installed on most new PCs is called Outlook Express, and it's very easy to learn and use.

The Outlook Express Window

The basic Outlook Express window is divided into three panes, as shown in Figure A6.1. The pane on the left is called the Folder List, and it's where you access your Inbox and other message folders. The top pane is the Message pane, and it lists all the messages stored in the selected folder. The bottom pane is the Preview pane, and it displays the contents of the selected message.

FIGURE A6.1

Use Outlook Express to send and receive e-mail.

Composing a Message

To create a new e-mail message, click the New Mail button on the Outlook Express toolbar. This launches a New Message window, similar to the one shown in Figure A6.2.

FIGURE A6.2

Use the New
Message window
to compose a
new e-mail
message.

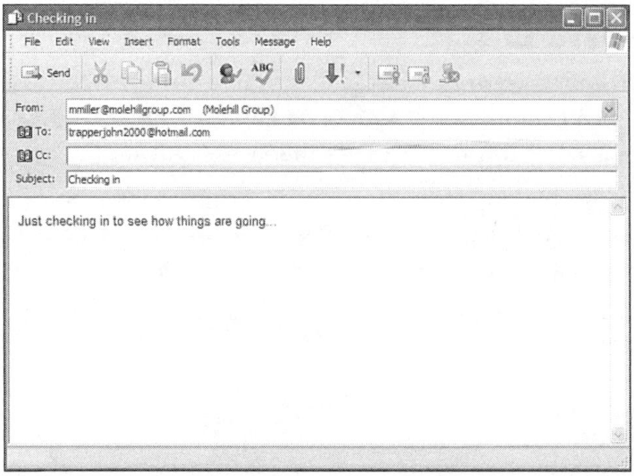

Enter the e-mail address of the recipient(s) in the To field and the address of anyone you want to receive a carbon copy in the Cc box. Separate multiple addresses with a semicolon (;), like this: `mmiller@molehillgroup.com;gjetson@sprockets.com`.

For the purposes of this activity, enter your own e-mail address in the To field.

After you've entered your address, move your cursor to the main message area and type your message. When your message is complete, send it to the Outbox by clicking the Send button.

Tip

You can also use e-mail to send computer files to other users. See Activity 64, "Send a File via E-mail," for more details.

Sending the Message

Now you need tosend the message from your Outbox over the Internet to the intended recipient (you!). You do this by clicking the Send/Recv button on the Outlook Express toolbar.

Reading New Messages

When you receive new e-mail messages, they're stored in the Outlook Express Inbox. To display all new messages, select the Inbox icon from the Folders list. All waiting messages now appear in the Message pane.

To read a specific message, select its header in the Message pane. The contents of that message are displayed in the Preview pane. (You also can double-click a message header to display it in a separate window.)

Replying to a Message

To reply to an e-mail message, select the message header in the Message pane and then click the Reply button on the Outlook Express toolbar. This opens a Re: window, which is just like a New Message window except with the text from the original message "quoted" in the text area.

The e-mail address of the recipient (the person who sent the original message) is preentered in the To field. Enter your reply text and click the Send button to execute your reply.

LIST YOUR FRIENDS IN AN ADDRESS BOOK

WHAT YOU NEED

- Windows Address Book
- Outlook Express
- Internet connection
- Basic computer system

Goal

Add a new contact to your Address Book, and then send an e-mail to that contact.

Opening the Address Book

Windows includes a contact manager application, called *Address Book*, that you can use to store information about your friends, family, and business associates. You can store individual names, addresses, phone numbers, e-mail addresses, birthdays, and other important information and then import your contacts into Outlook Express (to send e-mail), Microsoft Works Calendar (to remind you of birthdays), and Microsoft Word (to personalize letters and address envelopes and labels).

Address Book is incorporated into both Outlook Express and Microsoft Works Suite. You can launch Address Book from within Outlook Express, from the Works Task Launcher, or from the Windows Start menu.

Adding New Contacts

To add a new contact to your Address Book, click the New button on the Address Book toolbar and then select New Contact.

When the Properties dialog box appears, as shown in Figure A7.1, select the Name tab. Enter the contact's name (first, middle, and last), title, display name (how you want to list the name in the Address Book), nickname, and e-mail address.

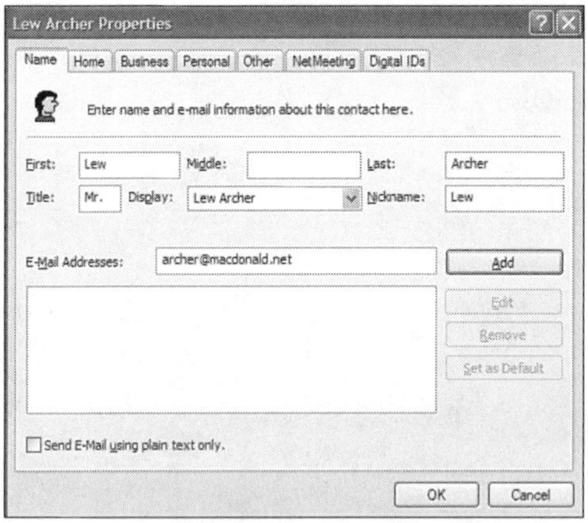

FIGURE A7.1

Entering information for a new Address Book contact.

The other tabs let you enter specific types of information about your contact:

- **Home**—To enter the contact's home address and phone number, select this tab.

- **Business**—To enter the contact's business address, phone, fax, and other work-related information, select this tab.

- **Personal**—To enter personal information about the contact (birthday, anniversary, names of spouse and children, and so on), select this tab.
- **Other**—To enter additional notes about this person, select this tab.

After you've entered all the information you know, click OK.

You don't have to enter all the information that can be entered into the Address Book. If all you know is a last name and e-mail address, you can still create a contact for that person. Just enter as much information as you know, and work from that.

You can also add contacts from any e-mail messages you receive. Just right-click the sender's name and select Add Sender to Address Book. This creates a new contact for that person; you can then go to the Address Book and add more detailed information later—as described next.

Editing Contacts

If you want to edit information for an existing contact, just select the contact name in the main Address Book list, and then click the Properties button. This displays the familiar Properties dialog box for that contact; change whatever information you want, and then click OK.

Sorting and Searching

By default, your Address Book list is sorted by contact name. You can sort your list by any of the other columns by clicking that column head. Click the head twice to sort in the reverse order.

You also can change the way Address Book displays the contact list. Pull down the View menu, and select from Large Icon, Small Icon, List, or Details (the default view).

If you have a *lot* of people in your Address Book, you might have trouble finding any single person. To search your Address Book, click the Find People button on the toolbar. When the Find People dialog box appears, enter either the name, e-mail address, street address, or phone number of the person you're looking for, and then click Find Now. Address Book will return a list of contacts matching your query.

Sending E-mail to a Contact

To send an e-mail to one of your contacts, select the contact, click the Action button, and then select Send Mail. This opens an Outlook Express New Message window; enter the subject and text of your message. Then click Send to send this message via the Internet, using Outlook Express.

Activity **8**

READ AND POST TO USENET NEWSGROUPS

What You Need
- Outlook Express
- Internet Explorer
- Internet connection
- Basic computer system

Goal
Search for a specific Usenet newsgroup, and read messages posted there.

Finding Newsgroups

In addition to being an e-mail program, Outlook Express also functions as a news-reader for Usenet newsgroups. A *newsgroup* is an electronic gathering place for people with similar interests—kind of like an online bulletin board. Within a newsgroup users post messages (called *articles*) about a variety of topics; other users read and respond to these articles. The result is a kind of ongoing, freeform discussion, in which hundreds of users can participate.

Understanding Newsgroup Names

There are more than 30,000 newsgroups available, organized by topic. A newsgroup name looks a little like a Web site address, with single words or phrases separated by periods. Newsgroup names are more logical, however, in that each break in the name signifies a different subset of the major topic.

So, as you read a newsgroup name, your focus moves from left to right, until you zero in on a very specific topic. For example, the `rec.arts.cinema` group tells you that the newsgroup is in the *recreational* section of Usenet and that it discusses the *art* of the *cinema*.

Searching for Newsgroups

To find a specific newsgroup, start by clicking the icon in the Outlook Express folder list for your particular news server. (This should have been set up when you first configured your computer for your particular Internet service provider.)

If this is the first time you've used Outlook Express's newsgroup function, you'll be prompted to view a list of all newsgroups. If not, you'll need to click the Newsgroups button on the toolbar to view a list of all available newsgroups.

When the Newsgroups dialog box appears (shown in Figure A8.1), click the All tab (at the bottom of the dialog box) and select a newsgroup from the main list. You can scroll through the list or search for a specific group by entering key words in the Display Newsgroups Which Contain box.

Reading Newsgroup Articles

When you find a newsgroup you want to read, click the Go To button. All the articles from that newsgroup will appear in Outlook Express's Message pane. Click a message header to read the contents of that article in the Preview pane.

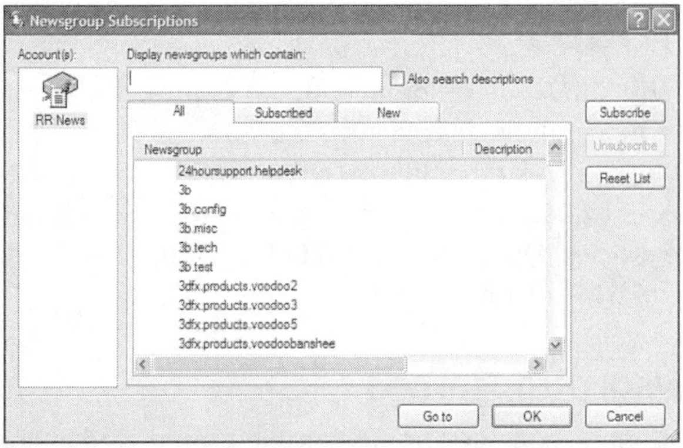

FIGURE A8.1
Search through more than 30,000 newsgroups for the topic you're interested in.

Creating and Posting Newsgroup Articles

To reply to an existing article, select the message in the Message pane and then click the Reply button. To create a new article, click the New Post button. Enter your message in the New Message window, and then click the Send button to post the message to the current newsgroup.

Searching for Newsgroup Articles

Normally, you use Outlook Express to browse through newsgroups and read individual newsgroup articles. If you're interested in viewing older articles, however, you need to search a newsgroup archive.

The best Usenet archive is found on the Web. The Google Groups Web site (groups.google.com) lets you search an extensive archive of newsgroup articles. Use Internet Explorer to go to the site; then enter one or more keywords in the search box. When you click the Search button, Google returns a list of articles in various newsgroups that contain your search phrase. Click an article to view the article.

There are so many newsgroup articles available, you probably should narrow your search as much as possible—either by including more specific keywords or by selecting specific newsgroups to search in.

Activity **9**

SEND AN INSTANT MESSAGE

What You Need
- Windows Messenger or MSN Messenger
- Internet connection
- Basic computer system

Goal
Find an online contact, and send him an instant message.

Getting Connected

Instant messaging lets you communicate one on one, in real-time, with your friends, family, and colleagues. It's faster than e-mail and less chaotic than chat rooms (discussed in Activity 10, "Chat with Friends Online"). It's just you and another user— and your instant messaging software.

Depending on your computer configuration, you probably have either MSN Messenger or Windows Messenger installed on your PC. Both programs work very similarly; Windows Messenger is really just an updated version of MSN Messenger.

You launch MSN/Windows Messenger from the Windows Start menu. The first time you use the program, you need to sign up for Microsoft's .NET Messenger service. The sign-up is free and lets you choose your own unique sign-in name that other users will know you by. Click the Click Here to Sign In link to register; then follow the onscreen instructions.

Note | The most popular instant messaging program is AOL Instant Messenger (AIM). You can download a copy of AIM from www.aim.com; it works pretty much the same as Windows Messenger, using lists of contacts (that AIM calls *buddies*). In addition, if you're a subscriber to the America Online service, you can use AOL's Buddy Lists feature, which is the private version of AIM.

Adding New Contacts

To send an instant message to another user, that person has to be on your Messenger contact list.

To add a contact to your list, click the Add button. This launches the Add a Contact Wizard. If you know the person's sign-in name or e-mail address, you can add them as a contact directly. If you don't know that information, select the option to search for contacts. If you try to add a contact who isn't yet a Messenger user, Microsoft sends an e-mail to that person inviting them to install Messenger, sign up for the service, and contact you.

After you add contacts to your list, they appear in the main Messenger window, as shown in Figure A9.1. Contacts who are currently online are listed in the Online section; those who aren't are listed as Not Online. To remove a contact from your list, right-click the name and then select Delete Contact.

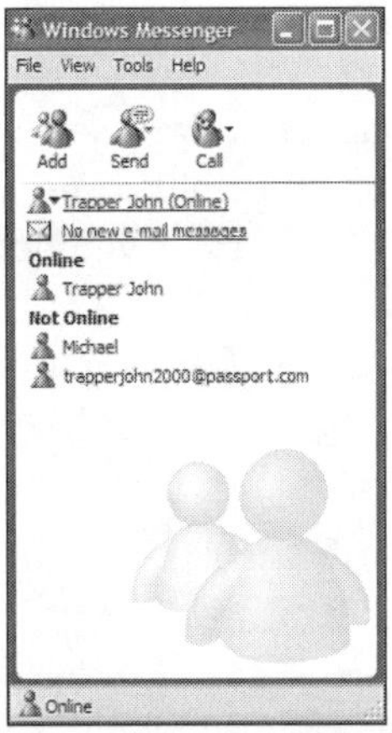

FIGURE A9.1

Choose a
contact to
send an instant
message to.

Sending a Message

To send an instant message to another user, double-click a name in your contact list.
When the Conversation window opens (see Figure A9.2), enter your message in the
lower part of the window, and then click the Send button (or press Enter). Your message will appear in the top part of the window, as will your contact's reply.

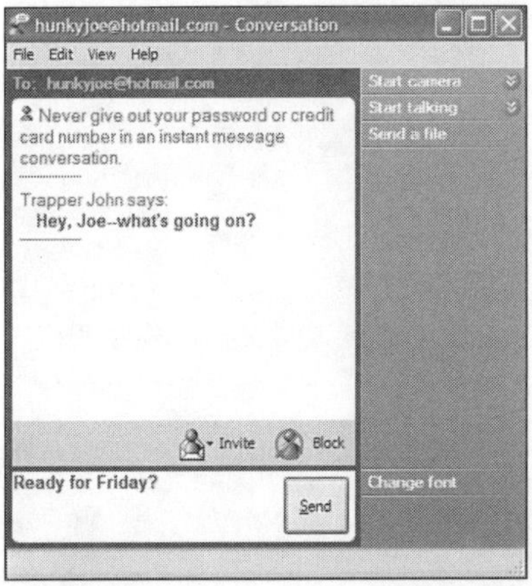

FIGURE A9.2

Send and receive
instant messages
via the
Conversation
window.

Continue talking like this, one message after another. Your entire conversation is displayed in the top part of the window, and you can scroll up to reread earlier messages.

Tip

You can change the font face, color, style, and size of your message by clicking the
Change Font link. When the Change My Message Font dialog box appears, select the
settings you want; then click OK. The next message you send will reflect the new formatting you selected.

Receiving a Message

When someone else sends you an instant message, Windows lets out with a little bleeping sound and then displays an alert in the lower-right corner of your screen. To open and reply to the message, click the alert. (Naturally, you have to be connected to the Internet to receive these messages.)

If you happen to miss the alert, Windows displays a flashing message button in the taskbar. You can click this button to read your message.

CHAT WITH FRIENDS ONLINE

What You Need
- Internet Explorer
- Internet connection
- Basic computer system

Goal
Join a group chat at Yahoo! Chat.

Understanding Chat

Chatting online is one of the most popular activities for Internet users. That's because most people like to talk to other people, even if that "conversation" is entirely text-based and facilitated by a computer keyboard.

An online chat is different from an instant message. Whereas instant messaging describes a one-to-one conversation between two users, online chat involves real-time discussions between large groups of users. These chats take place in public *chat rooms* (sometimes called *chat channels*).

You can find chat rooms at any number of Web sites, accessible via Internet Explorer or any other Web browser.

Another type of online chat, called *Internet Relay Chat*, uses special software programs and chat servers. Most users prefer Web-based chat because its easier to use and doesn't require any special software.

Chatting at Yahoo!

One of the most popular chat sites is Yahoo! Chat, which is part of the giant Yahoo! portal. You access Yahoo! Chat by clicking the Chat link on the Yahoo! home page or by going directly to chat.yahoo.com.

The first time you visit Yahoo! Chat, you'll be prompted for your Yahoo! ID and password; if you don't yet have a Yahoo! ID, take this opportunity to register. (It's free.)

The main Yahoo! Chat page is your home page for all of Yahoo!'s chat activities. From here you can access featured chat rooms and chat events or click the Complete Room List link for a list of all available Yahoo! Chat rooms.

After you select a chat room, Yahoo! has to load special chat software into your Web browser. This is done automatically, using Java technology.

When you enter a chat room, you see the screen shown in Figure A10.1. All messages are displayed in the Chat pane; everyone chatting in the room is listed in the Chatters pane.

You enter your messages in the Send box and then click the Send button or press Enter to send the message to the room. After you send a message, it appears in the Chat pane, listed in-line with all the other messages.

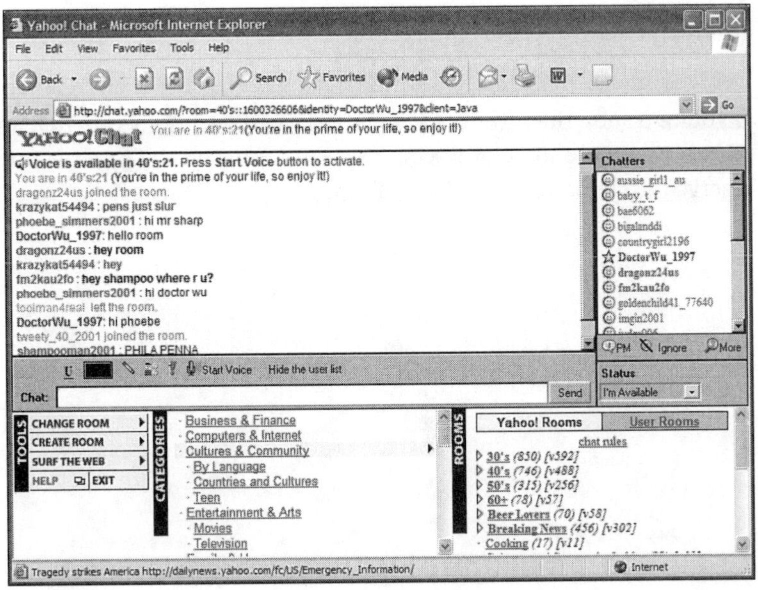

FIGURE A10.1

A typical Yahoo! chat room—enter a message in the Send box, and then chat away!

Everybody else in your chat room is listed in the Chatters list. In addition, you can display a list of all the participants in every Yahoo! Chat room by clicking the Who's Chatting button in the Tools section.

If you want to change chat rooms, click the Change Room button in the Tools section. When you click this button, Yahoo! displays the chat room list; click a room name to change to that room.

Tip

To send a Private Message to someone in your chat room, select that person's name in the Chatters list and then click the PM button. When Yahoo! displays the PM window, enter your private message and click the Send button. Keep the PM window open to continue your private conversation.

Other Chat Sites

If you're serious about online chat, you might want to check out some of the other major chat communities on the Web. These sites include:

- Excite Chat (chat.excite.com)
- Internet TeleCafe (www.telecafe.com)
- Lycos Chat (chat.lycos.com)
- MSN Chat (chat.msn.com)

- Talk City (www.talkcity.com)
- Worlds Chat (www.worlds.net)

If you're a subscriber to America Online, you can also access AOL's proprietary chat rooms. These are some of the busiest chat rooms on the Internet, and they're reserved exclusively for AOL members.

PART V

DO IT NOW: WORKING WITH NUMBERS

CREATE AND FORMAT A SPREADSHEET

What You Need
- Microsoft Works Spreadsheet (or Microsoft Excel)
- Basic computer system

Goal
Create a new spreadsheet, enter data, and perform basic formatting.

Understanding Spreadsheets

A *spreadsheet* is nothing more than a giant list. Your list can contain just about any type of data you can think of—text, numbers, and even dates. You can take any of the numbers on your list and use them to calculate new numbers. You can sort the items on your list, pretty them up, and print the important points in a report. You can even graph your numbers in a pie, line, or bar chart!

In a spreadsheet, all your data are stored in *cells*. Your spreadsheet is divided into lots of these cells, each located in a specific location on a giant grid made of *rows* and *columns*. Each single cell represents the intersection of a particular row and column.

As you can see in Figure A11.1, each column has an alphabetic label (A, B, C, and so on). Each row, on the other hand, has a numeric label (1, 2, 3, and so on). The location of each cell is the combination of its column and row locations. For example, the cell in the upper-left corner of the spreadsheet is in column A and row 1; therefore, its location is signified as A1. The cell to the right of it is B1, and the cell below A1 is A2.

FIGURE A11.1

The Works
Spreadsheet—use
the toolbar
and pulldown
menus to perform
most tasks.

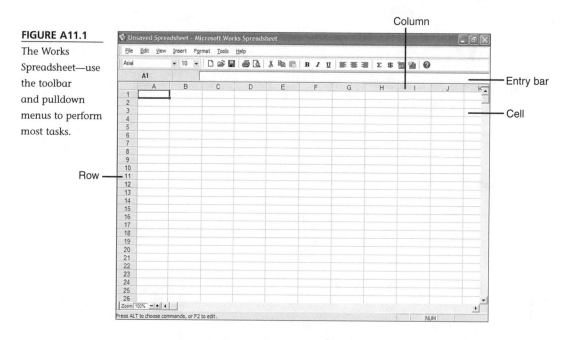

The Entry bar at the top of the workspace echoes the contents of the selected, or *active*, cell. You can type data directly into the active cell or into the Entry bar.

Creating a New Spreadsheet

If you have Microsoft Works Suite installed on your new PC, you can use the Works Spreadsheet for all your spreadsheet needs. Works Spreadsheet is fairly easy to use, and is compatible with the more fully featured Microsoft Excel spreadsheet program included with Microsoft Office.

| Note | The instructions in this section are specific to Works Spreadsheet. If you're using Excel, you might need to translate a few steps here and there because Excel does some things somewhat differently than Works. |

As with most Works Suite applications, you can start Works Spreadsheet either from Windows or from the Works Task Launcher.

To open a blank spreadsheet in the Works Spreadsheet workspace, click the New button on the toolbar. A blank spreadsheet is now loaded into the workspace, ready to accept any text or numbers you want to enter.

Entering Data

Entering text or numbers is easy. Just remember that data is entered into each cell individually—you can fill up a spreadsheet with hundreds or thousands of cells filled with their own individual data!

To enter data into a specific cell, select the cell you want to enter data into, and then type your text or numbers into the cell. What you type will be echoed in the Entry bar at the top of the screen. When you're done typing data into the cell, press Enter.

Applying Number Formats

When you enter a number into a cell, Works applies what it calls a "general" format to the number—it just displays the number, right-aligned, with no commas or dollar signs. You can, however, select a specific number format to apply to any cells in your spreadsheet that contain numbers.

Just select the cell (or cells) you want to format; then pull down the Format menu and select Number. When the Format Cells dialog box appears, make sure the Number tab is selected; then check one of the options in the Format list. If the format has additional options (such as decimal points or various date or time formats), configure these as desired; then click OK.

Formatting Cell Contents

You can apply a variety of formatting options to the contents of your cells. You can make your text bold or italic, change the font type or size, or even add shading or borders to selected cells.

To format a cell (or range of cells), select the cell (or range) and then apply the formatting from either the toolbar or the Format menu.

Inserting and Deleting Rows and Columns

To insert a new row or column in the middle of your spreadsheet, click the row or column header *after* where you want to make the insertion. Then, pull down the Insert menu and select either Insert Row or Insert Column. Works now inserts a new row or column either above or to the left of the row or column you selected.

To delete a row or column, click the header for the row or column you want to delete. Then, pull down the Insert menu and select either Delete Row or Delete Column. The row or column you selected is deleted, and all other rows or columns move up or over to fill the space.

USE SIMPLE FORMULAS

What You Need
- Microsoft Works Spreadsheet (or Microsoft Excel)
- Basic computer system

Goal
Perform algebraic calculations on spreadsheet data.

Basic Math

Any given cell can contain a piece of text, a date, a number, or a formula.

Works Spreadsheet lets you enter just about any type of algebraic formula into any cell. You can add, subtract, multiply, divide, and perform any nested combination of those operations.

Creating a Formula

When you enter an equal sign (=) into any cell, Works knows you're starting a formula. You start your formula with the equal sign and enter your operations *after* the equal sign.

For example, if you wanted to add 1 plus 2, you'd enter this formula in a cell: =1+2. When you press Enter, the formula disappears from the cell—and the result, or *value*, is displayed.

Basic Operators

Table A12.1 shows the algebraic operators you can use in Works Spreadsheet formulas.

Table A12.1   Works Spreadsheet Operators

Operation	Operator
Add	+
Subtract	-
Multiply	*
Divide	/

Working with Other Cells

To perform calculations using values from cells in your spreadsheet, you enter the cell location into the formula. For example, if you wanted to add cells A1 and A2, you'd enter this formula: =A1+A2.

An even easier way to perform operations involving spreadsheet cells is to select them with your mouse while you're entering the formula. To do this, select the cell that will contain the formula, and then enter =. Now click the first cell you want to include in your formula; that cell location is automatically entered in your formula. Next, enter an algebraic operator, and then click the second cell you want to include in your formula. Press Enter when your formula is complete.

Quick Addition with AutoSum

The most common operation in any spreadsheet is the addition of a group of numbers. Works Spreadsheet makes summing up a row or column of numbers easy via the AutoSum function.

All you have to do is select the cell at the end of a row or column of numbers, where you want the total to appear, and then click the AutoSum button on the Works toolbar. Works automatically sums all the preceding numbers and places the total in the selected cell.

Using Functions

In addition to the basic algebraic operators previously discussed, Works Spreadsheet also includes a variety of *functions* that replace the complex steps present in many formulas. For example, if you wanted to total all the cells in column A, you could enter the formula =A1+A2+A3+A4. Or, you could use the *SUM* function, which lets you sum a column or row of numbers without having to type every cell into the formula.

In short, a function is a type of prebuilt formula.

You enter a function in the following format: =function(argument), where function is the name of the function and argument is the range of cells or other data you want to calculate. Using the last example, to sum cells A1 through A4, you'd use the following function-based formula: =sum(A1:A4).

Works Spreadsheet includes more than 100 separate functions. You can access and insert any of Works's functions by selecting the cell where you want to insert the function, pulling down the Insert menu, and then selecting Function. When the Insert Function dialog box (shown in Figure A12.1) appears, select a function category; then select a function. When you click the Insert button, the function is inserted in the current cell. You can then manually enter the cells or numbers into the function's argument.

FIGURE A12.1

Choose from more than 100 separate functions in the Insert Function dialog box.

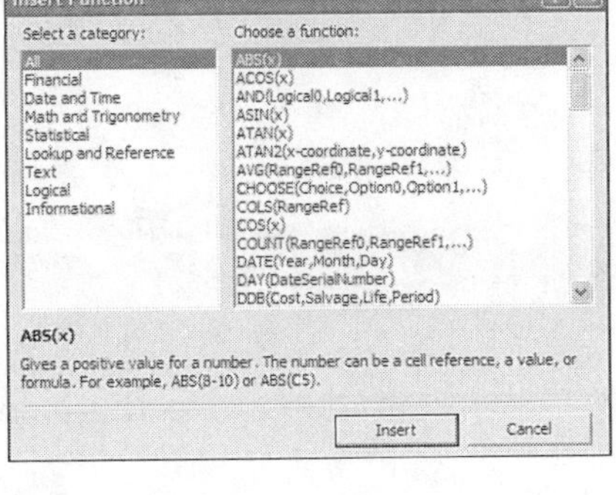

SORT AND ANALYZE YOUR NUMBERS

What You Need

- Microsoft Works Spreadsheet (or Microsoft Excel)
- Basic computer system

Goal

Perform basic sorting and analysis on a range of cells in a spreadsheet.

Sorting a Range of Cells

If you have a list of either text or numbers, you might want to reorder the list for a different purpose. Works lets you sort your data by any column, in either ascending or descending order.

To sort a range of cells, start by selecting all the cells you want to sort. Then, pull down the Tools menu and select Sort.

Note If Works asks whether you want to sort the highlighted information or whether you want to sort *all* the information in your spreadsheet, choose to sort only the highlighted information.

When the Sort dialog box appears, as shown in Figure A13.1, select whether your list does or doesn't have a header row. Then, pull down the first Select the Column You Want to Sort By list, and select which column you want to sort by. You also can choose to sort in either Ascending or Descending order. Click the Sort button to sort the data.

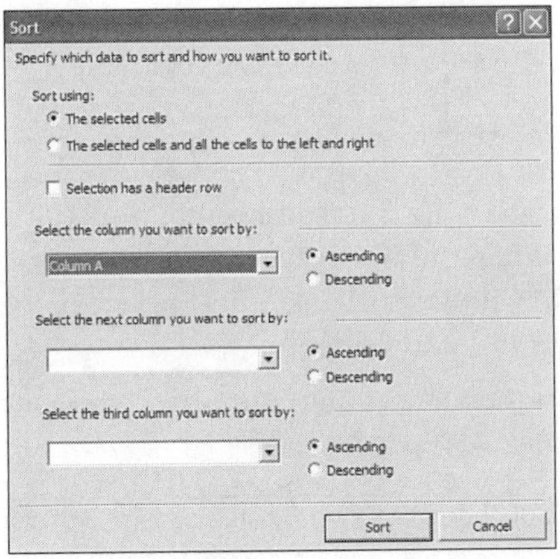

FIGURE A13.1

Sort your list by any column, in any order.

![Sort dialog box]

Sort

Specify which data to sort and how you want to sort it.

Sort using:
- ● The selected cells
- ○ The selected cells and all the cells to the left and right

☐ Selection has a header row

Select the column you want to sort by:
[Column A ▼]   ● Ascending   ○ Descending

Select the next column you want to sort by:
[▼]   ● Ascending   ○ Descending

Select the third column you want to sort by:
[▼]   ● Ascending   ○ Descending

[Sort]   [Cancel]

Note If you want to sort the information in your list by more than one column, you can use the second and third Select the Column You Want to Sort By lists in the Sort dialog box.

Creating a Task-Based Spreadsheet

If you have a specific task in mind, you might be able to use one of Works's task-based spreadsheet templates. These templates give you a good head start for entering and analyzing specific types of data.

For example, the Home Improvement Budget template (shown in Figure A13.2) has been preformatted for the task at hand. All you have to do is edit your own personal data, and everything else is calculated automatically.

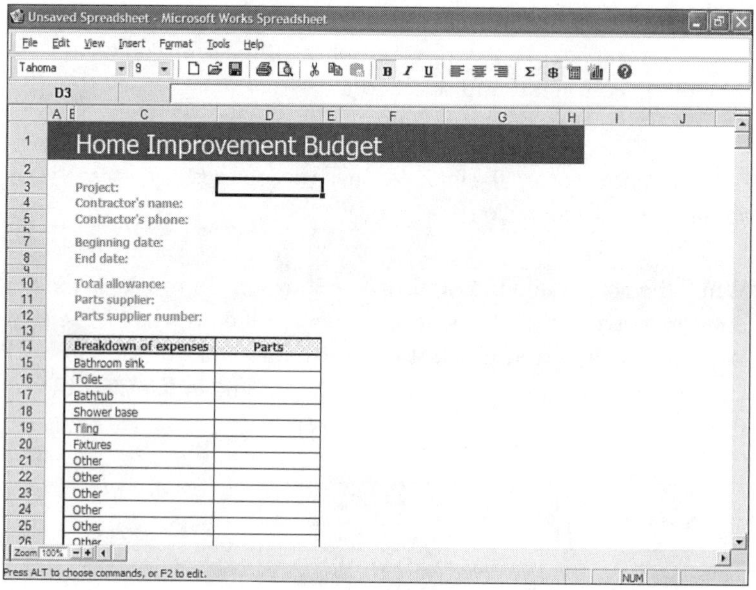

FIGURE A13.2

Use a preformatted spreadsheet template to automate many common tasks.

To use a template or wizard to create a spreadsheet for a specific task, pull down the File menu and select New. When the Works Task Launcher appears, make sure you're on the Programs tab (with Works Spreadsheet selected); then select a task from the Tasks list, and click the Start button.

The template you selected is then loaded into the Works workspace. Be sure to save this spreadsheet as a new file.

> **Tip**
>
> Some task templates are launched via a step-by-step wizard. Answer the questions and fill in the blanks, and your spreadsheet will be completed automatically.

CREATE A CHART

What You Need

- Microsoft Works Spreadsheet (or Microsoft Excel)
- Basic computer system

Goal

Create various types of charts from existing spreadsheet data.

Creating a Chart

Numbers are fine, but sometimes the story behind the numbers can be told better through a picture. The way you take a picture of numbers is with a *chart*, such as the one shown in Figure A14.1.

FIGURE A14.1

Some numbers are better represented via a chart.

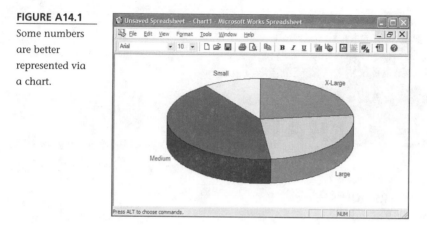

You create a chart based on numbers you've previously entered into your Works spreadsheet. Start by selecting the range of cells you want to include in your chart. If the range has a header row or column, include that row or column when selecting the cells.

Now click the New Chart button. This displays the New Chart dialog box, shown in Figure A14.2.

FIGURE A14.2

Create one of a dozen types of charts to visually represent your data.

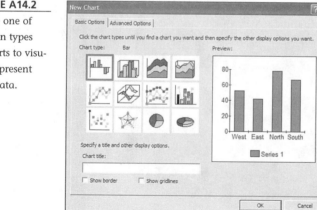

Select the Basic Options tab, and then select a chart type. A preview of the chart of your data appears in the Preview section.

Now you can select some basic formatting options. If you want your chart to have a title, enter the title in the Chart Title box. To display a border around your chart, check the Show Border option. If you want to show gridlines within your chart, check the Show Gridlines option.

When you're done, click OK. Your chart now appears in a new, separate, unnamed, and unsaved spreadsheet. You should pull down the File menu, select Save As, and save this chart file now.

Changing the Chart Type

You can accept this new chart as-is, or you can tweak the chart type to some degree.

To change the chart type completely, pull down the Format menu and select Chart Type. When the Chart Type dialog box appears, select the Basic Types tab, select a new type, and then click OK.

There's a second tab on the Chart Type dialog box—the Variations tab. This tab contains a number of popular variations on the selected basic chart type. For example, if you select Pie as your basic chart type and then click the Variations tab, you see six types of pie charts—with labels, without labels, with values, without values, with exploded slices, and without exploded slices. Select the variation you want, and then click OK.

Formatting the Chart

To change thedetailed formatting of your new chart, pull down the Format menu. Here you can find a variety of chart items to format, including the font, shading and color, and each axis of the chart.

 Different types of charts present different items to format.

PART VI

DO IT NOW: MANAGING YOUR FINANCES

SET UP A HOUSEHOLD BUDGET

What You Need

- Microsoft Money
- Information about planned or expected income and expenses
- Basic computer system

Goal

Set up a budget to forecast your household income and expenses.

Personal Finance Software

Most new computers come with at least one personal finance program installed. That program might be Microsoft Money, or it might be some variation of Quicken. Both programs work similarly, but for purposes of this book we're going to look at Money because it's fully integrated into the Microsoft Works Suite program.

Microsoft Money is a full-featured personal finance program. You can use it to manage your bank accounts, track your investments, pay your bills, and plan your budget. You can start Money from either the Windows Start menu or the Works Task Launcher.

Creating a New Budget

The easy way to plan your budget and track your progress is to use Money's built-in Budget Planner. It's easy to use, so all you have to do is follow the onscreen instructions—and then stick to the budget you create!

To launch Money's Budget Planner, pull down Money's Planner menu and select Budget Planner. When the main Budget Planner page appears, click the Create a Budget Link.

The Budget Planner now leads you step-by-step through nine screens of information. Each screen in the Budget Planner focuses on a particular budgeting task; complete all the screens to finish your budget.

Entering Your Income

Use the Enter Your Income screen to answer the question, "Where does your income come from?"

On this screen you should enter all your scheduled deposits, by category. You add new income categories by clicking the Add button and following the step-by-step onscreen instructions. You can view a graph of your income by clicking the View Income button.

Expenses

Use the Enter Your Expenses screen to answer the question, "How do you spend your money?"

On this screen you should enter all your scheduled expenses, by category. To add a new scheduled transaction, double-click the expense category and make a new entry in the Edit dialog box. You can view a graph of your income by clicking the View Spending button.

Savings Goals

Use the Savings Goals screen to answer the question, "What do you want to put into long-term savings?"

For most people, this is a simple screen. You can select either to Spend All Excess Income or to Save Some or All Excess Income Towards Goals. If you select the second option, you can then enter specific savings goals.

Budget Overview

This screen does just what it says: It provides a visual overview of your income, expenses, and savings goals.

Reviewing Your Current Budget Status

This screen lets you review how your actual income and spending compare to your budget. You can choose to view the status of your budget for the current month; current year; or a forecast for future weeks, months, and years. The information is displayed in a table that compares your actual income and expenses with your budgeted numbers; the difference between actual and budget is also displayed.

Budget Reports

There are two budget reports available from the Budget Planner screen. Both are accessible by selecting View Reports on the Common Tasks sidebar:

- **How I'm Doing on My Budget**—Displays a detailed, line-by-line itemization of your actual and projected budgets.
- **This Year's Budget**—Displays the line-by-line, month-by-month details of your current-year budget.

Other reports within Money can help you track how you're earning and spending your money. Pull down the Reports menu, and select Reports Gallery; you'll see the list of reports shown in Figure A15.1. You can create reports that detail your spending habits, net worth (What I Have), bills and debts (What I Owe), investments, and taxes. You also can create your own customized reports and access them as necessary.

Updating Your Budget

To update your budget at any time, open the Budget Planner and select Edit Budget from the Common Tasks sidebar.

MANAGE YOUR BANK ACCOUNT

What You Need

- Microsoft Money
- Account numbers and balances for your existing checking and savings accounts
- Internet connection
- Basic computer system

Goal

Use Microsoft Money for all your basic banking transactions.

Setting Up Your Accounts

The first time you start Money you're presented with the Setup Assistant. This assistant walks you step-by-step through setting up your Money accounts—including your existing banking accounts.

Before you run the Setup Assistant, however, you should gather all your important financial records. You'll be asked to input account numbers and balances, so make sure you have this information handy—for every checking account, savings account, credit card, bill payee, money market fund, and stock investment.

To add or change information after your initial setup, pull down the Accounts & Bills menu and select Account Setup. From here you can add a new account, close an existing account, permanently delete an account from your system, set up an online account, or change an account you've already created.

Entering Transactions

Money makes entering transactions into your checking and savings accounts easy. You do this from the account register. Open the account register by pulling down the Accounts & Bills menu and selecting Accounts and Bills Center. Click the name of a specific account, and Money displays the register for that account.

As you can see in Figure A16.1, you can perform three types of transactions: withdrawals, deposits, and transfers. Just click the transaction tab at the bottom of the workspace and enter the appropriate information, as follows:

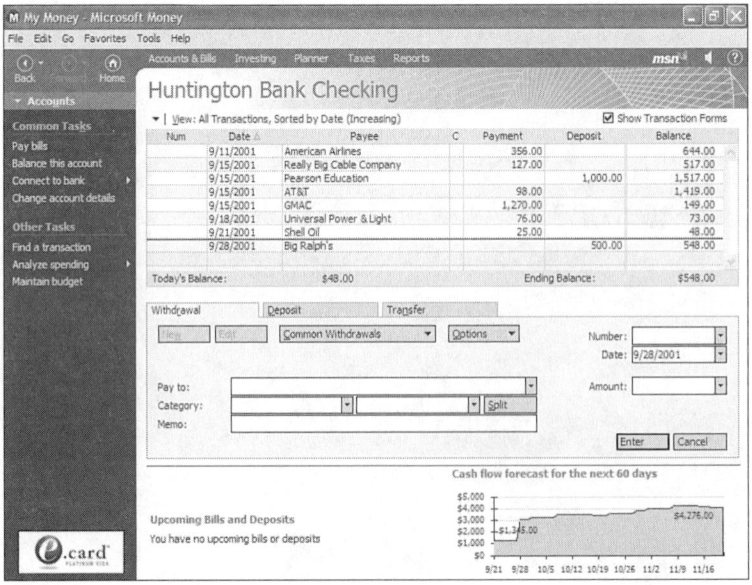

FIGURE A16.1

Enter banking transactions in the account register.

- **Registering a withdrawal**—Select the payee from the Pay To list, select a transaction category from the Category list, enter any memo text for this transaction, select a numbering option from the Number list, enter the Date of the transaction, and then enter the Amount of the withdrawal.

- **Registering a deposit**—Select the payer from the From list, select a transaction category from the Category list, enter any memo text for this transaction, select a numbering option from the Number list, enter the Date of the transaction, and then enter the Amount of the deposit.

- **Registering a transfer between accounts**—Select the appropriate accounts from the From and To lists, enter any memo text for this transaction, select a numbering option from the Number list, enter the Date of the transaction, and then enter the Amount of the transfer.

Balancing Your Checkbook

When you receive your monthly statement from your bank, you can have Money automatically reconcile your accounts to your statement—which is a lot easier than trying to do it by hand! Just go to that particular account register, and then click Balance an Account from the Common Tasks sidebar.

When the Balance Wizard appears, enter the following information from your monthly statement: statement date, starting balance, ending balance, service charges (if any), and interest earned (if any). Click Next to proceed.

Money now displays a balance page for the selected account. Compare the transactions in the Money register with the transactions on your monthly statement. Click the C column to clear each matching transaction. If a transaction doesn't match, click the transaction and edit it accordingly. If you're missing any transactions (the primary cause of accounts not balancing), click the New button to enter them as new.

Online Banking

An even easier way to handle your banking needs is to let Money do it automatically, by downloading all your transactions from the Internet. This way you don't have to enter much of anything—Money interfaces with your bank to track all your transactions.

Before you set up Money to work with your bank's online banking services, you'll need to confirm that your bank offers Money-compatible services. You also might need to sign up for those services (they're not always free) and obtain any necessary account numbers and passwords.

Then, from within Money, open the account register for your bank and select Connect to Bank, Services from the Common Tasks sidebar. When the next page appears, click Set Up Online Services. Money now tells you whether your bank offers online banking; if so, click the Set Up button and follow the onscreen instructions.

Not all banks offer online banking, and not all online banking services are compatible with Microsoft Money. Some banks let you perform online transactions only from their own Web pages; these banks are not compatible with Money's online banking feature.

PAY YOUR BILLS

What You Need

- Microsoft Money
- Blank check forms
- Account information for all your recurring payees
- Basic computer system
- Printer

Goal

Use Microsoft Money to write checks and pay bills online.

Working with Recurring Payments

The best way to use Money for bill paying is to set up a list of your recurring transactions—those bills you pay month after month. After you've entered a recurring payee, all you have to do is click a few buttons to pay that bill each month, every month.

Scheduling the Payment

To add a payee to your scheduled bills list, pull down the Accounts and Bills menu and select Bills and Deposits Setup. When the Schedule Your Upcoming Bills and Deposits screen appears, click the New button to display the Create New Schedule Transaction Wizard. Check the Bill option, and follow the onscreen instructions to set up the recurring payment.

Paying the Bill

After you've set up a recurring payment, you can easily write a check and enter that transaction in the Money register. All you have to do is pull down the Accounts & Bills menu and select Accounts & Bills Center. This screen displays your bank accounts and any upcoming bills you need to pay.

To pay a bill, select Pay a Scheduled Bill from the Common Tasks sidebar. When the Pay Bills screen appears, double-click the bill you want to pay. When the Record Payment dialog box appears (as shown in Figure A17.1), enter the correct payment amount; then pull down the Number list and select Print This Transaction. When you click the Record Payment button, this transaction is entered in your account register and the check is sent to Money's "to-do" list for printing at a later time.

FIGURE A17.1

Entering a payment.

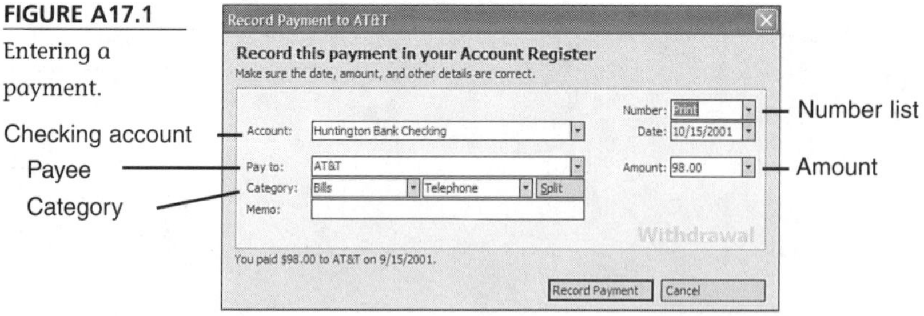

Checking account

Payee

Category

Number list

Amount

> Record Payment to AT&T
>
> **Record this payment in your Account Register**
> Make sure the date, amount, and other details are correct.
>
> Account: Huntington Bank Checking
> Number: Print
> Date: 10/15/2001
>
> Pay to: AT&T
> Amount: 98.00
> Category: Bills | Telephone | Split
> Memo:
>
> Withdrawal
>
> You paid $98.00 to AT&T on 9/15/2001.
>
> Record Payment | Cancel

Note

The first time you choose to print a check to a specific payee, Money displays the Print Address dialog box. Enter the appropriate information here, and then click OK.

Printing the Check

You have to manually choose to print all waiting checks. To do this, pull down the File menu and select Print Checks. When the Print Checks dialog box appears, select which checks you want to print (all or selected), what type of check forms you're using, the number of the first check form in your printer, and how many checks are on the first page. Click Print to print the selected check(s).

You can't print checks on plain white laser paper; you have to purchase special check forms to use with your specific banking accounts. You should be able to find Money-compatible check forms at your local office supply store, or you can order them directly from Microsoft at 800-432-1285.

Writing Checks Manually

If you want to write checks by hand and then enter those withdrawals into your Money register, follow the same procedure as for paying a recurring bill, but when you pull down the Number list in the Record Payment dialog box, *don't* select Print This Transaction. Instead, select Next Check Number or just enter a check number. When you click the Record This Transaction button, the transaction will be entered in the register—but you'll have to write the check yourself.

Paying Bills Online

Assuming that you've set up Money for online banking with your banking institution (as explained in Activity 16, "Manage Your Bank Account"), you can also choose to pay your bills electronically—and never write or print a paper check again!

Money calls this type of electronic payment an *Epay*. You specify an electronic payment in the Record Payment dialog box. Just pull down the Number list and select Electronic Payment (Epay).

The first time you enter an Epay for a payee, Money prompts you for certain details, such as the payee's name, address, and account number. Be sure you enter the correct information (typically available on your most recent bill from that payee), and then click OK.

Any bills you choose to pay electronically are sent to Money's to-do list. To send these electronic payments, go to your checking account register screen and select Connect to Bank from the Common Tasks sidebar. Money now connects to the Internet—and to your financial institution—and transmits your electronic bill payments.

GET THE LATEST STOCK QUOTES

What You Need

- Internet Explorer
- Microsoft Money
- Internet connection
- Basic computer system

Goal

Use the Internet to obtain information about your stocks and securities.

Getting Stock Quotes Online

The Internet is a great place to find up-to-the-minute information about stocks and other securities. Several sites and services specialize in providing real-time (or slightly delayed) stock quotes—for free!

Financial Sites

Here's a short list of financial Web sites that provide free stock quotes. You can access any of these sites with your Internet Explorer Web browser:

- CBS Marketwatch (cbs.marketwatch.com)
- CNNfn (money.cnn.com)
- FT.com (www.ft.com)
- Motley Fool (www.fool.com)
- MSN MoneyCentral (moneycentral.msn.com)
- Yahoo! Finance (finance.yahoo.com)

Portals

In addition, you can look up stock quotes at any of the major portals. Even better, most of these portals let you create your own customized start page, complete with your personalized list of stocks to track.

The portals you can customize in this fashion include

- AOL Anywhere (my.aol.com)
- My Excite (my.excite.com)
- My Lycos (my.lycos.com)
- My MSN (www.msn.com)
- My Netscape (my.netscape.com)
- My Yahoo! (my.yahoo.com)

Finding In-Depth Financial Information on the Web

If you want more than just quotes, a number of Web sites offer a wide variety of valuable financial advice and information. These sites help you plan your investment strategy and research individual investments.

The best of these sites includes

- **Annual Reports Library** (www.annualreportslibrary.com)—Collection of more than a half-million annual reports from corporations, foundations, banks, mutual funds, and public institutions

- **BigCharts** (www.bigcharts.com)—Up-to-date financial charts of all shapes and sizes

- **CBS Marketwatch** (cbs.marketwatch.com)—Financial news and information, plus research and streaming TV and radio news

- **CNNfn** (cnnfn.cnn.com)—Full-service finance site from the CNNfn cable financial network

- **FreeEDGAR** (www.freeedgar.com)—SEC documents in an easy-to-read HTML format

- **FT.com** (www.ft.com)—The online version of the *Financial Times* newspaper and a lot more, including information on specific markets, industries, and companies

- **Hoovers Online** (www.hoovers.com)—Detailed corporate news, financial, and other information; one of the most informative sites on the Web

- **Investorama** (www.investorama.com)—Full-service finance site

- **Motley Fool** (www.fool.com)—Full-service finance site; great message boards and company analysis

- **MSN MoneyCentral** (moneycentral.msn.com)—Full-service personal finance and online banking site from Microsoft

- **Multex Investor** (multex.multexinvestor.com)—Subscription site providing a massive database of company and industry research reports, usually for a charge

- **QuoteCom** (www.quote.com)—Full-service finance site from Lycos

- **SEC EDGAR Database** (www.sec.gov/edgar/searchedgar/webusers.htm)— Official corporate financial filings, including quarterly reports, annual reports, and IPO filings

- **Yahoo! Finance** (finance.yahoo.com)—Full-service finance site with terrific message boards, from Yahoo!

If you don't know where to start, two sites serve as good portals to the financial Web. InvestorLinks (www.investorlinks.com) is a huge directory of links to other financial sites, and Corporate Information (www.corporateinformation.com) functions as a kind of index to the financial Web. Both sites are good home pages in your search for corporate data.

Using Microsoft Money to Track Your Investments

You also can obtain stock quotes and information from within Microsoft Money, in conjunction with the MSN MoneyCentral Web site. Just pull down the Investing menu and select Investing Center. From here you can perform a variety of investing-related activities, including creating and managing your own investment accounts

BUY AND SELL STOCKS ONLINE

What You Need

- Internet Explorer
- Microsoft Money
- Internet connection
- Basic computer system

Goal

Choose an online broker, open an account, and start buying and selling stocks.

How Online Investing Works

More and more investors, both big and small, are executing their transactions over the Internet, via online brokerages. A large number of online brokerages let you buy and sell securities right from your personal computer—and some of these firms even offer special services just for day traders.

Setting Up an Account

Before you use an online broker, you must establish an account with that firm. You typically do this *offline*; you'll need to print out some forms, fill them in, sign them, and then mail them back to the broker. (Some brokers also require you to make an initial deposit of funds before you can initiate trading.) After all the paperwork is filled out and registered, you'll be given a user ID and password, and you're then ready to begin your online trading.

Making a Trade

Online trading is actually fairly easy. You use your Web browser to log on to the brokerage site, navigate to the trading section, and specify how many shares of which security you want to buy or sell. You can specify whether you want to trade at the market price (the current stock price) or at limit, which is a price you specify.

After the trade is consummated, funds generated from a sale are deposited in your account, and funds due from a purchase are noted. (You typically have to pay for any securities purchased within three working days.)

Most transactions come at a fixed cost, and this cost varies wildly from broker to broker—as do the individual services offered. You should shop around for the combination of price and service that best suits your investment style.

Choosing an Online Broker

Almost every major traditional brokerage has an online equivalent—and there are a number of online-online brokers. Be sure you check out all the fees and services before you select a specific broker; here's a list of the most popular of the bunch:

- Accutrade (www.accutrade.com)
- American Express Brokerage (finance.americanexpress.com/finance/ brokerage.asp)
- Ameritrade (www.ameritrade.com)
- Charles Schwab (www.schwab.com)

- CSFBdirect (www.csfbdirect.com)
- Datek Online (www.datek.com)
- E*TRADE (www.etrade.com)
- Fidelity.com (www.fidelity.com)
- Investrade (www.investrade.com)
- Legg Mason (www.leggmason.com)
- Merrill Lynch Direct (www.mldirect.ml.com)
- Morgan Stanley Online (www.online.msdw.com)
- Mydiscountbroker.com (www.mydiscountbroker.com)
- Net Investor (www.netinvestor.com)
- Piper Jaffray (www.piperjaffray.com)
- Prudential Securities (www.prufn.com)
- Quick & Reilly (www.quickandreilly.com)
- Salomon Smith Barney (www.salomonsmithbarney.com)
- TD Waterhouse (www.tdwaterhouse.com)
- UBS PaineWebber (www.painewebber.com)

If you want more information before you choose an online broker, check out the rankings at Gomez (www.gomez.com). This site gives you the scoop about which site is best for various types of investors.

Online Trading with Microsoft Money

You also can use Microsoft Money to connect to your online broker and manage your transactions. Pull down the Investing menu, and select Investing Center; then click the Brokers link (at the top of the screen). Money automatically connects to the Internet and downloads a list of brokers it works with.

When you select your broker from this list, Money connects you to your broker's Web site. From there you can log in and transact your business, as normal. You can then download your transaction information from your broker directly to Microsoft Money, so it can be entered and tracked in the appropriate account register.

APPLY FOR A LOAN ONLINE

What You Need

- Internet Explorer
- Internet connection
- Basic computer system

Goal

Use the Internet to find the best rates for home and auto loans.

Mortgages

Buying a new home is stressful enough as it is—and then you have to worry about obtaining a mortgage. You have to deal with the awkward questions, complex paperwork, and confusing terminology about balloons and ARMs and jumbos and points. Then, of course, there's the tension-filled period of waiting to see whether you've been approved.

Even though the Internet can't eliminate this process, it can take some of the pain out of it. You can use the Web to calculate how big a mortgage you can afford, shop around for the best possible rate, and apply for the mortgage you want. The best online mortgage sites lead you step-by-step through the entire process, from prequalification to application to approval to closing—and they're all completely safe and secure.

Shopping for Loans Online

The steps for choosing and completing a mortgage online are relatively simple:

1. Use a mortgage calculator to determine how large a loan you can afford.
2. Shop around for the best interest rate.
3. After you've decided on a particular lender, use the online forms to prequalify for the mortgage.
4. Decide on the home you want, and complete a sales contract.
5. Have the new home inspected and appraised.
6. Formally apply for the mortgage.
7. On approval, schedule the mortgage closing.
8. Close the loan, and get ready to move into your new house!

Note that although you can be prequalified online (based on basic information you supply), you can't actually apply online. This is because you need to supply a variety of paperwork, such as tax returns, a copy of the sales contract, credit information, and the like. Some companies let you fax copies of these documents to speed up the process; others require you to mail copies. In any case, there's still a bit of offline activity involved in online mortgages, so don't expect everything to happen with the click of a mouse.

The Best Online Mortgage Sites

If you're looking for a new home loan, the following sites can help you shop for the best possible mortgage rates:

- Anyloan Company (www.anyloan.com)
- Bankrate.com (www.bankrate.com)

- Current Mortgage Information (www.hsh.com)
- E-Loan (www.e-loan.com)
- GetSmart. com (www.getsmart.com)
- HomePath.com (www.homepath.com)
- Homestore. com (www.homestore.com/finance/)
- InfoLoan.com (www.infoloan.com)
- iOwn.com (www.iown.com)
- LendingTree (www.lendingtree.com)
- LoaningZone (www.loaningzone.com)
- LoanSurfer (www.loansurfer.com)
- Mortgage 101 (www.mortgage101.com)
- MSN HomeAdvisor (homeadvisor.msn.com)
- Quicken Loans (quickenloans.quicken.com)
- Yahoo! Finance Loan Center (loan.yahoo.com)

Auto Loans

Obtaining an automobile loan online is very similar to obtaining an online mortgage—if not simpler because the loan amounts are smaller and there isn't as much paperwork involved. In addition, many of the online auto loan services offer both better rates and faster loan approval than you get with a typical bank loan.

Here's a list of the most popular auto loan sites on the Web:

- Anyloan Company (www.anyloan.com)
- Auto Loan Finder (www.autoloanfinder.com)
- Auto Loan Online (www.auto-loan.com)
- Autoloan. com (www.autoloan.com)
- Bankrate.com (www.bankrate.com)
- Car Financing Direct (www.car-financing-direct.com)
- Carlender.com (www.carlender.com)
- Dealerloans.com (www.dealerloans.com)
- E-Loan (www.e-loan.com)
- GetSmart.com (www.getsmart.com)

- LendingTree (www.lendingtree.com)
- Rev-n-GO (www.revngo.com)
- Yahoo! Finance Loan Center (loan.yahoo.com)

In addition, most of the major automotive Web sites—such as Cars.com (www.cars.com), Carpoint (carpoint.msn.com), and Auto-By-Tel (www.autobytel.com)—also offer deals on auto loans and leases.

PART VII

DO IT NOW: FILING AND REPORTING

STORE IMPORTANT ITEMS IN A DATABASE

What You Need

- Microsoft Works Database
- Basic computer system

Goal

Create a simple database in Microsoft Works.

Working with Works Database

If a spreadsheet is a giant list, a database is a giant file cabinet. Each "file cabinet" is actually a separate database file, and contains individual index cards (called *records*) filled with specific information (arranged in *fields*).

You can use Works Database, included with Microsoft Works Suite, to create and store anything that includes a large amount of data. For example, you can create a database that contains all your favorite recipes or the contents of your CD or video collection.

You launch Works Database the same way you launch most other Works Suite applications, from either the Windows Start menu or the Works Task Launcher.

Creating a Preformatted Database

Works Database includes several preformatted database applications. These include a CD and tape library, home inventory, and recipe book. All these databases include ready-made forms and reports specific to that application.

To base your new database on one of these applications, open the Works Task Launcher, select the Programs screen, select Works Database, and then select the application you want.

Creating a Blank Database

You also can use Works Database to create your own customized applications. This means, of course, that you have to design your own fields, forms, and reports.

When you launch Works Database, you're presented with the Create Database dialog box. Now you're faced with some immediate choices. (Don't worry—if you don't like the choices you make, you can always go back and change them later.)

First, you need to decide how many fields to include in your database. In general, you should create one field for each type of information you want to store. If you're creating a database for your movie collection, for example, you might create fields for Title, Lead Actor, Lead Actress, Director, Running Time, and Year.

Each field you add is assigned a specific *format*. You can select from the following formats: General, Number, Date, Time, Text, Fraction, and Serialized (for automatic consecutive numbers). Select the format that best fits the type of data you'll enter into that field.

After you've finished adding fields to your database, click the Exit button. Works now creates a database, based on your specifications.

Changing Views

You can view your new database in two distinct ways.

The default view, called the *List view*, makes your database look a little like a spreadsheet. As you can see in Figure A21.1, the rows are your records, and the columns are your fields.

FIGURE A21.1

Viewing a database in List view.

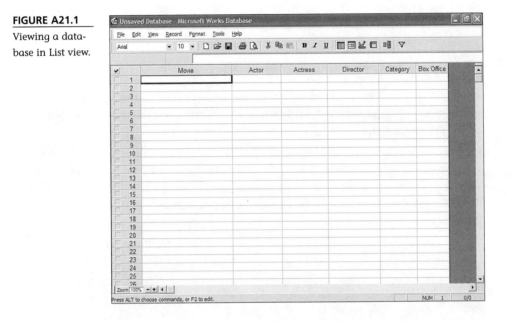

The *Form view* lets you look at one record at a time. You can flip from one record to another by using the arrow keys at the bottom of the screen.

You switch views by using the view buttons on the Works Database toolbar or by pulling down the View menu and selecting either List or Form.

Adding Data

No matter which view you're using, adding data to your database is easy.

If you're in List view, you add data to your database as you'd add data to a spreadsheet. Move your cursor to any particular field, and type your data. Use the Tab key to move to the next field in a record; use the Enter key to move to the next record.

You might prefer to add data one record at a time, as you'd enter data on an individual card in a file cabinet. Switch to Form view, and enter all the data for the fields in the current record. Use the Tab key to move from field to field; when you reach the end of one record, pressing Tab moves you to the first field of the next record.

Adding New Records

If you're in List view, adding a new record is as simple as starting to type in the first empty record row. If you're in Form view, just click the Insert Record button; a new blank record appears in the workspace.

Adding New Fields

After you get going in a database, you might discover that you want to include more information for each record. Going back to our movie database example, you might decide that you want to add a field for Category/Genre.

Fortunately, adding new fields to existing databases is easy. All you have to do is switch to List view and position your cursor anywhere in the field before where you want to insert the new field. Then, pull down the Record menu and select Insert Field, After. When the Insert Field dialog box appears, enter a name and format for the new field, and then click Add.

Works now adds the new field(s) to every record in your database. This field will be blank, of course, so you'll have to go back through your existing records and fill it in, as appropriate.

SORT AND FILTER SELECTED ITEMS

What You Need

- Microsoft Works Database
- Basic computer system

Goal

Learn how to work with the data in your database.

Sorting Data

You can add records to your database in any order. You don't have to insert new records alphabetically because you can have the program itself re-sort all the records for you.

You use List view to display all the records in your database. By default, these records are listed in the order in which they're entered. However, you can sort these records by any field—in either ascending or descending order.

Begin by pulling down the Records menu and selecting Sort Records. When the Sort Records dialog box appears, select the first field by which you want to sort from the Sort By list, and select whether you want to sort in Ascending or Descending order. You also can select a second or third field from which to sort, within the original sort.

Click OK, and Works re-sorts your database as directed.

Filtering Data

Another option you have in Works Database is to display only those records that match a specific criteria. This is sometimes necessary if your database contains a lot of records and you want to view only a subset of them. This process is called *filtering* the database, and it's easy to do.

For example, in your movie database you might want to display only Humphrey Bogart movies. You would create a filter that looks for all records containing Humphrey Bogart as an actor and displays only those records.

You begin the filtering process by switching to List view. Next, pull down the Tools menu and select Filters. Works displays the Filter Name dialog box; enter a name for the filter, and then click OK.

When the Filter dialog box appears, as shown in Figure A22.1, pull down the first Field Name box and select the first field you want to filter. Pull down the first Comparison list and select a criteria (is equal to, does not contain, and so on) for the filter. Then, in the first Compare To box, enter the value for the selected criteria. Repeat these steps to apply additional parameters for this filter; then click the Apply Filter button.

Using the movie database example, if you wanted to display only Humphrey Bogart movies, you'd select Lead Actor as the Field Name, pull down the Comparison list and select Contains, and then enter `Humphrey Bogart` in the Compare To box. Works Database looks for those records where the Lead Actor field contains Humphrey Bogart and displays only those records.

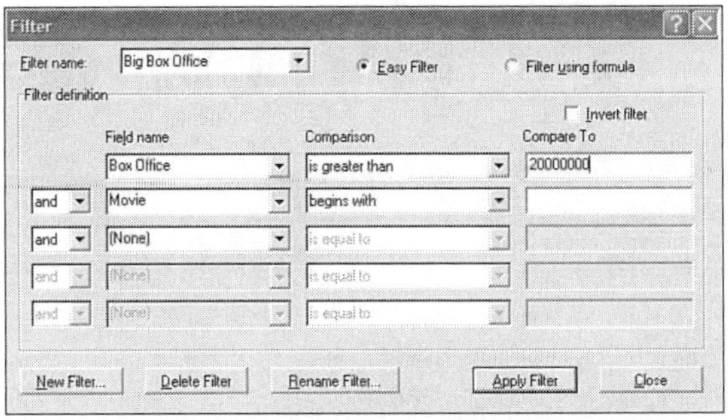

FIGURE A22.1

Filtering your data to display only selected records.

CREATE A REPORT

What You Need

- Microsoft Works Database
- Basic computer system
- Printer

Goal

Create useful output from the data in your database.

Printing a List

If you want to view all the fields in all the records in your database, all you have to do is print the list of records as they appear in List view. You do this by switching to List view and then clicking the Print button on the toolbar.

Tip

> Don't forget to sort your records before you print!

If you prefer, you can print only selected records by filtering your database, as explained in Activity 22, "Sort and Filter Selected Items." Apply the filter, and then print the resulting list of records.

If you just want to print a single record, you don't have to apply some draconian filter. Instead, switch to Forms view, navigate to the record you want to print, and then click the Print button. Works will print only the current form.

Using ReportCreator to Create a Report

Even more useful than printing a list is Works's capability to analyze and summarize the contents of a database in a customized *report*. Works Database includes a special ReportCreator tool that makes creating custom reports a snap.

To create a report, pull down the Tools menu and select ReportCreator. When the Report Name dialog box appears, enter a name for your report and click OK.

Now Works displays the ReportCreator dialog box, as shown in Figure A23.1. You create your report by moving from tab to tab and entering the appropriate information, as follows:

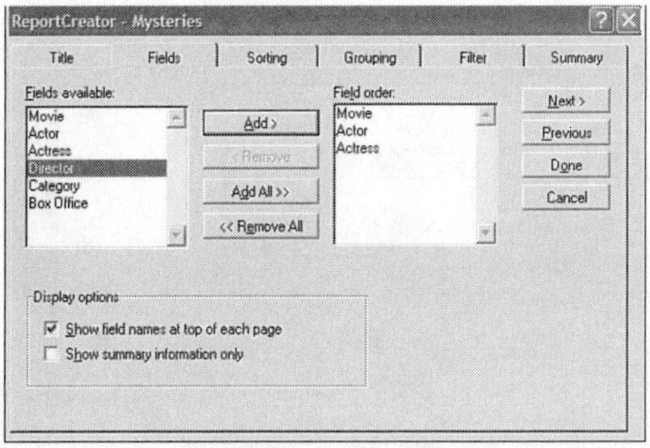

FIGURE A23.1

Use ReportCreator to create custom reports about your database.

- **Title**—Enter or edit the report title, and select an orientation and a font.

- **Fields**—Select those fields you want to include in your report, in the order that you want them to appear, and then click Add. If you want to display the field names at the top of your page, check the Show Field Names at Top of Each Page option; if you want to summarize the data in your fields, check the Show Summary Information Only option.

■ **Sorting**—Select which fields you want to sort by, in either Ascending or Descending order.

■ **Grouping**—Select any fields you want to group or subtotal and how you want them grouped.

Note

Only sorted fields are available for grouping.

■ **Filter**—Select any previously created filter from the Select a Filter list, or click the Create New Filter button to create and apply a new filter.

■ **Summary**—Select any fields you want to summarize, how you want to summarize (sum, average, count, and so on), and where you want to display the summaries (under each column, at the end of the report, and so on).

When you reach the Summary tab and finish your input, click the Done button. You're now asked whether you want to preview or modify the report. Click Preview.

Your report is now displayed onscreen in Preview mode, as shown in Figure A23.2. If you like what you see, click Print. If you don't, click Cancel and edit your report using the report commands on the Tools menu.

FIGURE A23.2

Summarize and analyze your database with custom-created reports.

		Movies - Mysteries			
Director	**Movie**	**Actor**	**Actress**	**Box Office**	
Alfred Hancock	Fear Me Lovely	Roger Mitchell	Ruth Greene	$22,500,000	
GROUP TOTAL Box Office:		$22,500,000			
Curtis Michaels	Deadly Kisses	Humphrey Lorre	Delores Rogers	$37,000,000	
Curtis Michaels	The Big Kiss	Michael Andrews	Sharon Lawrence	$27,000,000	
GROUP TOTAL Box Office:		$64,000,000			
Howard Walsh	Love Me Barely	Mitch Rogers	Lana Fonda	$26,000,000	
Howard Walsh	Kiss Me Softly	Steven Roberts	Greta Bergman	$25,000,000	
Howard Walsh	Kill Me Deadly	Andrew Michaels	Lauren Stone	$15,000,000	
GROUP TOTAL Box Office:		$66,000,000			
Raoul Hawks	The Big Fear	Robert Stevens	Ingrid Garbo	$20,000,000	
Raoul Hawks	The Big Kill	Peter Bogart	Ginger Del Rio	$18,000,000	
GROUP TOTAL Box Office:		$38,000,000			
TOTAL Box Office:		$190,500,000			

Movies - Microsoft Works Database

Page 1
Previous
Next
Zoom In
Zoom Out
Print
Cancel

PART VIII

DO IT NOW: READING THE LATEST NEWS

READ THE LATEST NEWS HEADLINES

What You Need

- Internet Explorer
- Internet connection
- Basic computer system

Goal

Find the most useful Web sites for news headlines and analysis.

Network News

The Internet is a great place to find both news headlines and in-depth analysis. Most news-related Web sites are updated in real-time, so you're always getting the latest news—on your computer screen, when you want it.

Some of the biggest, most popular news sites on the Web are run by the major broadcast and cable news networks. You can turn to these sites to get the latest headlines, and—in many cases—live audio and video feeds from the networks themselves.

The major network news sites include

- ABC News (www.abcnews.com)

- CBS News (www.cbsnews.com)

- CNN (www.cnn.com)

- Fox News (www.foxnews.com)

- MSNBC (www.msnbc.com)

Newspapers

Other good sources of national and international news are the Web sites of the big national newspapers. Most of these sites feature the equivalent of the entire printed edition online—and often for free.

Here are the best of the national newspaper Web sites:

- *Boston Globe* (www.boston.com/globe/)

- *Chicago Tribune* (www.chicagotribune.com)

- *Denver Post* (www.denverpost.com)

- *Detroit Free Press* (www.detroitfreepress.com)

- *Los Angeles Times* (www.latimes.com)

- *Miami Herald* (www.miami.com/herald/)

- *Minneapolis Star Tribune* (www.startribune.com)

- *New York Times* (www.nytimes.com)

- *San Jose Mercury News* (www.mercurycenter.com)

- *San Francisco Chronicle* (www.sfgate.com)

■ *USA Today* (www.usatoday.com)

■ *Wall Street Journal* (www.wsj.com)

■ *Washington Post* (www.washingtonpost.com)

 Tip   Your local paper probably has a Web site, too. Use Google (www.google.com) or another search engine to search for your paper's Web site address.

News Magazines

In addition, almost all the major weekly newsmagazines have first-rate Web sites, chock-full of informative content. Here are a few of the more popular news magazine sites on the Web:

■ *Business Week* (www.businessweek.com)

■ *Harper's* (www.harpers.org)

■ *National Review* (www.nationalreview.com)

■ *Newsweek* (www.newsweek.com)

■ *The New Republic* (www.tnr.com)

■ *Time* (www.time.com)

■ *U.S. News and World Report* (www.usnews.com)

News Archives

What if you want to find news about something more obscure, or about something that happened several months—or years—in the past?

When you're looking for older articles, turn to one of the many news archives on the Web. Some of these sites archive articles in their own databases, and some simply link to the archives of individual news sources. For the best news archives, be prepared to pay for access.

Here's a list of the top news archives on the Web:

■ 1st Headlines (www.1stheadlines.com)

■ AJR NewsLink (ajr.newslink.org)

- News and Newspapers Online (`library.uncg.edu/news/`)

- News Index (`www.newsindex.com`)

- NewsCentral (`www.all-links.com/newscentral/`)

- NewsHub (`www.newshub.com`

- NewsLibrary (`www.newslibrary.com`)

- Newspapers Online (`www.newspapers.com`)

- NewsTrawler (`www.newstrawler.com`)

- Northern Light Current News Search (`www.northernlight.com/news.html`)

- TotalNews (`www.totalnews.com`)

Tip

For a good compendium of *current* news headlines from all around the Internet, check out the Drudge Report site (`www.drudgereport.com`), run by notorious newshound Matt Drudge.

Entertainment News

After you get past the more serious news, it's time for something more entertaining—the serious business of entertainment! Here are some of the more interesting and informative sites for entertainment news and information:

- Ain't It Cool News (`www.aint-it-cool-news.com`)

- E! Online (`www.eonline.com`)

- Entertainment Weekly (`www.ew.com`)

- Film.com (`www.film.com`)

- Hollywood.com (`www.hollywood.com`)

- People.com (`www.people.com`)

- TV Guide Online (`www.tvguide.com`)

Activity 25

GET TODAY'S SPORTS SCORES

What You Need

- Internet Explorer
- Internet connection
- Basic computer system

Goal

Find the best Web sites for sports scores and stories.

Sports Portals

The Web is a great resource for sports fans of all shapes and sizes. Whether you're a fan or a participant, there's at least one site somewhere on the Web that focuses on your particular sport.

The best sports sites on the Web resemble the best news sites—they're actually portals to all sorts of content and services, including up-to-the-minute scores, post-game recaps, in-depth reporting, and much more. If you're looking for sports information online, one of these portals is the place to start:

- CBS SportsLine (www.sportsline.com)

- CNN/Sports Illustrated (sportsillustrated.cnn.com)

- ESPN.com (espn.go.com)

- FOXSports (www.foxsports.com)

- NBC Sports (www.nbcsports.com)

- The Sporting News (www.sportingnews.com)

- Sports Illustrated for Kids (www.sikids.com)

- Sports.com (world.sports.com)

- SportsNetwork.com (www.sportsnetwork.com)

- Yahoo! Sports (sports.yahoo.com)

If you follow a particular sports team, check out that team's local newspaper on the Web. Chances are you'll find a lot of in-depth coverage there that you won't find at these other sites.

Major League Sports

Each of the major sports leagues runs its own official Web site. Here you'll find team information, player stats, and the opportunity to deplete your wallet by purchasing all sorts of official league and team merchandise.

Here are the Web sites for each of the major sports leagues:

- Major League Baseball (www.mlb.com)

- Major League Soccer (www.mlsnet.com)

- National Basketball Association (www.nba.com)

- National Football League (www.nfl.com)

- National Hockey League (www.nhl.com)

- Professional Golfer's Association (www.pga.com)

- Women's National Basketball Association (www.wnba.com)

- World Wrestling Federation (www.wwf.com)

In addition, most teams have their own Web sites—often linked-to from the general league sites listed here.

Tip

If you're interested in college sports, a good place to start is NCAA Online, at www.ncaa.org. This site offers news, statistics, and an online hall of champions.

Participatory Sports

If you'd rather play than watch, there are Web sites for you, too. All the major participatory sports are well represented on the Web, as you can see from the following list:

- **Amateur and extreme sports**—Amateur-Sports.com (www.amateur-sports.com), Athlete.com (www.athlete.com), Bxtreme.net (www.bxtreme.net), ExtremeSports.com (www.extremesports.com), InfoSports.net (www.infosports.net), Mysportsguru.com (www.mysportsguru.com)

- **Baseball**—Full Count (www.3and2.com)

- **Basketball**—Basketball Highway (www.bbhighway.com), DtrainBasketball.com (www.dtrainbasketball.com)

- **Bowling**—Bowl.com (www.bowl.com)

- **Golf**—FreeGolfInfo (www.freegolfinfo.com), Golf 101 (www.golf101.com), Golfonline (www.golfonline.com), GolfREVIEW (www.golfreview.com)

- **Gymanastics**—Gymnastics Routines Directory (www.gym-routines.com), Gymn-Forum.com (www.gymn-forum.com)

- **Hockey**—Hockey Phreak (www.hockeyphreak.com), USA Hockey (www.usahockey.com)

- **Outdoor sports**—Boating America (www.boatingamerica.com), CampNet America (www.campnetamerica.com), GORP (www.gorp.com), The Fishing Network (www.the-fishing-network.com), thebackpacker.com (www.thebackpacker.com), WorldwideAngler.com (www.worldwideangler.com)

■ **Running**—Kick! (www.kicksports.com), realrunner.com (www.realrunner.com)

■ **Snow skiing**—OnTheSnow.com (www.onthesnow.com), SkiNet.com (www.skinet.com)

■ **Soccer**—Soccer. com (www.soccer.com)

■ **Swimming**—Swimmersworld.com (www.swimmersworld.com), WebSwim (www.webswim.com)

■ **Tennis**—Tennis Server (www.tennisserver.com), TennisONE (www.tennisone.com)

FIND OUT TODAY'S WEATHER FORECAST

What You Need

- Internet Explorer
- Internet connection
- Basic computer system

Goal

Find the best Web sites for weather reports and forecasts.

Weather Sites

Weather reports and forecasts are readily available on the Web; most of the major news portals and local Web sites offer some variety of weather-related services. There are also a number of dedicated weather sites on the Web, all of which offer local and national forecasts, weather radar, satellite maps, and more.

Here are the most popular weather sites on the Web:

- AccuWeather (www.accuweather.com)

- EarthWatch (www.earthwatch.com)

- Intellicast (www.intellicast.com)

- National Weather Service (www.nws.noaa.gov)

- USA Today Weather (www.usatoday.com/weather/)

- Weather Underground (www.wunderground.com)

- Weather.com (www.weather.com)

- WeatherDesk.org (www.weatherdesk.org)

- Wild Weather (www.wildweather.com)

Most of these sites also offer international weather forecasts—which are great if you're planning a vacation abroad and don't know what type of clothing to pack!

The number-one weather site on the Web, Weather.com (www.weather.com), is run by the Weather Channel. As you can see in Figure A26.1, Weather.com includes the largest variety of forecasts and maps anywhere, including local forecasts and activity-specific weather information.

FIGURE A26.1

The best weather on the Web— the Weather Channel's Weather.com.

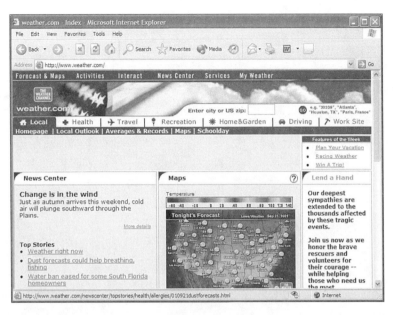

Personalized Weather Forecasts

There is a new type of Internet-based weather service available that promises a more personalized forecast—in terms of both time and location. These services will send you e-mails several times a day (or enable access to a special Web page) detailing the precise weather forecast for your specific ZIP code on an hour-by-hour basis.

All you have to do is go to one of these sites and input your ZIP code (or city and state, or latitude and longitude). In return, you'll receive an extremely accurate forecast, fine-tuned for your particular activities.

There are several of these personalized forecast sites. The best of the bunch are

- My-Cast (www.my-cast.com)
- AWS WeatherBug (www.weatherbug.com)
- Travelforecast.com (www.travelforecast.com)

Climate Data

Interested in weather conditions elsewhere in the world? Want to know what the average July high temperature is in Aberdeen? Or the record low temperature in Zimbabwe? Then, check out these two sites that present a variety of climate data for locations all around the globe:

- Weatherbase (www.weatherbase.com)
- WorldClimate (www.worldclimate.com)

PART **IX**

DO IT NOW: SEARCHING AND RESEARCHING

SEARCH FOR WEB SITES

What You Need

- Internet Explorer
- Internet connection
- Basic computer system

Goal

Use Google, Yahoo!, and other search sites to find specific information on the Web.

How to Search

The World Wide Web contains literally billions of different pages. There's a lot of good information out there, but it's extremely difficult to find—almost like finding a needle in a haystack.

Fortunately, there are numerous sites that help you search the Web for the specific information you want. While these sites all have their own proprietary methods of finding Web pages, they all work in pretty much the same fashion.

Basic Components

You'll find two basic components on every one of these sites—a *search box* and a *search button*. You enter your query—one or more *keywords* that describe what you're looking for—into the search box, and then click the Search button (or press the Enter key) to start the search. The search site then returns a list of Web pages that match your query; click any link to go directly to the page in question.

Constructing a Query

How you construct your query determines how relevant the results will be that you receive. In particular, focus on the keywords you use because the search sites look for these words when they process your query. Your keywords are compared to the Web pages the search site knows about; the more keywords found on a Web page, the better the match.

You should choose keywords that best describe the information you're looking for—using as many keywords as you need. Don't be afraid of using too many keywords; in fact, using too *few* keywords is a common fault of many novice searchers. The more words you use, the better idea the search engine has of what you're looking for.

If you're searching for a specific phrase, enclose that phrase in quotation marks. For example, to search for Monty Python, enter `"Monty Python"` and *not* `Monty Python`; the first query returns pages about the comedy troupe, while the second returns pages about snakes and guys named Monty.

Using Wildcards

But what if you're not quite sure which word to use? For example, would the best results come from looking for *auto*, *automobile*, or *automotive*? Many search sites let you use *wildcards* to "stand in" for parts of a word that you're not quite sure about.

In most instances, the asterisk character (*) is used as a wildcard to match any character or group of characters, from its particular position in the word to the end of that word. So, in the previous example, entering `auto*` would return all three words—auto, automobile, *and* automotive (as well as automatic, autocratic, and any other word that starts with "auto").

Additional Features

Beyond the basic search capabilities, some sites have additional features that let you exert more control over your searches. For example, HotBot includes a number of pull-down lists and check boxes you can use to narrow your search parameters.

Many of the major sites offer *advanced search modes* or pages. In most cases, the advanced search is the only place where you can perform Boolean and other operations that help to fine-tune your search. If you're having trouble finding relevant results, you should probably check out the advanced search mode—just to see if it helps.

Where to Search

Now that you know how to search, *where* should you search?

Directory Searching with Yahoo!

There are two ways to organize the information on the Web. One way is to physically look at each Web page and stick it into a hand-picked category. After you get enough Web pages collected, you have something called a *directory*.

A directory doesn't actually search the Web—in fact, a directory catalogs only a very small part of the Web. But a directory is very organized, and very easy to use, and lots and lots of people use Web directories every day.

The most popular Web directory is Yahoo! (www.yahoo.com). When you access Yahoo!'s main page, you can choose to search the Yahoo! directory or to browse through the directory's main categories. Since Yahoo! is so well-organized, clicking through the categories is a good way for less-experienced users to find what they want.

Note   Some search directories supplement their listings with results from search engines. For example, Yahoo! supplements its directory listings with results from the Google search engine.

Index Searching with Google

The other way to organize the information on the Web is to use a *search engine*. Unlike a directory, which is organized by people, a search engine isn't powered by human hands. Instead, a search engine uses a special type of software program (called a *spider* or *crawler*) to roam the Web automatically, feeding what it finds back to a massive bank of computers. These computers hold *indexes* of the Web, hundreds of millions of pages strong—many more pages than are found in the typical Web directory.

When you enter a query at a search engine site, your query is sent to the search engine's index. (You never actually search the Web itself, you only search the index that was created by the spiders crawling the Web.) The search engine then creates a list of pages in its index that match, to one degree or another, the query you entered.

The best search engine today is Google (`www.google.com`). Google is easy to use, is fast, and returns highly relevant results. That's because it indexes more pages than any other site. While Google's results aren't as well-organized as Yahoo!'s, you'll receive a lot more pages that match your query.

Other Good Search Sites

While Yahoo! and Google are the best directory and search engine, respectively, there are lots of other search sites that also provide more (or just different) results. These search sites include

- About.com (`www.about.com`)
- AltaVista (`www.altavista.com`)
- Ask Jeeves! (`www.askjeeves.com`)
- Dogpile (`www.dogpile.com`)
- Excite (`www.excite.com`)
- HotBot (`hotbot.lycos.com`)
- FAST Search (`www.alltheweb.com`)
- Lycos (`www.lycos.com`)
- MetaCrawler (`www.metacrawler.com`)
- Northern Light (`www.northernlight.com`)

SEARCH FOR NAMES AND ADDRESSES

What You Need

- Internet Explorer
- Internet connection
- Basic computer system

GOAL

Use Web-based white pages directories to look up people's names, addresses, and phone numbers.

Using White Pages Directories

As good as the search sites discussed in Activity 27, "Search for Web Sites," are for finding specific Web pages, they're not that great for finding people. When there's a person (or an address or a phone number) you want to find, you need to use a site that specializes in people searches.

People listings on the Web go by the common name of *white pages directories*, the same as traditional white pages phone books. These directories typically enable you to enter all or part of a person's name and then search for his address and phone number. Many of these sites also let you search for personal e-mail addresses and business addresses and phone numbers.

The best of these directories include

- 411Locate (www.411locate.com)

- AnyWho (www.anywho.com)

- Bigfoot (www.bigfoot.com)

- InfoSpace (www.infospace.com)

- PeopleSearch (www.peoplesearch.net)

- Switchboard (www.switchboard.com)

- The Ultimates (www.theultimates.com)

- WhitePages.com (www.whitepages.com)

- WhoWhere (whowhere.lycos.com)

- Worldpages (www.worldpages.com)

- Yahoo! People (people.yahoo.com)

Searching for E-mail Addresses

E-mail addresses are different from street addresses—and they're harder to track. While there are a handful of e-mail directory sites, these sites list only those e-mail addresses they know about—which typically means addresses provided by major Internet service providers and commercial online services. (Unfortunately, there is no central Web directory of e-mail addresses.)

The best of these e-mail directories include

- Internet Address Finder (www.iaf.net)
- World Email Directory (www.worldemail.com)

In addition, many of the Internet white pages directories also let you search for e-mail addresses.

Don't be surprised, however, if you can't find the e-mail address you're looking for. The best way to find a person's e-mail address, after all, is to ask that person for it.

Searching for Personal Home Pages

A surprisingly large number of people have created their own personal home pages on the Web. (You'll learn how to do this in Activity 46, "Create a Personal Web Page.") Because of this proliferation of personal pages, you have another place to look for people on the Internet.

When you're searching for someone's personal home page, follow this advice:

- Start your search at the WhoWhere Personal Home-Pages Directory (homepages.whowhere.com). This is simply the most comprehensive home pages search engine and directory on the Web.

- You can also search the various home page communities that host personal Web pages. Start with Yahoo! GeoCities (geocities.yahoo.com), which is the biggest. Next in size are Tripod (tripod.lycos.com), AngelFire (angelfire.lycos.com), Hometown AOL (hometown.aol.com), Homestead (www.homestead.com), and iVillage (www.ivillage.com/memberwebsites/).

- You can also use Google and other traditional search engines to search for personal home pages. Just add the words `personal home page` to your query, to help narrow the results.

Searching for Genealogical Information

While we're on the topic of searching for people, let's talk for a minute about genealogy and genealogy-related Web sites. There are thousands of Web sites devoted to genealogical research, and a tremendous amount of information is available online. You can find things like surname databases, the Social Security death index, some directories of public records, and tons of other links and data.

When you're looking for genealogical information, check out these sites:

- Ancestry.com (www.ancestry.com)
- Cyndi's List of Genealogy Sites on the Internet (www.cyndislist.com)
- FamilySearch (www.familysearch.org)
- Genealogical Research at the National Archives (www.nara.gov/genealogy/genindex.html)
- Genealogy Home Page (www.genhomepage.com)
- Genealogy.org (www.genealogy.org)
- Genealogy.com (www.genealogy.com)
- GenSource.com Common Threads (www.gensource.com/common/)
- Rootsweb (www.rootsweb.com)
- Vital Records Information (www.vitalrec.com)

Activity 29

SEARCH FOR HOMEWORK HELP

What You Need

- Internet Explorer
- Internet connection
- Microsoft Encarta
- Basic computer system

Goal

Guide your kids to the best Web sites to help them with their schoolwork.

Homework Help on the Web

If you have kids, they have homework. If they're having trouble with their homework, there are numerous Web sites they can access that provide targeted homework help. Most of these sites let users either browse through a list of topics or search the site for specific types of help.

The best of these homework-helper sites include

- A+ Homework Machine (thehomeworkmachine.com)
- Awesome Library (www.awesomelibrary.org)
- bigchalk (www.bigchalk.com)
- BrainMania (www.brainmania.com)
- DiscoverySchool.com (school.discovery.com)
- Grammar Lady (www.grammarlady.com)
- Homework Center (www.factmonster.com/homework/)
- Homework Help (www.startribune.com/education/homework.shtml)
- Kid Info (www.kidinfo.com)
- KidsClick (www.kidsclick.org)
- MadSci Network (www.madsci.org)
- StudyWEB (www.studyweb.com)
- Word Central (www.wordcentral.com)

Online Libraries

Another good source of information for school-age children is the online equivalent of the traditional library. These online libraries are either branches of existing bricks-and-mortar libraries or Internet-specific collections that can be used for research purposes.

Help your kids check out the following online library sites:

- Argus Clearinghouse (www.clearinghouse.net)
- Berkeley Digital Library SunSITE (sunsite.berkeley.edu)
- CyberStacks (www.public.iastate.edu/~CYBERSTACKS/)

- Digital Library Net (www.digitallibrary.net)

- Electric Library (www.elibrary.com)

- Internet Public Library (www.ipl.org)

- Library of Congress (lcweb.loc.gov)

- LibrarySpot (www.libraryspot.com)

- Michigan Electronic Library (mel.lib.mi.us)

- New York Public Library Digital Library Collection (digital.nypl.org)

- Refdesk.com (www.refdesk.com)

- Smithsonian Institution Libraries (www.sil.si.edu)

- World Wide Web Virtual Library (www.vlib.org)

Kid-Safe Searching

Of course, you could just let your kids do their research using Google, Yahoo!, and other traditional search sites. Unfortunately, searching on a standard search site often produces results that link to inappropriate content.

The solution is to use a site that offers kid-safe searching. These sites work by applying filters to weed out inappropriate content and then present their results via either a search or directory interface.

Kid-safe search sites are often good to use as the start page for your children's browser, since they are launching pads to guaranteed safe content.

The best of these kid-safe search sites include

- AltaVista—AV Family Filter (www.altavista.com; click the Family Filter link in the Search For section)

- Apple EdView (edview.apple.com)

- Ask Jeeves for Kids (www.ajkids.com)

- Family Web Files (www.familywebfiles.com)

- Fact Monster (www.factmonster.com)

- OneKey (www.onekey.com)

- Yahooligans! (www.yahooligans.com)

Homework Help with Encarta

Most new computers include a free version of Microsoft Encarta, an electronic encyclopedia. You can use Encarta to research all sorts of projects—including homework and school reports.

You launch Encarta from the Windows Start menu. You can browse through Encarta's many categories or use the Find function to search for specific information. Most articles include links to related articles, as well as additional information on the Web. Updates for the encyclopedia are available online.

Note

Although Encarta is the most-used encyclopedia software, several other well-known encyclopedias are also available on CD-ROM, including Compton's (www.learningco.com), Encyclopedia Britannica (store.britannica.com), Grolier (go.grolier.com), and World Book (store.worldbook.com/wb/).

There's also an online version of Encarta, located at encarta.msn.com. This free site includes more than 16,000 articles and links to other relevant Web sites. Use the search function at the Encarta site to find the information you're looking for.

SEARCH FOR HEALTH AND WELLNESS INFORMATION

What You Need

- Internet Explorer
- Internet connection
- Basic computer system

Goal

Look up valuable health-related information on the Web.

General Health Information

The Internet is a fount of information of all different types. It's a particularly good research tool for health-related information.

A number of Web sites offer detailed information about illnesses, diseases, and medicines. Many of these sites focus on preventive medicine and wellness, and almost all help you match symptoms with likely illnesses and treatments. Indeed, some of these sites provide access to the same medical databases used by most physicians—without waiting for an appointment!

The top medical sites on the Web include

- Achoo (www.achoo.com)
- drkoop.com (www.drkoop.com)
- healthAtoZ.com (www.healthatoz.com)
- HealthAnswers (www.healthanswers.com)
- HealthLinks.net (www.healthlinks.net)
- Healthtouch Online (www.healthtouch.com)
- kidsDoctor (www.kidsdoctor.com)
- MedExplorer (www.medexplorer.com)
- Medical World Search (www.mwsearch.com)
- Medicine Online (www.medicineonline.com)
- MedicineNet (www.medicinenet.com)
- Medscape Today (www.medscape.com)
- National Library of Medicine (www.nlm.nih.gov)
- Planet Wellness (www.planetwellness.com)
- Virtual Hospital (www.vh.org)
- WebMD Health (my.webmd.com, shown in Figure A30.1)
- Yahoo! Health (health.yahoo.com)

FIGURE A30.1

Use WebMD Health to search for in-depth medical information.

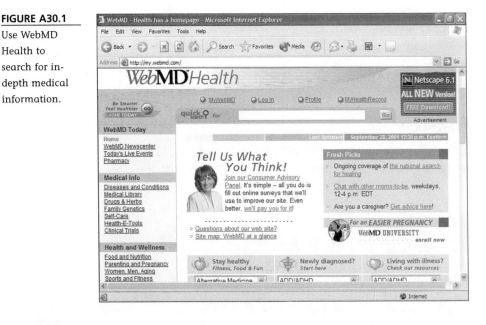

As useful as these health sites are, they should not and cannot serve as substitutes for a trained medical opinion.

Physician Directories

Many physicians, medical groups, HMOs, and hospitals have put their own sites on the Web. Most often these sites are informational only, but some let you schedule appointments from the convenience of your Web browser.

You can also use the Web to search for a new or specialist physician in your area. Some of the best physician search sites include

■ AMA Physician Select (www.ama-assn.org/aps/)

■ Best Doctors (www.bestdoctors.com)

■ DoctorDirectory.com (www.doctordirectory.com)

- MedAvenue.com (www.medavenue.com)

- mydoctor.com (www.mydoctor.com)

- Yahoo! Find a Doctor (health.yahoo.com/health/physicians/)

Senior Health

As we grow older, health issues increase in importance. For that reason, several Web sites focus exclusively on senior's health. These sites include

- AgeNet (agenet.agenet.com)

- Longevity 101 (www.longevity101.com/tableof.htm)

- LovingCare.net (www.lovingcare.net)

- Seniors Wellness (www.seniorswellness.com)

- Thriveonline Senior Nutrition (thriveonline.oxygen.com/ nutrition/seniors/senior.index.html)

- World Health Network (www.worldhealth.net)

In addition, there are numerous general Web sites for seniors that offer superb health resources. These sites include

- MySeniors.com (www.myseniors.com)

- RetireCentral (www.retirecentral.com)

- Senior Information Network (www.senior-inet.com)

- Senior Women Web (www.seniorwomen.com)

- Senior Surfers (www.seniorsurfers.org)

- Senior.com (www.senior.com)

- ThirdAge (www.thirdage.com)

- Today's Seniors (www.todaysseniors.com)

PART **X**

DO IT NOW: BUYING AND SELLING ONLINE

SHOP ONLINE

What You Need

- Internet Explorer
- Internet connection
- Credit card
- Basic computer system

Goal

Find and order quality merchandise from online retailers.

How to Shop

For many users, shopping online is easier than shopping at traditional "bricks-and-mortar" retailers. You can sit down in front of your computer screen at any time of the day or night, dressed or undressed, and use your PC to search the Web for just the right item you want to buy—you don't have to get dressed or start your car or bother with boisterous crowds.

To purchase an item online, all you have to do is enter your name, address, and credit card number, and the online merchant will arrange to have the item delivered directly to your house within a matter of days. It's that easy!

The big online retailers are just as reputable as traditional retailers, offering safe payment, fast shipping, and responsive service. Just to be safe, look for the following features before you shop at a given site:

- Payment by major credit card.

- A *secure server* that encrypts your credit card information.

- Good contact information—e-mail address, street address, phone number, fax number, and so on.

- A stated returns policy and satisfaction guarantee.

- A stated privacy policy that protects your personal information.

- Information *before you finalize your order* that tells you whether the item is in stock and how long it will take to ship.

Some users worry about how safe it is to shop online. They shouldn't. Providing your credit card information to a secure Web site is much safer than handing your credit card to a complete stranger dressed as a waiter in a restaurant or giving it over a cordless phone. The reality is that it's very difficult to steal the bits and bytes of your encoded card number on the Web.

In addition, all major credit card companies limit your liability if your card gets stolen, whether that's on the Web or in the so-called real world. So, go ahead and use your credit card online—there's nothing to worry about!

Shopping Directories and Comparison Services

When it comes to finding a specific online merchant, you can turn to one of the many Internet shopping directories—kind of online malls full of various types of online stores. You can also use a shopping search engine, many of which employ special software that scours the Web, looking for the best deals on particular merchandise.

Here are some of the best online shopping directories and comparison shopping services:

- Active Buyer's Guide (www.activebuyersguide.com)

- BizRate.com (www.bizrate.com)

- Buyer's Index (www.buyersindex.com)

- CyberMall.com (www.cybermall.com)

- Excite Shopping (shopping.excite.com)

- InternetMall (www.internetmall.com)

- Lycos Shop (shop.lycos.com)

- mySimon (www.mysimon.com, shown in Figure A31.1)

- PriceGrabber.com (www.pricegrabber.com)

- Smartshop.com (www.smartshop.com)

- StoreScanner (www.storescanner.com)

- ValueFind (www.valuefind.com)

- Yahoo! Shopping (shopping.yahoo.com)

FIGURE A31.1

Use mySimon to search for the best bargains on the Web.

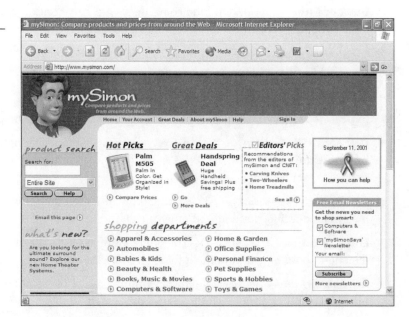

> **Tip**
>
> When it comes to finding the best merchants in a particular category, visit Gomez (`www.gomez.com`). Gomez ranks the biggest online retailers in selected categories (such as travel, apparel, auctions, and so forth), by a variety of criteria.

The Biggest—and the Best—Online Retailers

Even though there are thousands and thousands of merchants on the Web, a handful of online retailers garner the most user traffic—and sales. When you're looking for the best of the best, these are the online merchants to turn to:

- **800.com** (`www.800.com`)—Offering CDs, DVDs, videotapes, video game consoles, digital cameras, cordless phones, home video and audio equipment, and car audio equipment

- **Amazon.com** (`www.amazon.com`)—The world's largest online shopping site, offering books, CDs, videotapes, DVDs, video games, computer hardware, electronics, toys, and other types of consumer merchandise

- **Barnes and Noble.com** (`www.bn.com`)—The online branch of the largest bricks-and-mortar bookstore, selling books, CDs, DVDs, videotapes, and video games

- **Buy.com** (`www.buy.com`)—Offering computers, wireless phones, video games, office products, consumer electronics products, sporting gear, and more

- **CDNow** (`www.cdnow.com`)—Offering CDs, DVDs, and videotapes

- **Eddie Bauer** (`www.eddiebauer.com`)—The online branch of the popular catalog merchant, offering clothing and other merchandise

- **Express.com** (`www.express.com`)—Offering DVDs, CDs, and video games

- **J&R Music & Computer World** (`www.jandr.com`)—Offering computer hardware and software, CDs, DVDs, cameras, and a variety of consumer electronics equipment

- **L.L. Bean** (`www.llbean.com`)—The online branch of the popular catalog merchant, offering clothing and other merchandise

- **Land's End** (`www.landsend.com`)—The online branch of the popular catalog merchant, offering clothing and other merchandise

- **Nordstrom** (`store.nordstrom.com`)—The online branch of the popular department store, offering shoes, clothing, and other merchandise

- **Roxy.com** (`www.roxy.com`)—Offering cellular phones, digital satellite systems, audio, video, and other consumer electronics products

RESEARCH MAJOR PURCHASES

What You Need

- Internet Explorer
- Internet connection
- Basic computer system

Goal

Use the Internet to shop for a new home or automobile.

Buying a Home

The biggest single purchase most people make in their entire lives is their home. Numerous home-buying resources are available on the Internet, offering everything from real estate listings to mortgage information. You can use these sites to research what kind of home you want (and can afford), and then search for a new or resale home in a particular region and price range.

Some of the more popular home-buying sites include

- **eRealty.com** (www.erealty.com)—Offering home buying and selling services in select cities

- **FSBO.com** (www.fsbo.com)—Lists of homes for sale by owner (FSBO)

- **HomeFox.com** (www.homefox.com)—Home brokerage services for buying and selling residential and commercial real estate

- **Homes.com** (www.homes.com)—A one-stop shop for resale homes, apartments, and new-home builders

- **HomeScape.com** (www.homescape.com)—A true "home" portal, offering access to residential real estate, apartments, new homes, moving services (via MovingCenter), and financing

- **Homestore.com** (www.homestore.com)—A virtual portal for home-related activities, including homes for sale, apartments for rent, moving services, home improvement, lawn and garden, and more

- **iHomeowner.com** (www.ihomeowner.com)—Information and services for home buying, selling, and moving

- **iOwn** (www.iown.com)—A site that lets you shop for and apply for a mortgage online, as well as find a real estate agent

- **MSN HomeAdvisor** (homeadvisor.msn.com)—A full-service home-buying site, from Microsoft

- **NewHomeNetwork.com** (www.newhomenetwork.com)—One of the largest sites for new home construction on the Web

- **RealHome.com** (www.realhome.com)—A highly rated resource for buying, financing, improving, and selling your home

- **Realtor.com** (www.realtor.com)—As shown in Figure A32.1, the largest site for resale residential real estate on the Web, from the National Association of Realtors

- **Realty Online.Net (www.realtyonline.net)**—Direct access to resale homes, apartments, commercial properties, and foreclosures

- **Realty.com (www.realty.com)**—Online resources for selling your home, finding an agent, making home improvements, and so on

- **Yahoo! Real Estate (realestate.yahoo.com)**—An impressive collection of online listings and services for buying, selling, renting, improving, financing, and moving

FIGURE A32.1

Find a new place to live at Realtor.com.

Buying a Car

There are a number of Web sites that offer all sorts of information about new and used cars—including dealer cost information that can help you negotiate a better purchase price. Most of these sites offer some combination of new-car buying guides, reviews, dealer pricing information, and used-car classifieds; some even direct your inquiry to local car dealers, who offer special Internet-only pricing to online shoppers.

When you visit one of these sites, you'll be prompted to search for a particular car by manufacturer and model. You can read reviews and specifications for particular cars and then compare prices and specs between different models.

Here are the best of the Web's auto-research sites:

- Auto-By-Tel (www.autobytel.com)

- AutoNation.com (www.autonation.com)

- AutoSite (www.autosite.com)

- AutoVantage.com (www.autovantage.com)

- Autoweb (www.autoweb.com)

- CarPrices.com (www.carprices.com)

- CarReview.com (www.carreview.com)

- Cars.com (www.cars.com)

- CarsDirect.com (www.carsdirect.com)

- DealerNet.com (www.dealernet.com)

- DriversSeat.com (www.driversseat.com)

- Edmunds.com (www.edmunds.com)

- Kelley Blue Book (www.kbb.com)

- MSN CarPoint (carpoint.msn.com)

MAKE TRAVEL RESERVATIONS

What You Need

- Internet Explorer
- Internet connection
- Credit card
- Basic computer system

Goal

Find and book airline, hotel, and rental car reservations for your next business trip or vacation.

How to Make a Reservation

Savvy travelers use the Internet to book all their travel reservations—plane tickets, hotel rooms, rental cars, and more. To book reservations, all you need to know is where you're going and when—and all the numbers from your favorite charge card.

When you visit an online travel site, you'll have to enter some key information before you search for and book your reservations. You'll need to enter *when* you're traveling (your departure and return dates), *how many* people are traveling, *how much* you want to pay (full fare or discount fare), *what kind* of arrangements and accommodations you want, and any *special considerations* you have for your trip.

Armed with this information, the travel site will search for the flights (and rooms and cars) that best match your requirements. From there, finalizing your arrangements is as simple as clicking a few buttons and providing your credit card number.

Some Web sites give you the option of receiving a regular printed ticket or an electronic ticket *(e-ticket)*. While e-tickets purport to be more convenient than regular tickets, they can be difficult to exchange for a ticket on another airline if you're forced to change flights at the last moment. For that reason, many experienced travelers prefer to have traditional tickets delivered. If you choose e-ticketing, make sure you print copies of your confirmation and itinerary to take with you to the airport—you'll need them to pass security and check in.

Where to Make a Reservation

The Web's general travel sites all offer similar content and services, including the ability to book airline tickets, hotel rooms, and rental cars all in one place. Most of these sites let you search for the lowest rates, or for flights and lodging that match your specific requirements.

Here are the best of these "online travel agents":

- American Express Travel (travel.americanexpress.com)

- Arthur Frommer's Budget Travel Online (www.frommers.com)

- Biztravel (www.biztravel.com)

- CheapTickets.com (www.cheaptickets.com)

- Expedia (www.expedia.com)

- Orbitz (www.orbitz.com)

- Priceline (www.priceline.com)

- TicketPlanet.com (www.ticketplanet.com)

- TravelNow.com (www.travelnow.com)

- Travelocity (www.travelocity.com)

- TravelWeb (www.travelweb.com)

- Trip.com (www.trip.com)

- Yahoo! Travel (travel.yahoo.com)

 When you make reservations online, look for a site that employs real people behind the scenes—and offers a 24/7 800-number to contact those people if something goes wrong. Expedia and Travelocity both offer live customer support, which is a real lifeline if you're stranded somewhere without a reservation.

You can also make reservations from within Microsoft Works Suite. Open the Works Task Launcher, select the Tasks tab, select E-mail & Internet, and then select Flight Reservations on the Web. Works launches Internet Explorer and connects to the Expedia Web site, where you can make all your reservations.

Making Maps and Getting Directions

How do you find your way around a new city after you leave the airport? For that matter, how do you get to a specific city if you're traveling by car?

What you need is a map and some driving directions—both of which are readily available on the Web. There are several major map-making sites you can use, all of which also generate turn-by-turn driving directions when you input your starting and ending addresses.

Here are the major Web map sites:

- Expedia Maps (maps.expedia.com)

- MapBlast! (www.mapblast.com)

- MapQuest (www.mapquest.com)

- Yahoo! Maps (maps.yahoo.com)

Researching Before You Go

Before you decide where to go on your vacation, you may want to research several likely destinations. Traditionally, you'd do this with a printed travel guide by Frommer's, Fodor's, or a similar publisher. While those books are still available (and still popular), most travel publishers now have Web sites that offer the same information—in an easily searchable format.

Here are the sites you can use to research your trip before you go:

- Concierge.com (www.concierge.com)
- Fodors (www.fodors.com)
- GORP.com (www.gorp.com)
- Lonely Planet (www.lonelyplanet.com)
- Rough Guides (www.roughguides.com)
- VirtualTourist.com (www.virtualtourist.com)

BID ON AN ONLINE AUCTION

What You Need

- Internet Explorer
- Internet connection
- Basic computer system

Goal

Place a winning bid on eBay, the world's largest online auction site.

The Biggest Online Auctions

An *online auction* is, quite simply, a Web-based version of a traditional auction. You find an item you'd like to own and then place a bid on the item. Other users also place bids, and at the end of the auction—typically a seven-day period—the highest bidder wins.

Far and away the largest online auction site is eBay (www.ebay.com). eBay has more items listed and more bidders than all the other auction sites combined, with more than five million individual listings on any given day. Do a search from eBay's main page, and you can find everything from rare collectibles and vintage sports memorabilia to the latest electronics equipment.

After eBay, there are two other large general-interest online auctions. Amazon.com Auctions (auctions.amazon.com) and Yahoo! Auctions (auctions.yahoo.com) both offer a variety of merchandise in all popular categories, and all operate in pretty much the same fashion as eBay.

How Online Auctions Work

All online auctions work in a similar fashion:

1. The seller places an ad.
2. The buyer searches for an item.
3. The buyer makes a bid.
4. The bidding continues . . . .
5. The high bidder wins.
6. The seller contacts the high bidder with a final price (including shipping and handling).
7. The high bidder sends payment to the seller.
8. The seller ships the item to the high bidder.

Finding What You Want

eBay organizes its millions of items into a variety of categories. You can browse through the categories from eBay's main page; remember to click through the sub-categories within each major category.

Given the huge number of items up for auction, it might be more productive to search for a specific type of item. You can use the Search box on eBay's main page or click the Search link for more advanced search items.

Making a Bid

After you've found an item you want, it's time to bid. To make a bid, you have to enter your eBay user ID and password and the *maximum bid* you are willing to make.

It's important that you enter the maximum amount you'd be willing to pay, even if the current bid is much lower than that theoretical maximum—and even though you hope the bidding doesn't go up that high. That's because eBay uses automated bidding software. The software won't bid your maximum unless it absolutely has to; it actually enters the current bid amount as your bid, and holds your higher number in reserve for future bids, if necessary.

Some auctions have a *reserve price*. The high bid must be above this price (which is hidden) to actually win the auction. If bids don't reach the reserve, the seller is not obligated to sell the item.

As the auction continues and other users place their bids, it's possible that your maximum bid will be outbid. When this happens, you'll receive an e-mail from eBay; you can then choose to make a higher bid or to bow out of the bidding.

To increase your chances of winning an auction, use a technique called *sniping*. When you snipe, you hold your bid until the very last seconds of the auction. If you bid high enough and late enough, other bidders won't have time to respond to your bid—and your high bid will win!

Winning—and Paying

If you're the high bidder at the end of the auction, you win! You should receive a confirmation e-mail from eBay, as well as a message from the item's seller. The seller should provide you with the total price (your high bid plus shipping and handling charges), as well as information on where to send payment.

eBay doesn't charge any fees to its bidders—all eBay fees are paid by the sellers. High bidders, however, are typically responsible for the shipping and handling charges for the items they win.

How should you pay?

The least safe method of payment is to send cash; there's nothing to track, and it's very easy for someone to steal an envelope full of cash.

Also considered less safe (although better than cash) are cashier's checks and money orders—although these methods are preferred by many sellers. Like cash, they provide no money trail to trace if you want to track down the seller.

Paying by check gives you a minor trail to trace, but once the check is cashed, it's still pretty much a done deal. In addition, most sellers hold your merchandise for ten days or more for your check to clear your bank.

A safer way to pay is by credit card. When you pay by credit card, you can always go to the credit card company and dispute your charges if the item you bought never arrived or was misrepresented. The same safety measures typically apply to credit card payments made through PayPal, Billpoint, and other bill pay services that let you use your credit card for payment.

Receiving the Item—and Leaving Feedback

After you've received the auction item—and you're satisfied with your purchase—you need to leave feedback about the seller. Feedback can be either positive, neutral, or negative. Just go to the auction page for the item you just received, click the Leave Feedback link, and fill in the resulting form.

Check the seller's feedback rating before you bid. Avoid sellers with low feedback numbers or negative comments; if other buyers had trouble with that seller, you might, too.

SELL AT AN ONLINE AUCTION

What You Need

- Internet Explorer
- Internet connection
- Credit card
- Basic computer system

Goal

Place an item listing on eBay, and then conduct a successful auction for that item.

Placing Your Ad

To sell an item on eBay, you first have to register with the service and provide a credit card number. This is so eBay can charge you the appropriate fees for your item listing.

eBay makes its money by charging sellers two types of fees. *Insertion fees* are based on the minimum bid or reserve price of the item listed. *Final value fees* are charged when you sell an item, based on the item's final selling price. Fees are typically charged directly to the seller's credit card account.

You create an item listing by going to eBay's home page and clicking the Sell button. eBay displays a series of forms for you to complete; the information you enter into these forms is used to create your item listing.

You'll need to enter the following information:

- Category for your item listing

- A title and detailed description for the item

- The URL for an accompanying picture (optional)

- Your city and state

- The amount of your minimum (starting) bid

- The duration of your auction (3, 5, 7, or 10 days)

- What types of payments you'll accept

- Acceptable locations to ship to (you can opt not to ship outside the U.S., or only to specific regions)

- Who pays shipping (typically the buyer)

After you enter all the information, eBay creates and displays a preliminary version of your auction listing. If you like what you see, click OK and let your auction get started!

There are other options you can choose for your auction, including a reserve price (above the starting bid), listing enhancements, and so on. Most sellers skip these options and go with a straight 7-day auction.

Handling Payment

When you're listing an item for auction at eBay, you can choose what types of payment you'll accept from the winning bidder. This might seem like an easy decision, but each type of payment needs to be handled differently on your end:

- **Cash**—While it might be nice to receive cash in the mail, it's not very safe for your buyers; cash is too easy to rip off and virtually untraceable. Don't expect buyers to pay by cash—but if they do, it's okay to ship the item immediately on payment.

- **Personal checks**—This is the most common form of payment—it's very convenient for buyers. If you accept checks, make sure you wait for the check to clear (typically 10 business days) before you ship the item.

- **Money orders and cashier's checks**—To a seller, these are almost as good as cash. You can cash a money order immediately, without waiting for funds to clear, which means you can ship on payment.

- **Credit cards**—Because most individuals aren't set up to receive credit card payments, you can use a *bill pay service* to receive credit card payments on your behalf. These services, such as PayPal (www.paypal.com) and Billpoint (www.billpoint.com), accept the credit card payments for you and then deposit the money in your checking account. (They typically charge a slight fee for this service.) When you accept credit card payments in this fashion, you can ship items immediately on payment.

While PayPal remains the most popular bill pay service, Billpoint lets you sign up for its services directly from the eBay item listing form.

Ending the Auction

As soon as an auction ends, the auction site e-mails both the seller and the winning bidder. As soon as you receive this confirmation, you should send your own e-mail to the winning bidder. You should include the following information in this message:

- Total cost of the item, including shipping and handling

- What kind of payment you prefer

- Details on where the buyer should send the payment

- Details on the shipping method

The winning bidder should then respond to your e-mail and arrange payment. If the buyer *doesn't* respond to you within three business days, that high bidder forfeits her position as the winning bidder. You should then contact eBay about refunding your selling fees and relisting the item for sale.

Shipping the Item—and Leaving Feedback

After you receive payment, you need to pack it up and ship it out. Be sure you pack the item in an efficient yet sturdy manner, so the item doesn't get damaged in shipment. Then, take the item to the post office or one of the major shipping services and arrange shipment.

After you've shipped the item, e-mail the buyer that the item is on its way, log back onto eBay to leave feedback for the winning bidder, and congratulate yourself for a successful online auction!

PART **XI**

DO IT NOW: WORKING WITH PICTURES

MANAGE PHOTOS FROM A DIGITAL CAMERA

What You Need

- Digital camera
- Camera-to-PC cable
- Basic computer system

Goal

Connect your digital camera to your PC and upload pictures to your hard drive.

Connecting Your Digital Camera

Connecting a digital camera to your new PC is extremely easy, especially if your system uses the Windows XP operating system. Chances are your camera is Plug and Play–compatible and connects to your PC via a USB connection. Just use the cable that came with your camera to connect the camera to one of your PC's USB ports. When you turn on your camera (and switch it to "PC" or "transfer" mode), Windows automatically recognizes your camera and installs the appropriate software drivers.

If Windows does *not* recognize your camera, you can use the Scanners and Cameras utility to install the camera on your system. You open this utility by clicking the Windows Start button and selecting Control Panel. From the Control Panel, select Scanners and Cameras.

When the Scanners and Cameras utility appears, click the Add Device icon. This launches the Scanner and Camera Installation Wizard. Follow the onscreen instructions to identify the make and manufacturer of your camera, and then install the proper drivers.

When you exit the wizard, your new camera appears as a device in the Scanners and Cameras window.

Choosing a Picture Editing Program

If you want a particular picture editing program to launch whenever you upload pictures from your camera, open the Scanners and Camera utility, right-click your camera's icon, and then select Properties from the pop-up menu. When the Properties dialog box appears, select the Events tab, select an event from the Select an Event list, click the Start This Program option, and then select the application you want to link to the event.

Uploading Pictures to Your PC

When you connect your digital camera and activate its "transfer" mode, Windows displays the Choose Pictures to Copy dialog box. (You can also display this dialog box by opening the My Pictures folder and selecting the Get Pictures from Camera or Scanner task.)

At this point you can select from four actions:

- **Acquire Photos**—Choose this option to select photos to copy to your hard disk.

- **View a Slideshow of the Images**—Select this option and Windows displays a full-screen slideshow of the images currently stored in your camera. No copying of the images is necessary.

■ **Print the Pictures**—Select this option to print individual photos without first copying them to your hard disk.

■ **Open Folder to View Files**—Select this option when you want to view, delete, rename, or otherwise manage the camera.

When you select Acquire Photos (and click OK), the Scanner and Camera Wizard launches. You're presented with thumbnails of all the photos currently stored in your camera. You don't have to copy all these photos to your hard drive—although you can, by clicking the Select All option. Just select which photos you want to copy; then click the Next button.

Now you're presented with the Select a Picture Name and Destination screen. This is where you select the destination folder and filenames for your pictures. By default, Windows XP copies your pictures to the My Pictures folder.

Windows XP names all your photos with a common filename, followed by a unique number. So, for example, if you entered `Vacation` as the picture name, your photos would be named `Vacation 001`, `Vacation 002`, `Vacation 003`, and so on.

After you've entered all this information, click the Next button and the wizard copies your selected pictures to your hard disk.

Note   Some digital cameras come with their own image-management software. You can use your camera's software in lieu of Windows's image management functions, if you wish.

Working with Pictures in Your Camera

Interestingly, you don't have to copy photos from your camera to your hard disk to work with them. Windows XP also lets you work directly with the pictures currently stored in your digital camera.

When you connected your camera to your computer, you were presented with four options. (You can also display these options by selecting the camera icon in the Scanners and Cameras utility and clicking the Get Pictures option in the activity center pane.) You select the Acquire Pictures option to copy pictures to your hard disk, but you can select one of the other options to work with the pictures while they're still in your camera.

To print selected photos from your camera, choose the Print the Pictures option. All the photos in your camera will be displayed, and all you have to do is choose which photos you want to send to your picture.

To delete or rename the pictures in your camera, select the Open Folder to View Files option. This displays the contents of your camera in a My Pictures–like folder. You can use the commands in this folder to perform a full range of file-management tasks with your pictures.

If your camera contains any movie files, you can play these movies on your PC by selecting the Play the Video Files option. Because many digital still cameras also let you record short MPEG movies, this option is a nice way to view your movies without first copying them to your hard disk.

SCAN YOUR PHOTOS

What You Need

- Photo prints
- Scanner
- Basic computer system

Goal

Use a scanner to scan printed photos to your PC's hard drive.

Different Types of Scanners

A desktop scanner is an essential part of many users' PC systems. Scanners have come down in price to where they're quite affordable, and they're relatively easy to install and use.

If you're in the market for a new scanner for your computer system, you have three basic choices.

The most popular type of scanner is a *flatbed* scanner. This type of scanner lets you lay pictures and other items flat on a glass-top service. A flatbed scanner is easy to use, is versatile, and scans images in color.

A *sheet-fed* scanner requires you to feed the item to be scanned into some sort of mechanism. This type of scanner is typically incorporated into multifunction printers—those devices that combine printing, faxing, copying, and scanning into a single unit. Sheet-fed scanners are less versatile (you can't scan boxes or books) than flatbed scanners and often scan only in black and white.

The final type of scanner is a *handheld* scanner. While these devices are small and portable—so you can take them with you on the road—they're also somewhat difficult to use and don't always produce the best-quality scans.

Connecting and Configuring a Scanner

If you have the option, choose a scanner that connects via your computer's USB or FireWire port. USB and FireWire scanners require very little setup. When you connect the scanner, Windows recognizes it and begins the driver installation process.

If Windows does not recognize your scanner, you can add the scanner to your system via the new Scanners and Cameras utility. Just click the Scanners and Cameras icon in the Control Panel, and when the utility opens, click the Add Device icon. This starts the Scanner and Camera Installation Wizard, which walks you step-by-step through the installation.

The process of installing a scanner is identical to the process of installing a digital camera, discussed in Activity 36, "Manage Photos from a Digital Camera."

Choosing a Picture Editing Program

After your scanneris installed, you can link the scanner to a particular program. For example, you can configure Windows to automatically open a specific picture editing program when you click a scanned image anywhere on your system.

To configure Windows XP in this fashion, open the Scanners and Camera utility, right-click your scanner's icon, and then select Properties from the pop-up menu. When the Properties dialog box appears, select the Events tab, select an event from the Select an Event list, click the Start This Program option, and then select the application you want to link to the event.

Making a Scan

Some scanners come with their own scanning software. You can use this software to initiate a scan, or you can use the scanning features built in to Windows XP.

When you press the Scan button on your scanner, Windows senses this event and launches the Scanner and Camera Wizard. As you can see in Figure A37.1, the scanner part of this wizard lets you control how your picture is scanned.

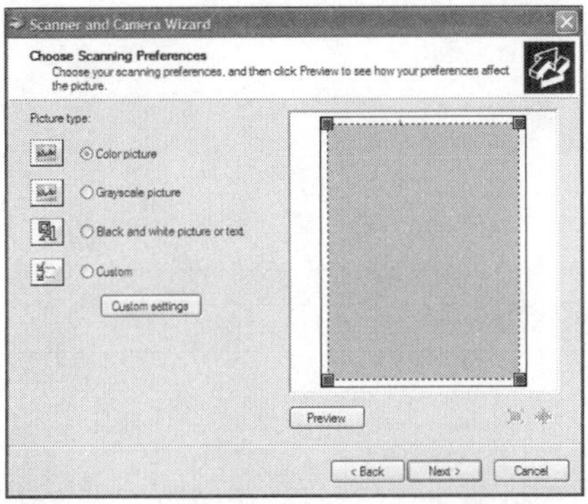

FIGURE A37.1

Use Windows XP to scan a photograph and preview your scan before you accept it.

Start by selecting one of the Picture Type options—Color Picture, Grayscale Picture, Black and White Picture or Text, or Custom. When you make a selection, the wizard displays a preview of what you're scanning.

If you like what you see, you can tell the wizard to finish the scan. If you don't like what you see, you can change the settings and look at another preview.

The wizard then saves your scan in the folder you select. By default, scanned photos are saved in the My Pictures folder.

If you have a bunch of photo prints you want to put on your computer, but *don't* have a scanner, all is not lost. Many photo-processing services and commercial printers (including Kinko's) offer scanning services. For a fee, they'll turn your prints (or, in some cases, your negatives) into JPG or TIFF files you can use on your computer.

TOUCH UP YOUR PICTURES

What You Need

- Digital photos
- Microsoft Picture It! Publishing (or similar photo editing software)
- Basic computer system

Goal

Fix blemishes in your pictures, and add simple special effects.

Managing Your Photos

By default, Windows XP stores all your picture files in the My Pictures folder. This folder includes a number of features specific to the management of picture files, found in the Picture Tasks panel. These features include

- View as a slide show

- Order prints online

- Print this picture

- Set as desktop background

You can also change the way files are displayed in this folder. To display a thumbnail of each file, pull down the View menu and select Thumbnails. To view the selected file as a large image with all the other files in a scrolling list, pull down the View menu and select Filmstrip. To view details about each picture (its size, when it was taken, and so on), pull down the View menu and select Dimensions.

Using Microsoft Picture It! Publishing

Not all the pictures you take are perfect. Sometimes the image might be a little out-of-focus or off-center, or maybe your subject caught the glare of a flash for a "red eye" effect. The nice thing about digital pictures is that you can easily edit them to correct for these and other types of flaws.

To fix the flaws in a picture, you use a picture editing program. The picture editing program built in to Microsoft Works Suite is called Microsoft Picture It! Publishing. You launch Picture It! Publishing from either the Windows Start menu or the Works Task Launcher.

Other popular picture editing programs include Adobe PhotoDeluxe (www.adobe.com/products/photodeluxe/), Corel Photo-Paint (www.corel.com), MGI PhotoSuite (www.mgisoft.com/photo/), and Micrografx Picture Publisher (www.micrografx.com/mgxproducts/picturepublisher.asp).

To open a specific picture for editing, click the My Pictures icon on the Welcome screen. When the next screen appears, click the My Documents icon, navigate to the My Pictures folder, and then select the picture you want to edit.

The picture appears onscreen, as shown in Figure A38.1. All open pictures are shown in the Tray at the bottom of the screen, and the Picture Options panel appears on the left side. (This panel changes based on which option you select.)

FIGURE A38.1

Edit your pictures
with Microsoft
Picture It!
Publishing.

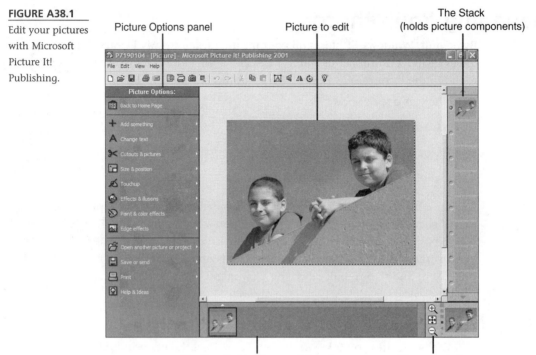

Picture Options panel   Picture to edit   The Stack
(holds picture components)

The Tray (holds all open pictures)   Zoom controls

Touching Up a Picture

To perform basic touch-up operations, select Touchup from the Picture Options
panel. You have several types of touch-ups to choose from:

- **Brightness and contrast**—Lets you lighten or darken your picture

- **Correct tint**—Lets you change the color level and tint

- **Fix red eye**—Removes the red tint caused by inappropriate flash

- **Repair**—Lets you remove dust, blemishes, scratches, and wrinkles

- **Touchup painting**—Lets you play around with the picture's colors, including
  colorizing black-and-white photos and applying transparency effects

- **Clone painting**—Lets you repeat images in your picture

Most of these tasks have an "automatic fix" option. When you click the Automatic
Fix button, Picture It! Publishing makes its best guess about what needs to be fixed
and then executes the changes. (And if you don't like the program's best guess, just
pull down the Edit menu and select Undo to undo the changes.)

Cropping a Picture

One of the more common picture flaws comes when the subject of the picture isn't ideally positioned. You can fix this type of flaw by *cropping* the picture to eliminate unwanted areas of the image.

To crop a picture with Picture It! Publishing, select Size & Position from the Picture Options panel, and then select Crop. You can pick a shape for your final image and then move and resize the final image onscreen. Click the Done button to complete the crop.

Adding Special Effects

Picture It! Publishing includes lots of other neat special effects you can add to your pictures—more than can be described here. You can find most of these special effects on the Picture Options panel, under the Effects & Illusions, Paint & Color Effects, and Edge Effects options. The best way to discover these effects is to experiment on your own—which can also be a lot of fun!

PRINT YOUR PHOTOS

What You Need

- Digital photos
- Microsoft Picture It! Publishing (optional)
- Color printer
- Basic computer system

Goal

Use your printer to create high-quality prints of your digital photos.

Choosing the Right Printer—and Paper

If you have a color printer, you can make good-quality prints of your image files. Even a low-priced color inkjet can make surprisingly good prints, although the better your printer, the better the results.

Some manufacturers sell printers specifically designed for photographic prints. These printers use special photo print paper and output prints that are almost indistinguishable from those you get from a professional photo processor. If you take a lot of digital photos, one of these printers might be a good investment.

The quality of your prints is also affected by the type of paper you use. Printing on standard laser or inkjet paper is okay for making proofs, but you'll want to use a thicker, waxier paper for those prints you want to keep. Check with your printer's manufacturer to see what type of paper it recommends for the best quality photo prints.

Printing from a Program

Any picture editing program will let you print your pictures from within the program—often with useful options. For example, Microsoft Picture It! Publishing lets you select the size of the final print, the orientation of the picture (portrait or landscape), and the print quality (the higher the quality, the slower the printing). To initiate printing from this program, pull down the File menu and select Print.

Using the Photo Printing Wizard

Windows XP also includes some useful options for printing pictures, via the Photo Printing Wizard. You launch this wizard by opening the My Pictures folder, selecting a picture, and then selecting the Print Pictures option in the Picture Tasks panel.

The Photo Printing Wizard, shown in Figure A39.1, walks you step-by-step through the printing process. Here are some of the options you can select:

- Which pictures to print

- Which printer to use

- Which layout to use—full-page fax print, full-page photo print, 35-print contact sheet, 8×10 prints, 5×7 prints, 4×6 cutout prints, 4×6 album prints, 3.5×5 wallet prints, or nine wallet prints

- How many prints to print

When you complete the wizard, the printing starts, just as you specified.

FIGURE A39.1

Print your pictures with Windows XP's Photo Printing Wizard.

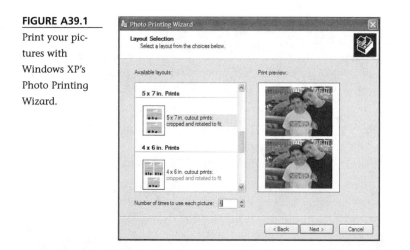

FIGURE A39.1

Print your pictures with Windows XP's Photo Printing Wizard.

E-mailing a Picture

Windows XP also gives you the option of e-mailing your pictures to others. E-mailing images can be tricky because you face a compromise between file size and quality. Higher-quality images create larger-sized files, which take longer for your recipients to download. Smaller files make for faster downloads but can also compromise image quality.

When you let Windows XP e-mail your pictures for you, you can choose to send the pictures at their original sizes or to make the pictures smaller for easier e-mailing. All you have to do is open the My Pictures folder, select the picture you want to e-mail, and then select E-mail This File from the File and Folder Tasks panel.

This displays the Send Pictures via E-mail dialog box, shown in Figure A39.2. The two basic options are Make All My Pictures Smaller and Keep the Original Sizes. When you click Show More Options, you can also select from Small, Medium, and Large options. Choose the best size for your recipient—in most cases, smaller is better.

FIGURE A39.2

Choose the right size for e-mailing your pictures.

Windows now launches your e-mail program (Outlook Express, by default), with a new message. This message already includes your selected picture as an attachment. Just enter the recipient's e-mail address, a subject for the message, and any desired message text. Click the Send button to send this message to your Outbox.

Note | Learn more about sending e-mail messages in Activity 6, "Send and Receive E-mail."

MAKE A FAMILY PHOTO ALBUM

What You Need

- Digital photos
- Microsoft Picture It! Publishing
- Color printer
- Basic computer system

Goal

Create and print an album of your digital photos.

Picking a Project

If you're really into digital photos, you'll end up with a ton of pictures stored on your computer's hard disk. Now you have the problem of how to share those photos with your friends and family. You can e-mail the pictures, of course—you learned how to do this in Activity 39, "Print Your Photos." A more traditional approach is to use your photos to create your own printed photo album.

Microsoft Picture It! Publishing includes lots of fun projects, including photo album pages. You can choose from a number of good-looking designs, add your own photos, and then print the pages on your color printer.

You start by picking a particular project and design. From Picture It! Publishing's Welcome screen, click the Pick a Design icon. When the Pick a Design screen appears, select Photo Projects; when the next screen appears, select Album Pages.

As you can see in Figure A40.1, you now can select from nine "themes" for your pages—Baby, Birthday, Family, General, Kids, Seasonal, Sports, Travel, and Wedding. Select a theme, and then choose a specific page template.

FIGURE A40.1

Choose from several album themes and templates.

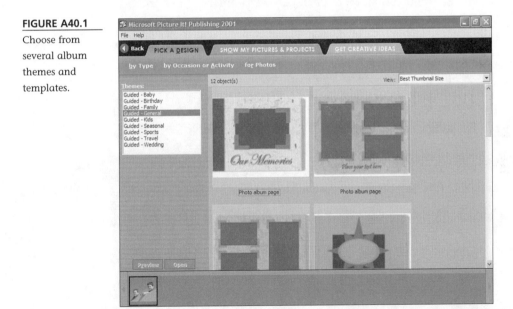

Loading the Tray

Your page template now appears onscreen. You'll need to fill this template with your own pictures—but before you do this, you have to add your pictures to the Tray at the bottom of the screen.

To do this, select Open a Picture from the Photo Album Pages panel and navigate to the folder that holds your pictures. Now drag the photo you want from the main window to the Tray. You can drag as many photos as you want—in fact, now is the time to fill up the tray with all the pictures you want to add to your album.

When you're done adding pictures, click the Done button. Picture It! Publishing returns you to the album page template screen.

Adding Pictures and Text

Now it's time to add those pictures to your template. This is as easy as dragging a picture from the Tray to a position on the template. You have to do this one page at a time, so when you fill up the first page, click the Next button.

You might have noticed that some of your pictures are either too big or too small for the cutout in the template. That isn't a problem because the next screen lets you resize and move your pictures to fit in the available space. Just select a picture in the template to display its *handles*, as shown in Figure A40.2. These are little green circles you can use to resize or stretch the picture.

FIGURE A40.2

Use the picture handles to move and resize your pictures within the template.

To resize the picture (and keep its original dimensions), select one of the corner handles and drag it in or out. To stretch the picture either vertically or horizontally, drag one of the handles on the top, bottom, or sides of the picture and move it in or out.

To move the picture so that it better fits in the template cutout, position the cursor over the picture until the cursor changes into a little hand. You can now drag the picture in any direction so that the best part of the picture is displayed in the cutout.

When you're done editing the pictures, click the Next button. This next screen lets you add or edit any text that appears on the album page. When you double-click a text box, the sidebar changes to the Edit Text panel. Type your text in the top part of the panel, select any formatting options (bold, italic, colors, and so on), and then click Done.

Saving and Printing

When you've finished editing this particular album page, click the Next button. You now have several options to choose from:

- To create additional album pages, select Create Another Album Page.
- To save your album, select Save It.
- To print your album pages, select Print It.

That's all there is to it. Create as many pages as you need; then print them, bind them into an album, and show them to your friends!

Activity  41

DISPLAY AND PRINT PHOTOS ONLINE

What You Need

- Digital photos
- Internet Explorer
- Microsoft Picture It! Publishing
- Internet connection
- Basic computer system

Goal

Upload your digital photos to an online photo processor, order prints, and create an online photo album.

Ordering Prints Online

If you don't have your own photo-quality printer, you can use a professional photo-processing service to print your photos. There are a number of ways you can create prints from your digital photos:

- Copy your image files to disk, and deliver the disk by hand to your local photo finisher.

- Go to the Web site of an online photo-finishing service, and transfer your image files over the Internet.

- Use the Order Prints from the Internet option in Windows XP's My Pictures folder.

The first option is kind of old-fashioned, and not always convenient. For many users, it's a lot less hassle to order photo prints from the comfort of their computer keyboards—however you do it.

Ordering from a Photo-Processing Site

There are dozens and dozens of Web sites offering photo-processing services. They all operate in pretty much the same fashion.

After you register with the site, you upload the pictures you want printed from your hard drive to the Web site. Most sites accomplish this by giving you a few buttons to click and forms to fill out; a handful of sites let you send them your picture files as e-mail attachments. After you upload the photos, you choose what size prints and how many copies you want, along with how fast you want them shipped. Enter your name, address, and credit card number, and your order is complete.

If you're looking for online photo services, here are some of the best and the biggest sites to consider:

- Club Photo (www.clubphoto.com)

- dotPhoto (www.dotphoto.com)

- FotoTime (www.fototime.com)

- Kodak PictureCenter (playground.kodak.com)

- Ofoto (www.ofoto.com)

- PhotoAccess (www.photoaccess.com)

- PhotoFun.com (www.photofun.com)

- PhotoPoint (www.photopoint.com)

- PhotoWorks (www.photoworks.com)

- PrintRoom (www.printroom.com)

- Shutterfly (www.shutterfly.com)

- Snapfish (www.snapfish.com)

- Webshots (www.webshots.com)

- YourPhotos.com (www.yourphotos.com)

Ordering from Within Windows XP

If your new PC is running the Windows XP operating system, you can order prints directly from the My Pictures folder. All you have to do is select the files you want to print and then click the Order Prints from the Internet option in the Picture Tasks panel.

This launches the Internet Print Ordering Wizard, shown in Figure A41.1. The wizard lets you pick which service you want to use, as well as what type of and how many prints to make. You have to fill in all the normal shipping and payment information, of course. But then, you'll receive your prints in a few days, just like you would if you ordered directly from that site via your Web browser.

FIGURE A41.1

Use Windows XP's Internet Print Ordering Wizard to order prints directly from the My Pictures folder.

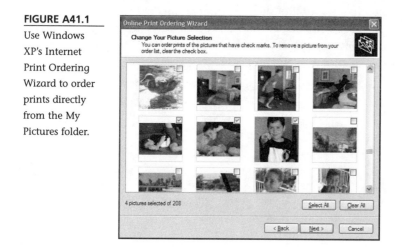

Displaying Pictures at a Photo Service Site

Many online photo sites also let you store copies of your pictures on their sites, in a kind of online photo album. You can then give the URL of your online album to friends and family, so they can go online and look at your pictures, too.

For example, Ofoto lets you create attractive online photo albums, like the one shown in Figure A41.2. Just upload your photos as directed onscreen, make any necessary edits and enhancements, and then share your album with your friends and family.

FIGURE A41.2

Create an online photo album at Ofoto.

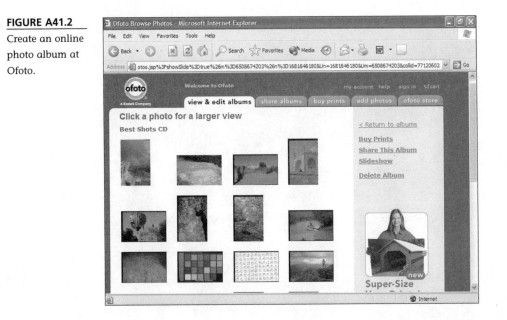

PART XII

DO IT NOW: CREATING FUN PROJECTS

FIND AND DOWNLOAD CLIP ART

What You Need

- Internet Explorer
- Internet connection
- Basic computer system

Goal

Search the Web for graphic images you can use in your custom documents and projects.

Searching for Images

If you need an image to include in a presentation or report, or to use as part of a crafts project, the Web is a good place to look. Literally hundreds of Web sites offer drawings (called *clip art*) or photographs for downloading, either for free or for a minimal charge. You can also use specialized image search engines to look for particular types of images across the entire Web.

Many software programs come with their own collections of clip art. For example, both Microsoft Word and Microsoft Picture It! Publishing come with built-in clip art galleries.

When you're searching for specific types of images, you want a search engine that specializes in image searching. With these image search engines, it's a *description* of the image that's indexed, so when you perform a text-based search, you're trying to match a particular image description.

There are several decent image search engines on the Web, as well as other sites that manually catalog image files. Most of these sites let you search by keyword; some also let you browse by image category.

There is little if any overlap between these image search engines and directories. You might need to go to multiple image search sites to find the exact image you want.

Here are some of the best of these image search engines and directories on the Web:

- Alta Vista Image Search (www.altavista.com/sites/search/simage/)
- Amazing Picture Machine (www.ncrtec.org/picture.htm)
- Diggit! (www.diggit.com)
- Ditto.com (www.ditto.com)
- Lycos Multimedia Search (multimedia.lycos.com)
- WebSEEk (www.ctr.columbia.edu/webseek/)
- Yahoo! Picture Gallery (gallery.yahoo.com)

For a good list of image search tools and directories for children, go to the Kids Image Search Tools page at KidsClick! (www.kidsclick.org/psearch.html).

Clip Art Collections

Clip art is the fancy term for line drawings or illustrations in the form of graphics files. There is much clip art to be found on the Internet, and much of it is free.

The best places to look for clip art are the big, Web-based clip art collections. Many of these collections offer clip art you can download for free; the better collections, however, charge for their art—either on a per-download or subscription basis.

If you need some pictures to spice up your Web page, check out these Web-based clip art collections:

- All Season Clipart (www.allseasonclipart.com)
- Art Today (www.arttoday.com)
- Clip Art Center (www.clip-art-center.com)
- Clip Art Review (www.webplaces.com/html/clipart.htm)
- Clipart Place (www.theclipartplace.com)
- Clipart.com (www.clipart.com)
- ClipArtNow (www.clipartnow.com)
- CoolGraphics.com (www.coolgraphics.com)
- GoGraph.com (www.gograph.com)
- MediaBuilder (www.mediabuilder.com)
- WebSpice.com (www.webspice.com)

Tip

When you download clip art or other graphics files to your computer's hard disk, save them in the My Pictures folder for easy access.

Photo Libraries

There are also a handful of sites that specialize in providing photographic images for your personal or professional use. The largest of these sites are commercial in nature, charging either on a subscription basis or for each picture purchased.

Here is a short list of some of the best general online photography collections:

- Corbis (www.corbis.com)
- Smithsonian Photo Archive (photo2.si.edu)
- Time Life Photo Sight (www.pathfinder.com/photo/)

Images from Web Pages

You don't have to go to a dedicated image site to download pictures from the Web; you can use your Web browser to download any picture you find on any Web page.

To download a picture displayed on a Web page, start by hovering your cursor over the image. Now, right-click your mouse and select the Save Picture As option from the pop-up menu. When the Save Picture dialog box appears, select a filename and location; then click the Save button.

The picture will now be downloaded from the Web and saved on your hard disk.

CREATE A BANNER

What You Need

- Microsoft Picture It! Publishing (part of Microsoft Works Suite)
- Color printer
- Basic computer system

Goal

Use your computer system to create and print a giant banner to hang up at your next party or function.

Choosing a Design

From the dawn of the personal computer era, people have been using their computers to create long banners for all sorts of occasions. In the old days, however, the banners were black and white and composed of letters and numbers on a dot-matrix printer. With today's graphics technology and color printers, you can create banners of near-professional quality—even though you still have to tape all the separate 8×11 pages together in a row!

The easiest way to create a banner is with a picture editing program, like Microsoft Picture It! Publishing. You can start Picture It! Publisher from the Windows Start menu or from the Works Task Launcher.

Start your banner project by selecting Pick a Design from the program's Welcome screen. When the Pick a Design screen appears, select Signs/Banners; then, select either the General or Occasions subcategory. When the next screen appears, select a theme, and then click the specific design you want to use.

Editing the Background and Text

Your basic banner now appears onscreen, as shown in Figure A43.1. If you like the banner as-is, skip ahead to pick the final printed size. Otherwise, take this opportunity to add your own text or edit the graphics on the banner.

FIGURE A43.1

Creating a fancy banner with Microsoft Picture It! Publishing.

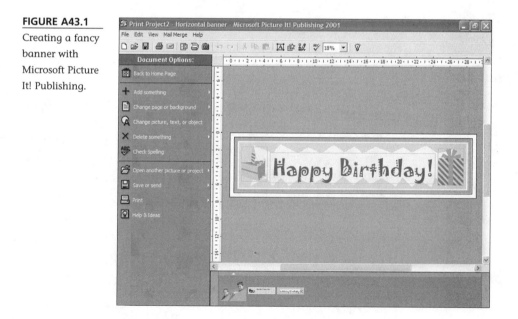

Adding Text and Graphics

To add text to your banner, select Add Something from the Document Options panel, and then select Text and either Plain Text or Shaped Text. The program places a text box in the middle of your banner. You can now type inside the box to add your text, or select one of the options on the Text Options panel to format your text. (For example, you'll probably want to select Change Formatting, Font to change the font size and type.)

You can also use the Add Something option to add a new graphic, line, or border to your banner.

Formatting Graphics

To change the appearance of your banner's graphics, select the graphic to change and then select one of the options from the Picture Options panel. You can do any of the following:

- Replace the picture with another picture (select Change Picture, Replace Picture).
- Crop the picture (select Size & Position, Crop).
- Rotate the picture (select Size & Position, Rotate).
- Add various special effects (select Effects & Illusions, Paint & Color Effects, or Edge Effects).

Changing the Size

Once your banner looks the way you want it to, you can then determine what size banner you want.

From the Document Options panel, select Change Page or Background, Poster or Banner Size. This displays the Set Dimensions dialog box, shown in Figure A43.2. From here you can select how wide and high you want the banner to be, measured in number of 8×11 pages. (You'll print out multiple pages and then tape them together to form the complete banner.) Make your selection; then, click OK.

FIGURE A43.2

Determine how big you want your banner to be.

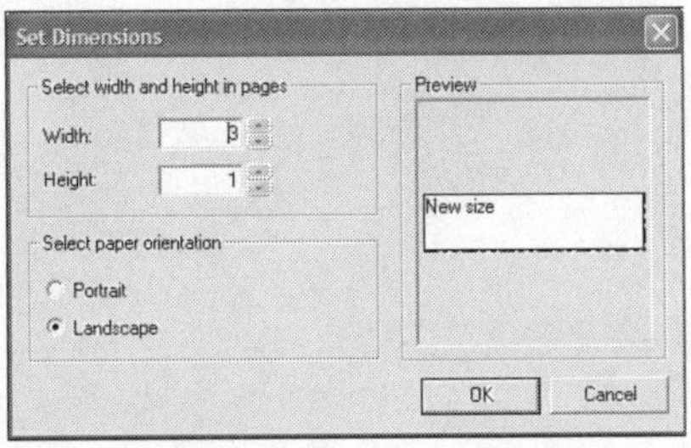

Printing the Banner

When you're doneediting and sizing your banner, you should save the file (select File, Save As), and then start printing.

You print this banner in a series of *tiles*. Each 8×11 page printed is a separate tile, and you tape the tiles together to form the complete banner.

Initiate printing by selecting Print, Print This Project from the Document Options panel. When the Print dialog box appears, you can choose to print all the tiles of your banner by selecting All and clicking OK.

To print only selected tiles, click the Print Specific Parts of a Project button to display the Select Pages to Print dialog box. Click which pages you want to print, and then click OK.

CREATE A PERSONALIZED HOLIDAY CARD

What You Need

- Digital photos
- Microsoft Picture It! Publisher
- Color printer
- Basic computer system

Goal

Combine a personal photograph with a predesigned template to create a custom greeting card.

Choosing a Design

Picture It! Publishing, like other picture editing programs, includes many fun projects for creating your own greeting cards. You can choose from projects that feature stock pictures or clip art, or you can insert your own digital photos to put your family's picture on the front of the card.

Start your greeting card project by selecting Pick a Design from the program's Welcome screen. When the Pick a Design screen appears, select Cards; then, select Photo Cards.

Tip

If you want to create a non-photo greeting card, select one of the other subcategories (Announcements, Baby, Birthday, and so on).

When the next screen appears, select the Guided Greeting Cards theme, and then click the specific design you want to use. (Note that the project typically displays both the front and back of the card, sometimes flipped or upside down.)

The card template now appears onscreen.

Adding Your Photo

The most important part of this project is adding your photograph to the template. To do this, you must first add your photo to the Tray. You do this by selecting Open a Picture from the Greeting Card panel, navigating to your picture, and using your mouse to drag it into the tray. Click the Done button when you're finished.

After your picture is in the tray, you can drag it onto the card template. You'll probably have to resize the picture a tad to make it fit the cutout, so go ahead and click the Next button.

Now, you can click the photo to display its editing handles, as shown in Figure A44.1. Drag the corner handles to resize the picture with its original dimensions intact, or drag the top, bottom, or side handles to stretch or squeeze the photo. You can also move the picture around by positioning your cursor directly on top of the picture and then dragging it to a new position.

FIGURE A44.1

Insert and edit your family photograph.

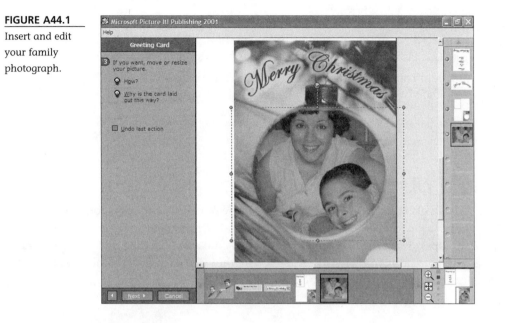

Editing the Text

Most greeting cards have a greeting and graphics on the front, a blank inside spread, and either a blank back or some generic greeting on the back. You can edit any of the text by clicking the Next button, selecting the text to edit, and then double-clicking that text. The text appears in the big text box in the Edit Text panel; you can delete this text, add your own text, or apply a variety of text formatting options. Click Done when you're finished editing that text, and click Next when you're done with all your editing.

Printing and Folding the Card

Before you print, think about what kind of paper you want to use. Most office supply stores sell heavier greeting card stock, in various colors and weights and textures. Pick a stock that fits your card design—and that will work with your color printer.

Now you're ready to print your cards. Select Print It from the Greeting Card panel; then, select your printing options (including how many copies to print) from the Print This Picture panel. Click the Print button to start printing.

After your cards are printed, you have to fold them into their final shapes. Pick up a pen to add a personal greeting, and you're ready to mail them!

Use the edge of a ruler to make a sharp and straight fold for your card.

Creating a Matching Envelope

You can also use Picture It! Publisher to create matching envelopes for your greeting cards. Just go to the Pick a Design screen and select Envelopes; then, select Card Envelopes. Select the appropriate theme and card size, and then design away. When it's time to print your envelopes, make sure that you've inserted blank envelopes of the right size into your color printer.

SEND AN ONLINE GREETING CARD

What You Need

- Internet Explorer
- Internet connection
- Basic computer system

Goal

Create and send an electronic greeting card to someone you love.

Choosing a Greeting Card Site

In Activity 44, "Create a Personalized Holiday Card," you learned how to create a traditional printed greeting card. In this electronic age, however, you don't have to send your cards the old-fashioned way—instead, you can send your cards electronically, over the Internet!

An electronic greeting card, like the one in Figure A45.1, is actually a Web page that contains a graphical message. You pick the greeting you want to relay, and then the online greeting card site sends the recipients an e-mail informing them of their new online card. Your friends and family use their Web browsers to access the special greeting card page, where they can view the greetings you sent them.

FIGURE A45.1

An electronic greeting card— online, viewed with your Web browser.

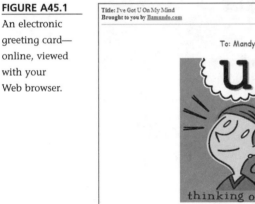

There are many online greeting card sites on the Web. The best of the best include

- 123Greetings.com (www.123greetings.com)
- Blue Mountain Arts (www.bluemountain.com)
- CardsAlive (www.cardsalive.com)
- E-Cards (www.e-cards.com)
- E-Greetings (www.egreetings.com)
- We Got Cards (www.wegotcards.com)
- Yahoo! Greetings (greetings.yahoo.com)

Sending a Greeting with Yahoo! Greeting

For this particular activity, we'll send a greeting card from Yahoo! Greetings. When you access the Yahoo! Greetings page (shown in Figure A45.2), you can choose from one of the featured greetings, or you can browse through the various greeting categories. After you've found the greeting you want to send, click the greeting to personalize it.

FIGURE A45.2

Browse through the categories, and choose a card from Yahoo! Greetings.

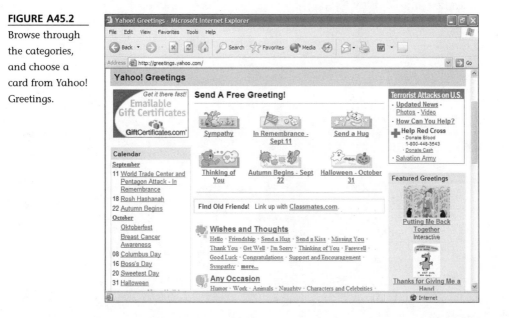

When the Personalize This Greeting page appears, scroll down and fill out all the appropriate boxes. You can send the same card to multiple recipients (up to 10 at a time) by entering multiple addresses in the To: field, separated by commas. You can also choose to receive notification when the card has been received by checking the Please Notify Me When the Recipient Views This Card option.

For the purposes of this activity, enter your own e-mail address in the To: field—so you'll be sending a greeting to yourself!

Click the Preview This Greeting button to see what your card looks like before you send it. If you like what you see, click the Send This Greeting button to send the card. (If you don't like what you see, click the Make More Changes button to return to the previous screen.)

Picking Up a Yahoo! Greeting

As soon as you click the Send This Greeting button, Yahoo! Greetings sends your recipients an e-mail notifying them that they have a greeting waiting on the Yahoo! Greetings site. (This means that you'll receive a notification for this test greeting.) This e-mail includes a link to the page containing the greeting; when they click this link, they jump directly to your greeting.

CREATE A PERSONAL WEB PAGE

What You Need

- Internet Explorer
- Microsoft Picture It! Publisher
- Internet connection
- Basic computer system

Goal

Learn how to create your own personal Web page—and post it to the Internet for everyone to see.

Creating a Simple Page at Yahoo! GeoCities

It seems like everybody and their brother has their own personal Web pages these days. If you want to keep up with the Joneses, you need to create a personal Web page of your own.

Home Page Communities

All Web pages are based on a special programming code, called the Hypertext Markup Language (HTML). Fortunately, you don't need to learn HTML to create a simple Web page. That's because many Web sites make it easy to generate good-looking pages without you having to learn any fancy programming. These *home page communities* even host your pages on the Web, so all your friends and family can visit them.

The most popular home page community is Yahoo! GeoCities (`geocities.yahoo.com`). Like most home page communities —including Angelfire (`angelfire.lycos.com`) and Tripod (`tripod.lycos.com`)—it's easy to use, and it's free.

Using PageWizards

Yahoo! GeoCities offers several ways to build a Web page. The easiest way is to use its PageWizard feature. To start this process, click the PageWizards link on the site's home page.

When the Yahoo! PageWizards page appears, select the page design you want to use. A new Quick Start Web Page Wizard window will now appear on your desktop. Click the Begin button to proceed.

The PageWizard, shown in Figure A46.1, leads you step-by-step through the creation of your Web page. You'll need to make a few choices and provide a few pieces of information, in the following order:

- Choose a look for your page.
- Enter your page title and text.
- Pick a picture to appear on your page.
- Enter your favorite links to your favorite Web pages.
- Enter your information, including name and e-mail address.
- Name your page.

FIGURE A46.1

Use the Yahoo! PageWizard to create your own personal Web page at GeoCities.

Keep clicking the Next button to move from page to page in the wizard. When you finish with the Name Your Page page, the wizard displays a Congratulations page. The URL for your new page is displayed here; write it down for future reference, or click the link to view your page.

Creating Personal Pages with Picture It! Publisher

You can also create a Web page from the Picture It! Publisher program and upload those pages to a home page community (such as Yahoo! GeoCities). The advantage to this approach is that you can create much more sophisticated pages than you can with the PageWizards utility.

Creating Your Pages

Begin by selecting Pick a Design from the Welcome screen and then selecting Web Pages from the Pick a Design page. When the next screen appears, select the type of Web page you want to design; then select a theme and particular template to use.

The template you selected now appears onscreen. You can use the program's various editing options to add new graphics and text, edit existing graphics and text, or delete unwanted page elements.

You can add links to other pages within any text box. Just double-click the text box and then select More Options, Hyperlink from the Text Options panel.

Each project consists of multiple Web pages; edit each successive page by clicking the page number at the bottom of the Document Options panel. Preview your pages as they will look on the Web by selecting Preview, All Pages from the Document Options panel.

Uploading Your Pages

When you're done creating your pages, you have to upload them to your chosen home page community. Make sure you've registered with that community before you proceed.

From the Document Options panel, select Save or Send, Publish to Web Site. This displays the Publish to Web dialog box. Pull down the Select a Web Site Host list, and select your home page community from the list. You have to enter the user ID/login name and password you got when you registered at the site and provide a Project Name for your pages. When you click the Next button, Picture It! Publisher converts your project to HTML, connects to the Internet, and uploads your pages to your home page community, all automatically.

If you *don't* have an account with a home page community, click the Sign Me Up button in the Publish to Web dialog box. The program connects to the Internet and leads you step-by-step through the registration process at the site of your choosing.

PART XIII

DO IT NOW: PLAYING GAMES

PLAY A PC GAME

What You Need

- Any commercial computer game
- Game controller
- Basic computer system

Goal

Prepare your system for playing the latest computer games.

Upgrading Your System to Play the Latest Games

Believe it or not, but the most demanding application for your new computer system is probably a game. With all those fancy graphics, gee-whiz sound effects, and high-speed action, computer games definitely put your computer system through its paces.

In fact, to get the *best* game play possible, you need a truly state-of-the-art computer system. If you purchased a low-end computer, you might find that it doesn't play the latest games quite as fast or as smoothly as you might have expected.

What can you do to beef up your system for better game play? Here are some things to keep in mind:

- If you're using an older PC, you might think about buying a new system with a fairly powerful processor. Think Pentium 4 or AMD Athlon, running at 1GHz or more.

- Whether you have a newer or an older PC, you'll want to increase its memory to at least 256MB.

- You'll also need a lot of hard disk storage because the newer games take up a lot of disk space. Go for at least a 40GB hard disk—bigger if you can afford it.

- You should also consider upgrading to a DVD drive because many new games come on single DVDs rather than multiple CDs.

- You might need to upgrade your sound card. Consider going with a high-quality 3D sound card, and be sure you have a quality speaker system, complete with subwoofer.

- The capability to handle rapidly moving graphics is essential. If your PC's original video card isn't quite up to snuff, upgrade to either a 32MB or 64MB 3D video card with graphics accelerator.

- Big games look better on a big screen, so think about a 17" or even a 19" video monitor, if you have the desktop space.

- Finally, you ,need something other than your mouse to control your games. You'll want to invest in a good-quality joystick or similar game controller.

Adding a Joystick

There are many brands and types of joysticks and game controllers available for use with PC games. Connecting a new device is as simple as plugging it in (and running the installation program, if there is one). Many joysticks still connect through the games port on the back of your system unit (actually part of the sound card), although some newer units connect to the USB port, which makes for an easier installation.

You can configure a new game controller by opening the Control Panel and selecting the Game Controllers icon. This opens the Game Controllers dialog box.

To test your new controller, select the controller you want to test. Click the Properties button; then, select the Test tab. Follow the onscreen instructions to move or press each control, including all the pads and buttons.

If your controller doesn't check out 100%, you might need to calibrate it. To do this, return to the Properties dialog box and select the Settings tab. Click the Calibrate button, and follow the onscreen instructions to calibrate this particular device.

Playing a New Game

Before you play a new PC game, you'll have to install the game software according to instructions. You might also, in some instances, need to keep the game CD in your PC's CD-ROM drive. (This is because many games access the CD to load images and sounds during the course of the game.)

You'll also need to have your game controller installed and connected, and then you're ready to play. You launch the new game from the Windows Start menu.

Every game operates a little bit differently. You typically are presented with some type of opening screen, sometimes in the form of an animated movie. Most games let you skip this animation by clicking somewhere (or anywhere) within the movie window.

Don't be *too* quick about bypassing the opening animation. Sometimes information essential to the game is presented in this movie.

After you get past the opening, you might need to configure various parameters for the game. For example, you might have to choose a user level (try starting with "beginner"), enter your player name, and so on. You should also take this opportunity to read the game's instructions, either onscreen (sometimes via the Help menu) or in an accompanying booklet.

When you've boned up on how the game works, it's time to start playing. Good luck!

Saving Your Game—and Resuming Play

Many games let you pause or save games in progress, so if you have to stop for the day, you can start up again tomorrow in the same spot. To save a game, follow the game's specific instructions to save your particular game file—typically by accessing some sort of "save" or "file" menu or function.

When you're ready to start playing again, all you have to do is load the previously saved game. This is typically accomplished as the game is loading, or via some type of "resume" or "file" menu. After the game is reloaded, you can resume play exactly where you stopped the day before.

Activity **48**

PLAY A SIMPLE
ONLINE GAME

What You Need

- Internet Explorer
- Internet connection
- Basic computer system

Goal

Find the best game sites on the
Web—and start playing, online.

Playing Games Online

You don't have to head to your local computer store to find a new game to play. Many sites on the Web offer all sorts of games to play online—often for free. Whether you're looking for a quick game of checkers or an evening-long session of Quake II, you can find dozens of sites to satisfy your craving for action and strategy.

You can play most online games by going to a gaming site and clicking the appropriate links. Everything you need to play the game is automatically loaded into your Web browser.

You'll need to read the instructions first, of course, especially if you need to find an online partner to play a particular game. Don't get too nervous about this; most sites make it extremely easy to play their most popular games.

Checking Out the Games

You'll find all sorts of games online, including games in the following major categories:

- **Arcade games**—Typically older games, such as Asteroids, Battlezone, Centipede, and Pong.
- **Board games**—Such as backgammon, chess, and checkers—as well as some commercial board games, such as Monopoly and Scrabble.
- **Card games**—Such as solitaire, bridge, euchre, gin rummy, and hearts.
- **Casino games**—Such as blackjack, poker, keno, and roulette.
- **Puzzle games**—Including jigsaw and sliding puzzles.
- **Trivia games**—In all manner of categories. Entertainment and sports trivia are the most popular variations.
- **Word games**—Including anagrams and other brain teasers.

The Best Game Sites on the Web

Most online games can be played free of charge. Many gaming sites even hand out prizes to winning players. You can log on to these sites with a minimal amount of pre-play registration and then start playing with a few clicks of your mouse.

If you're interested in playing some simple single-player online games, check out these Web sites:

- All Games Free (www.allgamesfree.com)
- ArcadeTown.com (www.arcadetown.com)
- BoxerJam.com (www.boxerjam.com)

- Flipside.com (www.flipside.com)
- Games Arena (www.thegamesarena.com)
- Games.com (play.games.com)
- Igames (www.igames.com)
- Internet Chess Club (www.chessclub.com)
- Internet Park (www.internet-park.com)
- Lycos Gamesville (www.gamesville.lycos.com)
- MSN Gaming Zone (zone.msn.com)
- Playsite (www.playsite.com)
- Pogo.com (www.pogo.com)
- Yahoo! Games (games.yahoo.com)

Playing at the Gaming Zone

The MSN Gaming Zone is one of the largest game sites on the Web. To play a game at the Gaming Zone, you first have to click the Games link on the home page. This gives you an alphabetical list of the 100+ games hosted on the site. Click a link for a specific game, and you'll see the main page for that game.

Each game works a little differently. Some single-player games drop you right into the game, which is displayed in your Web browser. Other games require that the game be downloaded and loaded into a separate browser window. Many games offer a number of different "rooms" you can enter to begin your play. You'll want to read and follow the instructions on the game's main page before you start playing.

As an example, one of the most popular games at the Gaming Zone is Backgammon. When you click the Backgammon link, you're presented with a list of rooms—some for casual play, and some for more serious, competitive play. When you click a link to enter a room, you're prompted to download the software necessary to play the game.

Note If you haven't yet signed up as a member of the Gaming Zone, you'll also be prompted to register. Registration is free, but necessary to proceed.

After the software is downloaded and installed, you can enter a room. As you can see in Figure A48.1, you can join a player waiting for an opponent or "sit down" at a table and wait for someone to join you. Just click a chair at the table you want, and proceed from there.

FIGURE A48.1

Waiting for an opponent to sit down at a Backgammon table at the MSN Gaming Zone.

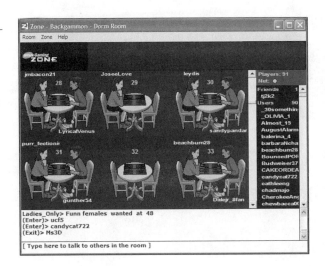

PLAY A MULTIPLAYER ONLINE GAME

What You Need

- Any commercial computer game with multiplayer option
- Internet Explorer
- Internet connection
- Basic computer system

Goal

Connect with other game players to play your favorite computer games online.

Playing Games—Against Other Players

Most PC games sold at retail today include a multiplayer option. This option lets you play the game against a human opponent. You can play another player on your local area network or find and play an opponent over the Internet. To play these multiplayer games, the game software has to be installed on your PC; then, you connect to a dedicated gaming site on the Web to network together with other players.

Most multiplayer gaming sites do more than just connect together opponents for multiplayer game play. Many of these sites host tournaments and post rankings and ladders of the best players. Some sites that host sophisticated role-playing games let dozens of players band together to both compete and cooperate within the game's environment.

Popular Multiplayer Games

Multiplayer functionality is common in most strategy, action, and role-playing games sold at retail outlets today. The most popular of these multiplayer games include

- Age of Empires/Age of Empires II
- Baldur's Gate/Baldur's Gate 2
- Combat Flight Simulator
- Command & Conquer/Command & Conquer: Red Alert
- Descent/Descent 2/Descent 3
- Diablo/Diablo Hellfire
- Doom/Doom II
- Duke Nukem 3D
- Forsaken
- Half-Life
- MechWarrior 2/MechWarrior 3
- Myth/Myth II
- Quake/Quake 2/Quake 3 Arena
- StarCraft
- Unreal/Unreal Tournament
- Warcraft/Warcraft II

Getting Connected

Setting up a multiplayer game is relatively straightforward. You start by launching the game on your computer; then you, connect to the Internet and log on to a specific Web site. This site can be hosted by the game manufacturer, or it can be a general gaming site that has licensing access to a particular game. In many cases, the site you need to log in to is hard-wired into the game software itself. All you have to do is pull down the menu and select the multiplayer option; then, the game automatically connects itself to the proper Web site, using your normal Internet connection.

After you're logged on to the site, you access the area of the site dedicated to your particular game. You can then choose to host a game (and look for other players) or join a game already in progress. You're then connected to the other player(s), and the game begins.

The faster your Internet connection, the smoother the game play you'll experience.

Multiplayer Game Sites

As you learned in Activity 48, "Play a Simple Online Game," there are dozens of gaming sites on the Internet. Most sites offering multiplayer gaming operate on a subscription basis—in other words, you have to pay to play. Subscription fees vary per site but are typically assessed on an hourly, a monthly, or a yearly basis. (Fees can run as low as $20 for lifetime access or as high as $2 per hour of play.) For this fee, you get the privilege of connecting to other users, as well as using the site's services to organize and coordinate both individual match-ups and tourneys.

The most popular of the multiplayer sites include

- Battle.net (www.battle.net)
- EA.com (www.ea.com)
- Gamerlink (www.gamerlink.net)
- GameSpy Arcade (www.gamespyarcade.com)
- MSN Gaming Zone (zone.msn.com)
- Net-Games (www.net-games.com)
- Ultimate Gamers (www.ultimategamers.com)

Multiplayer Game Networks

In addition to these general game sites, there are also several game networks you can use to play most multiplayer games.

The biggest of these networks is Kali (www.kali.net). To use Kali, you must pay a $20 one-time registration fee and then download and install the Kali software on your computer. You can then launch the Kali software, connect to a Kali server, and start looking for opponents. After you're connected, game play takes place just as it would on any other gaming site.

The other big multiplayer game network is Khan (www.kahncentral.net). It operates similarly to Kali, except the Khan software is free of charge, with slightly faster game play.

PART XIV

DO IT NOW: PLAYING AND RECORDING MUSIC

PLAY A CD ON YOUR PC

What You Need

- Audio compact disc
- Windows Media Player
- Basic computer system with CD-ROM drive
- Speaker system or headphones
- Internet connection (optional)

Goal

Turn your computer system into an audio system for playing compact discs.

Setting Up Your PC for CD Playback

Most new computer systems come complete with a CD-ROM drive. This drive reads computer CD-ROMs and plays back normal audio CDs.

In most cases this drive is installed and configured at the factory, so you don't have to do anything to use it. Just insert an audio CD, and wait for something to happen.

Some CD drives come configured so that they start automatically when you insert an audio CD. In this scenario, your drive should start spinning, some sort of media player program will launch, and your CD should start playing through your computer's speakers. If this describes how your system works, you don't have to do anything other than sit back and listen to the music.

If, on the other hand, your CD *doesn't* start playing automatically, you have to manually launch a media player program. Fortunately, Windows includes its own media player (which might or might not be the player that launches automatically on some systems), called the Windows Media Player.

Using Windows Media Player

Windows Media Player (WMP) is a great little program you can use for many purposes—playing CDs, recording CDs, listening to Internet radio broadcasts, watching Web casts, and playing DVDs. It works similarly to most other media players, so if you know how to use WMP, you should be able to figure out any other media player program.

Whether you're playing a CD, DVD, or digital audio file, you use the controls located at the bottom of the WMP window (shown in Figure A50.1). These are the normal transport buttons you find on a cassette deck or VCR, including Play/Pause, Stop, Rewind, and Fast Forward. WMP also includes Next and Previous track buttons, along with a volume control and Mute button.

The biggest part of the WMP window is an area which displays the picture when you're playing back DVDs. This area can also be used to display what Microsoft calls "visualizations" while you're listening to music. (Think of visualization as a kind of "live" wallpaper that moves along with your music.) You can choose which visualizations are displayed by pulling down the View menu, selecting Visualizations, and then making a choice.

To the right of the video/visualization window is the Playlist area. Individual tracks of a CD or DVD are listed here. This area also displays the songs in any playlists that you create from the song files stored on your hard drive.

FIGURE A50.1

Playing CDs and
other media with
the Windows
Media Player.

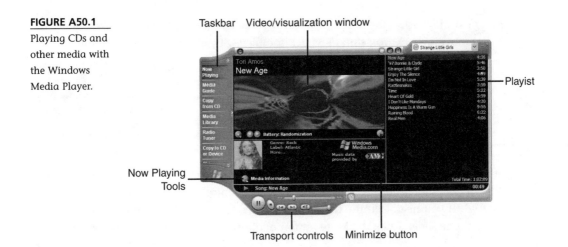

Between the playback controls and the video/visualization window is an area called
the Now Playing Tools area. This area typically displays information about the
currently playing CD or audio file.

Note

To display this information, your computer must be connected to the Internet. WMP
automatically goes out to the Internet to retrieve information about any CD or DVD
you're playing.

Finally, the seven buttons along the left of the window (contained in what is called
the Taskbar) link to key features of the player. Click a button and the entire player
interface changes to reflect the selected feature—Now Playing, Media Guide, CD
Audio, Media Library, Radio Tuner, Portable Device, or Skin Chooser.

By default, WMP is launched in its Full mode. If you'd rather display the player
without all the extraneous controls, you can switch to the more compact Skin mode
by clicking the Switch to Skin Mode button (or by pulling down the View menu and
selecting Skin Mode). When you're in Skin mode, a small anchor window appears at
the bottom left of your desktop; double-click this window to return to Full mode.

Playing a CD

If WMP doesn't start automatically when you load a CD into your PC's CD-ROM
drive, you can launch it manually from the Windows Start menu. You can then start
playback by clicking WMP's Play button.

To pause playback, click the Pause button (same as the Play button); click Play again to resume playback. You stop playback completely by clicking the Stop button.

> To play the songs on a CD in a random order, select Play, Shuffle. WMP will now shuffle randomly through the tracks on the CD.

Adjusting the Volume and Sound

If the sound is too loud (or not loud enough), you can change the volume by dragging the Volume slider—to the right of the transport controls—to the right (louder) or left (softer). If you need to mute the sound quickly, click the Mute button to the left of the Volume slider. Click the Mute button again to unmute the sound.

LISTEN TO INTERNET RADIO

What You Need

- Windows Media Player and/or RealPlayer
- Internet Explorer
- Internet connection
- Basic computer system
- Speaker system or headphones

Goal

Turn your computer system into an audio system that can receive radio broadcasts over the Internet.

Understanding Internet Radio

Many real-world radio stations broadcast over the Internet using what is called *streaming audio*.

In Activity 52, "Find and Download Music Files," you'll learn how to download audio files from the Internet to your hard disk. When you download a file, you can't start playing that file until it is completely downloaded to your PC. With streaming audio, however, playback can start before an entire file is downloaded. This also enables live broadcasts to be sent from the broadcast site to your PC.

Streaming audio broadcast over the Internet is informally called *Internet radio*. Some Internet radio programs are simulcasts of traditional radio stations. Other Internet radio programs are Web-only affairs. All Internet radio programs can be played through either Windows Media Player or RealPlayer software.

Listening with Windows Media Player

You can use WMP to listen to many Internet radio programs. You start by clicking the Radio Tuner button on the WMP taskbar. This automatically connects WMP to the Internet and displays a list of available Internet radio stations.

You can choose to listen to a station on your preset list or search for stations by format, band (AM or FM), language, location, callsign, frequency, or keyword. Double-click a station name to play that station.

To add a station to your list of presets, select the station and click the Add button. Your preset stations are displayed on the left side of the screen.

Listening to Internet radio or watching Webcasts can use up a lot of your connection bandwidth—and make anything else you're doing online (like downloading files) go a lot slower. Because of this, many businesses block or ban this type of activity over their corporate networks.

Listening with RealAudio

Another popular program for playing back Internet radio is RealPlayer. The RealPlayer program (available at www.real.com/player/) is the most-used streaming media player today. This is because the majority of Web sites use the RealMedia format to deliver their streaming media content. When you go to a Web site and click the link to start streaming audio or video playback, chances are that RealPlayer will launch automatically—it's probably already installed on your PC.

You might need to have both Windows Media Player and RealPlayer installed on your system. This is because Internet radio streamed in the RealMedia format can't be played with WMP.

Even though RealPlayer and WMP are somewhat incompatible, they both operate in pretty much the same fashion. The main RealPlayer window has a row of transport controls (Play, Pause, Stop, and so on) along the top, underneath the main menu bar. There's a big window on the right to display video broadcasts, and the My Channels pane on the left displays your favorite Internet radio stations.

To use RealPlayer to listen to Internet radio broadcasts, pull down the Radio menu and select Open Radio Tuner. This opens a separate Radio Tuner window, shown in Figure A51.1. You can click the Featured tab to choose from Real's current recommended stations; the Find a Station tab to search for specific stations by genre, language, city, state, country, or station name; or the My Stations tab to go directly to your favorite stations. Just click the link for a specific station to begin the streaming playback.

FIGURE A51.1

Listening to Internet radio with the RealPlayer Radio Tuner.

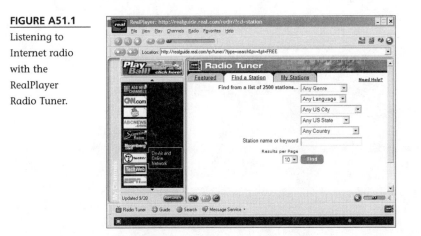

Finding an Internet Radio Station

When you're looking for Internet radio broadcasts (of which there are thousands, daily), you need a good directory of available programming. Here's a list of sites that contain links to traditional radio stations simulcasting over the Web:

- Internet Radio List (www.internetradiolist.com)

- Live@ (www.live-at.com)

- Radio Broadcast Network (www.radiobroadcast.net)

- Radio-Locator (www.radio-locator.com)

- Radiostations.mu (www.radio-stations.net)

- Web-Radio (www.web-radio.com)

In addition to sites that simulcast traditional radio stations over the Web, there are many sites that create their own original programming for Internet broadcast. Here's a short list of some of the most popular Internet-only radio sites:

- Akoo (www.akoo.com)

- ARTISTdirect radio (radio.artistdirect.com)

- Echo (www.echo.com)

- NetRadio.com (www.netradio.com)

- RadioMOI (www.radiomoi.com)

- SHOUTcast (yp.shoutcast.com)

Activity **52**

FIND AND DOWNLOAD MUSIC FILES

What You Need

- Internet Explorer
- Internet connection
- Basic computer system

Goal

Find digital music on the Web and download it onto your computer's hard drive.

Understanding Digital Audio

Anyone with a personal computer—and the right software—can make digital copies of music from CDs and then store these copies on their computer's hard disk. These digital audio files can also be traded with other users, over the Internet.

There are many different ways to make a digital recording, which results in many different file formats for digital audio. The two most popular file formats are MP3 and WMA (Windows Media Audio).

Note

Most media players—such as Windows Media Player—can play back files recorded in either MP3 or WMA formats. See Activity 53, "Play Digital Music on Your PC," for more information.

MP3 Audio

MP3 is the most popular digital audio format because it was the first widely accepted format that combined near-CD quality sound with reasonably small file sizes. These small file sizes are possible because the MP3 format uses a form of digital file compression; a typical three-minute song in MP3 format takes up only about 3MB of disk space.

File size is important not just because smaller files take up less space on your hard drive, but also because they take less time to download over the Internet. With a normal 56.6Kbps dial-up connection, a 3MB song takes about five minutes to download. This same song, uncompressed (as it originally appeared on CD), is a 32MB file—which would take more than a half-hour to download.

Windows Media Audio

MP3 isn't the only digital audio file format in use today. Microsoft is waging a strong campaign for its Windows Media Audio format, which offers similar quality to MP3, but with smaller files.

WMA also offers something that you might not want—copy protection. Files encoded in the WMA format can be configured to play back only on the system that recorded the files. This means you might find WMA files that were recorded on other computers and won't play back on your computer—or were recorded on your computer, but won't play back on your portable audio player.

So, while the music industry likes the fact that WMA protects its copyrights, most users prefer the MP3 format, which doesn't impose any copy protection on users.

Finding Digital Music to Download

In recent years there has been a flood of digital audio files available on the Internet. Some of these files are supplied by artists and record labels; other files are created by normal users who record songs from their own CD collections. (See Activity 54, "Make Copies of Your Favorite Songs," for more details on this practice.)

To find files to download, fire up Internet Explorer and navigate to one of these digital audio archive sites:

- ARTISTdirect (www.artistdirect.com)
- Liquid.com (www.liquid.com)
- MP3.com (www.mp3.com)
- MTV.com (www.mtv.com)
- sonicnet.com (www.sonicnet.com)
- Tunes.com (www.tunes.com)

You then search the site for the song you want to download and click some sort of "download now" button or link. You then specify where on your hard disk you want to store the downloaded file and start the download.

Tip

The big music labels have created their own Web sites for "official" downloading of their artists' music—for a fee. These sites are MusicNet (www.musicnet.com) and pressplay (www.pressplay.com).

Swapping Files with Other Users

In addition to these archives of digital music, there are also services that let you swap digital audio files directly with other users. These file-swapping services help you find other users who have the songs you want. You then connect directly to the user's computer and copy the file you want from that computer to yours.

(It works the other way, also. When you register with one of these services, other users can download digital audio files from *your* computer, as long as you're connected to the Internet.)

Among the most popular of these file-sharing services are

- AIMster (www.aimster.com)

- Audio Galaxy Satellite (www.audiogalaxy.com)

- KaZaA Media Desktop (www.kazaa.com)

- MusicCity Morpheus (www.musiccity.com)

- Napster (www.napster.com)

Most of these services require you to download a copy of their software and then run that software whenever you want to download. You use their software to search for the songs you want; the software then generates a list of users who have that file stored on their computers. You select which computer you want to connect to, and then the software automatically downloads the file from that computer to yours.

Downloading or copying copyrighted material without permission is against the law and deprives musicians of their hard-earned income. Let your conscience be your guide.

PLAY DIGITAL MUSIC ON YOUR PC

What You Need

- Digital audio files in MP3 or WMA format
- Windows Media Player or similar software
- Basic computer system
- Speaker system or headphones

Goal

Turn your computer system into an audio jukebox to play back your favorite songs from computer files.

Choosing a Media Player

After you've downloaded a fair number of MP3- or WMA-format digital audio files (as described in Activity 52, "Find and Download Music Files"), you probably want to listen to them. Just as you need a CD player to play your compact discs, you need a digital audio player program to play MP3 and WMA files on your computer.

> If you're more interested in making your own digital audio files, you need an *encoder* program. Many encoder programs are also CD *rippers*, which work in the other direction and record digital audio files onto CD-R discs. Read ahead to Activity 54, "Make Copies of Your Favorite Songs," and Activity 55, "Make Your Own CD," to learn more about encoding and ripping.

There are a number of digital audio players available, most for free and almost all downloadable over the Internet. The most popular of these players include

- RealPlayer (www.real.com/player/)

- Sonique Media Player (sonique.lycos.com)

- UltraPlayer (www.ultraplayer.com)

- WinAmp (www.winamp.com)

Aside from these popular programs, there's another digital audio player you might want to consider—because it's probably already installed on your PC. This player is the Windows Media Player (WMP), and we'll examine how to use WMP to manage all your digital audio files later in this activity.

> If you're more interested in recording your own MP3 files, check out MusicMatch Jukebox (www.musicmatch.com), RealJukebox (www.real.com/jukebox/), or RioPort Audio Manager (www.rioport.com/Software/).

Playing Digital Audio Files

Whichever audio player you use, you follow the same general steps to play an MP3 or WMA file. You start by launching the program; then, you pull down the File menu and select Open. (Some players have an Open button you can use, instead.) Select the file you want to play, and then use the player's transport controls to play, pause, and stop playback.

Some players let you create *playlists* of songs to play, one after another. You can create playlists from the files you have stored on your hard disk, in any order you want.

Using WinAmp

The most popular program for playing MP3 files is WinAmp. You can download a free copy of the WinAmp program at www.winamp.com; some new computers come with this program already installed.

As you can see in Figure A53.1, WinAmp is as easy to use as a conventional tape deck or CD player. To play an MP3 file with WinAmp, click the WinAmp button (in the upper left of the window) and select Play, File. When the Open File(s) dialog box appears, select the file to play and then click Open; the file will begin to play automatically.

FIGURE A53.1

Playing MP3s with the WinAmp player.

To load songs into a playlist, click the Add button and select Add URL (to add files from the Internet), Add Dir (to add all the files in a directory on your hard drive), or Add File (to add a specific file from your hard disk). To remove a song from your playlist, select the song, click the Rem button, and select Rem Sel. To save a playlist, click the List Opts button and select Save List; when the Save Playlist dialog box appears, assign a name and location to the list and click Save.

To load a previously saved playlist, click the List Opts button and select Load List; when the Load Playlist dialog box appears, select a playlist and click Open. Click Play to play the songs in your playlist, in sequential order.

Using Windows Media Player

You already know Windows Media Player from Activity 50, "Play a CD on Your PC," and Activity 51, "Listen to Internet Radio"; it's a versatile media player that's included free with Microsoft Windows.

To play back an MP3 or WMA file with WMP, you start by selecting the Now Playing tab. Pull down the File menu and select Open; then, select the file you want to play. The file you selected will start playing automatically.

WMP stores your favorite files in what it calls the Media Library. To add a file to the Media Library, pull down the File menu and select Add to Library; then, select Add Currently Playing Track, Add File (to add a file from your hard disk), or Add URL (to add a file from the Web).

Files in your Media Library can be combined into playlists. To create a new playlist, click the Media Library tab and then click the New Playlist button; when the New Playlist dialog box appears, enter a name for the playlist and click OK. To add a file to a playlist, select the file from the title listing, click the Add to Playlist button, and select Playlists; when the Playlists dialog box appears, select the playlist and click OK.

To play a playlist, go to the Now Playing screen, pull down the Playlist list, and select a playlist. The playlist should start playing automatically. If not, all you have to do is click the Play button. All the tracks in your playlist will play, one at a time, in the order listed.

Activity **54**

MAKE COPIES OF YOUR FAVORITE SONGS

What You Need

- Audio compact discs
- Windows Media Player or similar "ripper" software
- Basic computer system with CD-ROM drive
- Speaker system or headphones
- Internet connection (optional)

Goal

Copy songs from CDs to your computer's hard drive.

How to Rip

If you have a decent CD collection and a CD-ROM drive in your computer system, you can make your own MP3 or WMA files from the songs on your compact discs. You can then listen to these files on your computer, download the files to a portable audio player for listening on the go, or use these files to burn your own custom mix CDs. (You can also share these files with other users via one of the file-swapping services listed in Activity 52, "Find and Download Music Files"—even though it might not be entirely legal to do so.)

This process of copying files from a CD to your hard disk, in either MP3 or WMA format, is called *ripping*. You use an audio encoding program, such as Windows Media Player or MusicMatch Jukebox (www.musicmatch.com), to rip your files.

The ripping process is fairly simple. You start by inserting the CD you want to copy from into your PC's CD-ROM drive. Then you launch your encoder program and select which songs on your CD you want to rip. You'll also need to select the format for the final file (MP3 or WMA) and the *bit rate* you want to use for encoding; the higher the bit rate, the better the sound quality. (And the larger the file size!) After you've set everything up, click the appropriate button to start the encoding process.

After you start encoding, the song(s) you selected will be played from your PC's CD drive, processed through the encoder program into a WAV-format file, encoded into an MP3- or WMA-format file (your choice), and then stored on your hard disk.

After you've started the encoding process, do *not* use your computer to do anything else while encoding; doing so runs the risk of adding "skips" to your MP3s.

Ripping with Windows Media Player

Windows Media Player (WMP) not only plays back digital audio files, it can also create those files from the songs on a compact disc. The only drawback about using WMP to encode digital audio is that, by default, it doesn't encode in the MP3 format. While WMP can play back both MP3 and WMA files, it can encode only in the WMA format.

You can, however, add MP3-format encoding to WMP. You do this via an add-on software utility called the MP3 Creation Pack. This add-on pack is available (for about $30) in three versions, each using a different MP3 encoder. The three versions are marketed by CyberLink, InterVideo, and Ravisent, and one is as good as the other.

Setting the Format and Quality Levels

Before you begin copying, you first have to tell WMP what format you want to use for your ripped files—and which quality level you want to record at.

You do this by pulling down the Tools menu and selecting Options. When the Options dialog box appears, select the Copy Music tab. Then, in the Copy Settings section, pull down the File Format list and select either Windows Media Audio or MP3. (If you haven't installed the MP3 Creation Pack, you won't have a choice here—your only option will be Windows Media Audio.)

Now use the Copy Music at This Quality slider to set the bit rate for your ripped files. Move the slider to the left for smaller files and lower sound quality. Move the slider to the right for larger files and higher sound quality. Click OK when done.

When you're copying in the WMA format, either the 96Kbps or 128Kbps level should be a good compromise between file size and sound quality. When you're copying in the MP3 format, the 128Kbps rate is recommended—although higher bit rates produce noticeably better-sounding files.

Ripping the Files

After your settings are set, it's time to start ripping. Start by inserting the CD you want to rip into your PC's CD-ROM drive. Now connect to the Internet; this lets WMP download track names and CD cover art for the songs you're ripping.

Select the Copy from CD tab to show the contents of the CD, and then put a check mark by the tracks you want to copy. When you've selected which tracks to rip, click the Copy Music button.

WMP now begins to copy the tracks you selected, in the format you selected, and at the quality level you selected. Unless you specify otherwise in the Options dialog box, the tracks are recorded into your My Music folder, into a subfolder for the artist, and within that in another subfolder for this particular CD.

Ripping with MusicMatch Jukebox

MusicMatch Jukebox is the most popular MP3 encoding program because it's so easy to use—practically the entire process is automated. It also has MP3 encoding built in, so you don't have to buy or install any "add-on" software like you do with Windows Media Player. (You can download a free copy of MusicMatch Jukebox from www.musicmatch.com.)

To encode a song with MusicMatch Jukebox, you start by connecting to the Internet and launching the MusicMatch software. Next, you click the Record button, which starts the encoder program.

Now insert the CD you want to copy from into your PC's CD-ROM drive. MusicMatch will now synch up (over the Internet) with CDDB, an online database, to obtain track information.

To set the bit rate and format for recording, pull down the Options menu and select Recorder, Settings. When the next dialog box appears, select the Settings tab. In the Recording Quality section, select the desired bit rate and format; then, click OK.

Back in the main window, check the boxes next to the tracks you want to copy. When all is ready, click the Record button; MusicMatch now copies the selected files from your CD to the My Music folder on your hard disk.

MAKE YOUR OWN CD

What You Need

- Digital audio files in MP3 or WMA format
- Blank CD-R disc
- Blank CD labels
- Windows Media Player or similar "CD burner" software
- Microsoft Picture It! Publisher
- CD-R/RW drive
- Speaker system or headphones
- Color or black-and-white printer
- Basic computer system

Goal

Burn your own CDs from the MP3 files stored on your hard disk.

How to Burn a CD

One of the great things about having a recordable/rewritable CD (CD-R/RW) drive in your computer system is that you can make your own audio mix CDs. You can take any combination of songs on your hard disk (in either MP3 or WMA format) and "burn" them onto a blank CD—and then play that CD in your home, car, or portable CD player.

Unlike CD ripping, CD burning doesn't require you to set a lot of format options. That's because whatever format the original file is in, when it gets copied to CD it gets encoded into the CD Audio (CDA) format. All music CDs use the CDA format, so whether you're burning an MP3 or WMA file, your CD burner software translates it to CDA before the copy is made.

There are no quality levels to set, either. All CDA-format files are encoded at the same bit rate. So, you really don't have any configuration to do—other than deciding which songs you want to copy.

The easiest way to burn a CD full of songs is to copy an entire playlist. Assemble the playlist beforehand to get the timing right, and then send the entire playlist to your CD. You can record up to 74 minutes or 650MB worth of music, whichever comes first.

After you've decided which songs to copy, load a blank CD-R disc into your computer's CD-R/RW drive, launch your CD burner software, and then follow the program's instructions to start translating and copying the song files. After the ripping begins, the MP3 files on your hard drive are converted and copied onto a blank CD-R in standard CD Audio format.

To play your new CD in a regular (non-PC) CD player, record in the CD-R format and use a blank CD-R disc specifically labeled for audio use. (CD-RW discs will not play in most CD players.)

Burning CDs with Windows Media Player

Because most CD burner software works in pretty much the same fashion, you might as well use Windows Media Player (WMP) to burn your CDs.

You start by selecting the Media Library tab and creating a playlist of the songs you want to burn. Then you click the Copy to CD or Device tab, which displays the Music to Copy list. Click the Music to Copy section to display all your playlists; then, select the playlist or album you want to copy.

Now you insert a blank CD-R disc into your computer's CD-R/RW drive. Select your CD-R/RW drive from WMP's Music on Device list, and then click the Copy Music button.

WMP now inspects the files you want to copy, converts them to CDA format, and copies them to your CD. When the entire process is done, WMP displays a Closing Disk message for the last track on your playlist. The burning is not complete until this message is displayed.

Other popular CD burner programs include MusicMatch Jukebox (www.musicmatch.com) and RealJukebox (www.real.com/jukebox/).

Creating CD Labels

When you burn a custom CD, it's a good idea to create a label for the new CD—and maybe even a track listing for the CD jewelbox.

There are many label-creation programs available. Microsoft Picture It! Publishing, included with Microsoft Works Suite, lets you create some great-looking CD labels with just a few clicks of the mouse.

Other popular label-making programs include My CD Labeler (www.elibrium.com/ mysoftware/), cdrLabel (www.ziplabel.com), Visual Cover ++ (www.directlogic.com), and the Neato CD Labeler Kit (www.neato.com).

Begin by selecting Pick a Design from the Welcome screen, then selecting Labels/Stickers, and then selecting Guided Photo Labels. When the next screen appears, select the Labels theme, and then scroll down and select one of the round CD label templates. You can use the template as-is and add your own text, or you can replace the template's artwork with your own personal photo or graphics. When you're done editing the template, save and print the label on special CD label paper.

You can find round labels specially made for compact discs at your local computer or office supply store.

After you've created the CD label, return to the Pick a Design screen and select the corresponding CD sleeve template. Create both a front and back sleeve, with the title on the front and the track listing on the back. Print both sleeves on regular or slick paper; then, insert them into an empty CD jewelbox.

DOWNLOAD SONGS TO A PORTABLE PLAYER

What You Need

- Digital music files in MP3 format
- Windows Media Player or similar software
- Portable MP3 audio player with connecting cable
- Basic computer system

Goal

Transfer your favorite MP3 files from your computer to a portable MP3 player.

Choosing a Portable Audio Player

MP3 files are perfect for listening to on the go—especially through Walkman-type portable players. Most of these players are extremely compact devices, storing MP3 files in memory (often via removable memory sticks or cards) or on extremely small hard disks (called *microdrives*).

There are many portable MP3 files on the market today. If you're looking to buy a new player, look for models from these manufacturers:

- Casio (www.casio.com)

- Creative Labs (www.nomadworld.com)

- Frontier Labs (www.frontierlabs.com)

- Philips (www.expanium.philips.com)

- RCA (www.rca.com)

- Samsung (www.samsungelectronics.com)

- SONICblue (www.sonicblue.com)

- Sony (www.sel.sony.com)

Copying Files from Your PC to Your Portable Player

Transferring files from your computer to your portable audio player is very similar to copying files to a recordable compact disc. Just launch the appropriate software (often included with the portable player), connect your portable device, select the tracks or playlist you want to copy, and then click the "copy" or "transfer" button. Most players and software let you select from different quality levels for the copied files; the higher the quality, the fewer songs you can fit in the player's memory.

Using Windows Media Player to Copy Files

If your portable audio player came with its own software, you can use that software to transfer files to the device. You can also use Windows Media Player (WMP) to perform this task.

To start the downloading process, connect your portable audio player to your PC. Then launch Windows Media Player, and select the Copy to CD or Device tab.

Go to the Music to Copy pane, and select the playlist or files you want to copy. In the Music on Device pane, select your portable audio player; then. click the Copy Music button.

WMP now verifies that there is enough space on your portable audio player for the files you selected. If there's enough space, the files are copied. If not, you'll have to delete enough files to make everything fit.

Changing the Quality Level

In most cases, the portable audio player automatically determines the quality level (and the file size) of the files you copy to its memory. Most players are configured to provide the best compromise between playing time (determined by file size) and playback quality.

If you want to override this automatic setting, you can manually select the quality level for the files you copy to your portable player. Within Windows Media Player, pull down the Tools menu and select Options. When the Options dialog box appears, select the Devices tab, select your player from the Devices list, and click the Properties button.

When the Properties dialog box appears, select the Portable Device tab. To use your player's automatic settings, select the Select Quality Level Automatically option. To set your own settings, select the Select Quality Option and move the slider to the desired quality level.

Copying Licensed Files

You might run into problems copying some digital audio files—particularly WMA files—to your portable device. If the file is copy-protected or otherwise licensed, you might need to enter the serial number of your player before you can copy the file. It's also possible that the file isn't licensed for portable play; if this is the case, you won't be able to play the file in your portable device.

This licensing problem is specific to WMA-format files, which can incorporate a copy-protection scheme. MP3-format files, on the other hand, include no copy protection, and thus won't give you any playback problems when you copy them to your portable player. (This is one of the primary factors behind the popularity of the MP3 format.)

PART XV

DO IT NOW: WATCHING TV AND MOVIES

Activity **57**

PLAY A DVD ON YOUR PC

What You Need

- DVD movie
- DVD decoder software
- Windows Media Player
- Internet connection (optional)
- Basic computer system with DVD drive
- Speaker system or headphones

Goal

Turn your computer system into a miniature home theater system for playing DVD movies.

Playing a DVD Video

If you have a DVD-ROM drive in your computer and the proper DVD decoder software installed, it's a snap to play DVD movies on your computer monitor.

New PCs with DVD drives installed typically come all set up for movie playback, so no additional configuration is required. If you've just added a DVD drive to an existing computer, you'll need to be sure you install the appropriate DVD decoder software. If your system is running Windows XP, you can add DVD capability with one of the DVD Decoder Pack add-ins from CyberLink, InterVideo, or Ravisent. (These cost around $30 each and are available wherever Windows is sold.) These packs add DVD playback capability to Windows Media Player (WMP)—which is probably the best software to use to play back DVD movies.

Using Windows Media Player to Play DVDs

When you insert a DVD in your DVD drive, playback should start automatically. Your system should sense the presence of the DVD, launch Windows Media Player, and start playing the movie. (You can also initiate playback from within WMP by pulling down the Play menu and selecting DVD.)

As you can see in Figure A57.1, the picture from the DVD displays in WMP's video window. The individual tracks on the DVD are displayed in the Playlist area, and information about the DVD (including the DVD cover) is displayed beneath the video window.

FIGURE A57.1

Watching a DVD movie with Windows Media Player.

Video window   Movie chapters

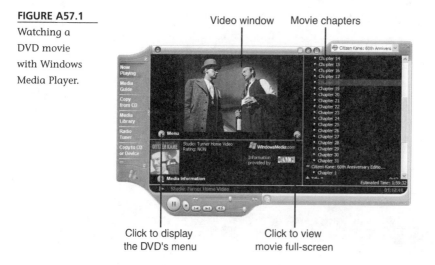

Click to display the DVD's menu

Click to view movie full-screen

| Note | You have to be connected to the Internet for WMP to find and display this DVD information and cover art. |

Changing Display Size

You can watch your movie in WMP's video window, or you can view the DVD using your entire computer screen. Just click the Full Screen button (at the lower-right corner of the video window) or pull down the View menu and select Full Screen, and the movie will enlarge to fill your entire screen. Press Esc to return to normal viewing mode.

Navigating DVD Menus

Almost all DVDs come with their own built-in menus. These menus typically lead you to special features on the disc and allow you to select various playback options and jump to specific scenes.

To display the DVD's main menu, pull down the View menu and select DVD Features, Title Menu. To display the DVD's special features menu, pull down the View menu and select DVD Features, Top Menu. When the special features menu is displayed, you can click any of the options onscreen to jump to a particular feature.

Changing Audio Options

Many DVDs come with an English-language soundtrack, as well as soundtracks in other languages. Some DVDs come with different types of audio—mono, Dolby Pro Logic surround, Dolby Digital 5.1 surround, and so on. Other DVDs come with commentary from the film's director or stars on a separate audio track.

You can select which audio track you listen to by pulling down the View menu and selecting DVD Features, Audio and Language Tracks. This displays a list of available audio options. Select the track you want to listen to, and then settle back to enjoy the movie.

Playing in Slow Motion—or Fast Motion

WMP provides a variety of special playback features. You can pause a still frame, advance frame-by-frame, or play the movie in slow or fast motion. To access these special playback features, you have to pull down the View menu and select Now Playing Tools, DVD Controls. This displays a set of special controls in the Now Playing Tools area of the WMP window. Use these tools to vary the playback speed or pause the movie on a still frame.

Displaying Subtitles and Closed Captions

Many DVDs include subtitles in other languages. To turn on subtitles, pull down the View menu and select DVD Features, Subtitles and Captions, and then select which subtitles you want to view.

Other DVDs include closed captioning for the hearing impaired. You can view closed captions by pulling down the View menu and selecting DVD Features, Subtitles and Captions, Closed Captions.

WATCH A WEBCAST

What You Need

- Windows Media Player or similar software
- Internet Explorer
- Internet connection
- Basic computer system
- Speaker system or headphones

Goal

Turn your computer system into a receiver for television and video broadcasts over the Internet.

Finding Webcasts on the Internet

When you add pictures to an Internet radio broadcast, you get Internet television—or what some people call *Webcasts*. Just as Internet radio broadcasts use streaming audio technology, Webcasts use streaming video to deliver both prerecorded and real-time pictures direct to your PC.

Many different sites offer different types of Webcast programming. Most Webcasts are simulcasts of traditional television programs or sporting events. There are also a variety of live concerts and special events broadcast in real-time over the Web.

To find a Webcast, check out the following sites:

- Feedroom (www.feedroom.com)

- LikeTelevision (www.liketelevision.com)

- mediaontap.com (www.mediaontap.com)

- RealGuide (realguide.real.com)

- StreamSearch (www.streamsearch.com)

- Yahoo! Broadcast (broadcast.yahoo.com)

In addition, most of the major news sites offer Internet television broadcasts of the latest news clips and headlines directly from their home pages. You can also find streaming video of selected sporting events at the major Web sports sites.

You really need a broadband Internet connection to watch Webcasts. A normal dial-up connection simply isn't add fast enough to watch high-bandwidth streaming video programming.

Watching Webcasts

There are actually three formats for streaming video over the Internet. Each format requires a different type of media player program, which means you will probably have to download and install all three programs on your PC.

Using Windows Media Player

You're familiar with Windows Media Player (WMP) because we've used it to perform a number of activities in this book. You should have a copy of WMP already installed on your PC; it comes free of charge as part of Microsoft Windows.

When you're using WMP to watch a Webcast, it's easy to change the size of the video display. Just pull down the View menu, select Zoom, and then choose from 50%, 100%, 200%, or Fit to Window. You can also display the video full-screen by pulling down the View menu and selecting Full Screen.

Caution

No matter which player you use, if you choose to display a Webcast at a larger-than-normal size, it's likely that the picture will start to look "blocky" and lose fine detail.

Using RealPlayer

You first learned about RealPlayer in Activity 51, "Listen to Internet Radio." Using RealPlayer to watch Webcasts is almost identical to using it to listen to Internet radio broadcasts.

You can change the size of RealPlayer's video display by using the Zoom control. Just click the Zoom button and select from Original Size, Double Size, or Full Screen.

Using QuickTime Player

Apple's QuickTime Player is a media player similar to WMP and RealPlayer, used primarily for playing QuickTime-format movies and video clips. You can download a copy of the player from `www.apple.com/quicktime/`.

QuickTime Player, shown in Figure A58.1, is a little different from RealPlayer or WMP in that if you open multiple movies at the same time, multiple viewing windows are displayed. You can change the size of the viewing window by pulling down the Movie menu and then selecting from Normal Size, Double Size, or Full Screen.

FIGURE A58.1
Watching movies with QuickTime Player.

SET UP YOUR OWN WEBCAM

What You Need

- PC camera, with connecting cables
- PC microphone (optional)
- Webcam software
- Server to host your Webcam pages
- Internet Explorer
- Internet connection
- Basic computer system

Goal

Configure your computer system to broadcast video signals to other users over the Internet.

All About Webcams

A *Webcam* is a PC camera that is hooked up to a personal computer and then linked to a Web page to provide continuous images or streaming video via the Internet. When you use Internet Explorer to browse a Webcam page, you get a live look at whatever the camera is pointing at. (If you're looking at a still image, that image will be updated periodically—typically once a minute or so.)

Some people have decided to put their entire lives on the Web, warts and all, via 24/7 Webcams. Some cities have traffic Webcams aimed at busy intersections or stretches of highway. You can even find Webcams installed at various vacation spots around the globe to entice you to visit on your next vacation.

Finding a Webcam to Watch

If you're more of a watcher than a doer, check out one of the many Webcam directories on the Internet. These sites list all different types of Webcams for your viewing pleasure, and include

- Camarades (www.camarades.com)

- Camville.com (www.camville.com)

- WebCam Central (www.camcentral.com)

- WebCam World (www.webcamworld.com)

- WebcamNow (www.webcamnow.com, shown in Figure A59.1)

- WebcamSearch. com (www.webcamsearch.com)

FIGURE A59.1

Go to
WebcamNow
to view other
users' Webcams
or set up one of
your own.

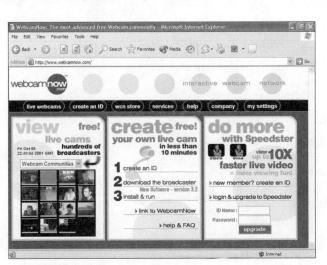

Setting Up Your Own Webcam

A Webcam is nothing more than a simple digital PC camera, attached to your computer. The camera connects to your PC, typically via the USB or FireWire port, and feeds images into a special Webcam software program. This program is configured to periodically grab single frames from the camera and save the pictures as JPG-format graphic files. The individual JPG files are then fed to a Web server, which embeds the pictures into a constantly refreshing Web page.

Choosing a PC Camera

The most popular PC cameras are priced in the $50–$250 range, and most deliver acceptable picture quality. These cameras usually don't have built-in microphones, so if you want to broadcast audio with your video, you will need to attach an external microphone to your PC.

Most PC cameras can plug into your computer's USB port (ideal), parallel port, or a proprietary interface board (only necessary with some higher-end models). The USB connection is the easiest to make and in most cases is trouble-free.

Selecting Webcam Software

Webcam software typically performs a variety of functions, including grabbing still frames from your camera, uploading those frames to a server or saving them to individual files, and managing streaming broadcasts for either Webcam or video conference use. You can find commercial Webcam software at your local computer store; there are also a number of freeware and shareware programs that you can download from the Web. (Some PC cameras come bundled with free Webcam software, too.)

Here are some of the most popular Webcam programs available:

- CoffeeCup WebCam (www.coffeecup.com/webcam/)
- Eyes&Ears (www.intech2.com)
- HomeWatcher (www.homewatcher.com)
- iVISTA (www.ivista.com)
- NOWencoder (www.nowonair.com)
- SoftCam (www.softcam.com)

Finding a Host

The final piece in the Webcam puzzle is the server that hosts your live Webcasts. That server might be in your home office (if you host your own server), it might be at a standard Web site hosting service, or it might be at a site that specializes in Webcam hosting.

Wherever your server is, you'll need a relatively persistent connection between your home computer and the host server. The connection has to be up all the time for your Webcam images to be constantly updated. This means you probably need a DSL or cable modem connection; a dial-up connection is less viable for Webcam use.

If you're new to the whole Webcam business, the best solution is one of the sites that specializes in hosting and listing Webcams. Most of the sites listed in the "Finding a Webcam to Watch" section, earlier in this activity, also offer Webcam hosting services and can serve as a one-stop shop when you're first getting set up.

Putting It All Together

After you've signed up with a Webcam host, you're all set to go live with your Webcam. You can use the software and services available at the host site to set up your Webcam page, or (if you're savvy with HTML) you can create your own Web page with a constantly refreshing Webcam image. Look for instructions at the Webcam host site for how to proceed.

EDIT A HOME MOVIE

What You Need

- Home movie on videotape
- Windows Movie Maker or similar video editing software
- Video capture board (for non-digital recorders)
- Basic computer system (with FireWire connection, for digital recorders)

Goal

Turn your computer system into a video production console for editing home movies on videotape.

Configuring Your System for Video Editing

If you have a camcorder and make your own home movies, you can use your computer system to make those movies a lot more appealing. With the right hardware and software, you can turn your PC into a video editing console—and make your home movies look a *lot* more professional.

All you have to do is connect your camcorder or VCR to your PC system unit and then install some form of video editing software. If your computer is running Windows XP, this software is already installed on your system, in the form of the Windows Movie Maker (WMM) program. You launch WMM by clicking the Start button and then selecting All Programs, Accessories, Windows Movie Maker.

As to connecting all your hardware, how you do this depends on what type of camcorder or VCR you have. If you have a VHS, VHS-C, SVHS, 8mm, or Hi8 recorder, you'll need to install an analog-to-digital video capture card in your PC. You'll plug your recorder into the jacks in this card, and it will convert the analog signals from your recorder into the digital audio and video your computer understands.

If you have one of the latest digital video (DV) recorders in the Digital8 or MiniDV formats, you don't need a video capture card. What you do need is an IE1394 FireWire interface, which is included with many new PCs. This type of connection is fast enough to handle the huge stream of digital data pouring from your DV recorder into your PC.

Understanding Windows Movie Maker

Windows Movie Maker works by dividing your home movie into scene segments it calls *clips*. You can then rearrange and delete specific clips to edit the flow of your movie.

The basic WMM window is divided into four parts, as shown in Figure A60.1. All the clips you can use appear in the Clips area in the middle of the screen. The movie you assemble from these clips appears in the Workspace at the bottom of the screen. You can view your movie-in-progress in the Monitor area.

FIGURE A60.1

Editing home
movies with
Windows Movie
Maker.

Collections   Clips   Monitor

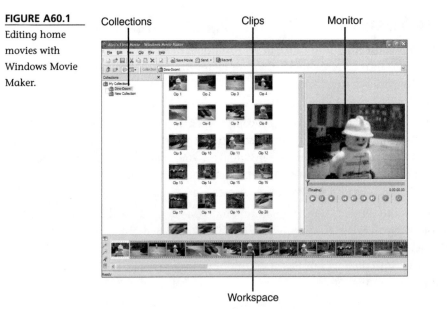

Workspace

Importing Your Source Material

The first step in editing your movie is to import your original home movie into Windows Movie Maker. After you have your camcorder or VCR connected, pull down WMM's File menu and select Record. When the Record dialog box appears, pull down the Record list and select the type of source material you want to record. Then pull down the Setting list and select the level of recording quality you want. (For most purposes, Medium Quality represents a good compromise between audio/video quality and file size.) Now check the Record Time Limit and Create Clips options, and click the Record button.

After your computer is set to record, click the Play button on your VCR or camcorder. Recording will now start and continue until you click WMM's Stop button (or two hours elapse, whichever comes first).

When recording is stopped, the Save Windows Media File dialog box appears. Enter a name and location for this file, and then click Save. The new clips you create now appear in the Clips area of the WMM window.

While most of your projects will consist primarily of movies recorded from videotape, you can also use other types of source material—including movie clips you download from the Internet, songs you rip from your favorite CDs, or title slides you create in a graphic editing program. Just pull down the File menu and select Import; then, navigate to and select the file you want to import. The files you import will appear as one or more clips in the Clips panel.

Editing Your Video

You create your movie by dragging clips into the Workspace area. You can insert clips in any order, and more than once if you want. After the clips are in the Workspace, you can drag them around in a different order. This is how you edit the flow of your movie.

By default, the Workspace is shown in Storyboard view. This view is easiest for seeing how all your clips fit together. When you get the basic flow of your movie in place, you can switch the Workspace to Timeline view (by clicking the Timeline/Storyboard button at the upper-left of the workspace). In this view you see the timing of each segment and can overlay background music and narration.

Adding Transitions

To make a more pleasing movie, you can add professional cross-fade transitions between scenes, where the last frames in the first clip fade out as the initial frames of the second clip fade in.

To create a transition, the Workspace must be in Timeline view. Then all you have to do is drag the second clip so that it overlaps the first clip. The shaded area indicates the length of the transition.

Saving—and Watching—Your Movie

When you're done editing, you save your project by pulling down the File menu and selecting Save Project. This does not save a movie file, however—it only saves the component parts of your project.

When your project is absolutely, positively finished you actually make the movie. Pull down the File menu and select Save Movie to display the Save Movie dialog box. From here you have to select the playback quality, enter a title, and click OK. Windows Movie Maker then creates your movie and saves it as a WMV-format file, which can be viewed with the Windows Media Player.

PART XVI

DO IT NOW: WORKING WITH FILES

MANAGE FOLDERS

What You Need

- Basic computer system
- Windows XP

Goal

Create and view folders to hold your document files.

Viewing Folders and Files

As you learned in Chapter 3, "Windows and Software Basics," all the documents and programs on your computer are stored in files. These files are then arranged into a series of folders and subfolders.

You use either My Computer or My Documents (both accessible from the Windows Start menu) to view the folders and files on your system. Both of these tools work similarly and enable you to customize the way they display their contents. (Figure A61.1 shows the various subfolders stored within the My Documents folder.)

FIGURE A61.1

Manage your folders and files with the My Documents folder.

View the last-viewed folder

View the parent folder

Folder

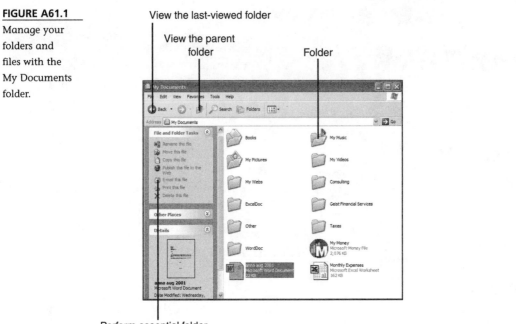

Perform essential folder and file operations

Changing the Way Files Are Displayed

You can choose to view the contents of a folder in a variety of ways. Just click the Views button from within any folder and select from Thumbnails, Tiles, Icons, List, or Details. Experiment with each view to determine which you like best.

Tip

Thumbnails view is best for working with graphics files. Details view is best if you're looking for files by date or size.

Sorting Files and Folders

When viewing files in My Computer or My Documents, you can sort your files and folders in a number of ways. To do this, pull down the View menu, select Arrange Icons By, and then choose to sort by Name, Size, Type, or Modified. (This last option sorts files by date and time last edited.)

Grouping Files and Folders

You can also configure Windows XP to group the files in your folder, which can make it easier to identify particular files. For example, if you sorted your files by time and date modified, they'll now be grouped by date (Today, Yesterday, Last Week, and so on). If you sorted your files by type, they'll be grouped by file extension. And so on.

To turn on grouping, pull down the View menu, select Arrange Icons By, and then check the Show in Groups option. Windows now groups your files and folders by the criteria you used to sort those items.

Saving Your Settings, Universally

By default, when you customize a folder, that view is specific to that folder. To apply a folder view to all the folders on your system, configure a folder the way you want; then, pull down the Tools menu and select Options. When the Folder Options dialog box appears, select the View tab, click the Like Current Folder button, and then click OK.

To return your folders to their original states, click the Reset All Folders button.

Navigating Folders

You can navigate through the folders in My Computer, My Documents, and other folders in several ways:

- To view the contents of a disk or folder, double-click the selected item.

- To move up the hierarchy of folders and subfolders to the next highest item, click the Up button on the toolbar.

- To move back to the disk or folder previously selected, click the Back button on the toolbar.

- To choose from the history of disks and folders previously viewed, click the down arrow on the Back button and select a disk or folder.

- If you've moved back through multiple disks or folders, you can move forward to the next folder by clicking the Forward button.

- Go directly to any disk or folder by entering the path in the Address Bar (in the format *x:\folder\subfolder*) and pressing Enter or clicking the Go button.

You can also go directly to any folder by clicking the Folders button to display the Folders pane and then selecting the folder in the Folders list.

Creating New Folders

The more files you create, the harder it is to organize and find things on your hard disk. When the number of files you have becomes unmanageable, you need to create more folders—and subfolders—to better categorize your files.

To create a new folder, start by navigating to the drive or folder where you want to place the new folder. Then select Make a New Folder from the File and Folder Tasks panel.

A new, empty folder now appears, with the filename New Folder highlighted. Type a name for your folder (which overwrites the New Folder name), and press Enter.

Activity  **62**

COPY AND MOVE FILES

What You Need

- Basic computer system
- Windows XP

Goal

Copy and move files from one folder to another.

Copying Files

Now it's time to address the most common things you do with files—copying and moving them from one location to another. These operations, like most file operations, can be accessed directly from the activity center pane in any Windows folder.

Copying is different from moving. When you *copy* an item, the original remains, in its original location. When you *move* an item, the original is no longer present in the original location.

The Easy Way to Copy

To copy a file (or a folder) with Windows XP, start by selecting the item you want to copy. Next, select Copy This File from the File Tasks list.

When the Copy Items dialog box appears, navigate to and select the new location for the item, and then click the Copy button. (If you want to copy the item to a new folder, click the New Folder button first.)

That's it. You've just copied the file from one location to another.

Other Ways to Copy

Windows provides several other methods to copy a file. For example, you can pull down the File menu and select Copy (or Copy to Folder). You can right-click a file and select Send To from the pop-up menu. You can hold down the Ctrl key and drag it from one location to another within the My Documents or My Computer folders. You can even drag the file with the *right* mouse button—when you drop the file into a new location, you see a pop-up menu that asks whether you want to move it or copy it.

Moving Files

Moving a file (or folder) is different from copying it. Moving cuts the item from its previous location and places it in a new location. Copying leaves the original item where it was *and* creates a copy of the item elsewhere.

In other words, when you copy something you end up with two of it. When you move something, you only have the one thing.

The Easy Way to Move

To move a file, start by selecting the item you want to move. Now select Move This File from the File Tasks list.

When the Move Items dialog box appears, navigate to and select the new location for the item, and then click the Copy button. (If you want to move the item to a new folder, click the New Folder button first.)

Other Ways to Move a File

Just as Windows provides several other ways to copy a file, you also have a choice of alternative methods for moving a file. For example, you can pull down the File menu and select Move (or Move to Folder). You can drag the file from one location to another. You can even do the right-drag trick discussed earlier. When you drop the file into a new location, you see a pop-up menu that asks whether you want to move it or copy it.

Working with Compressed Folders

Really big files can be difficult to move or copy. They're especially hard to transfer to other users, whether by floppy disk or e-mail.

Fortunately, Windows XP includes a way to make big files smaller. *Compressed folders* take big files and compress them down in size, which makes them easier to copy or move. After the file has been transferred, you uncompress the file back to its original state.

Compressing a File

Compressing one or more files is a relatively easy task from within any Windows folder. Just select the file(s) you want to compress, right-click the file(s) to display the pop-up menu, and then select Send to, Compressed Folder.

Windows now creates a new folder that contains compressed versions of the file(s) you selected. (This folder is distinguished by a little zipper on the folder icon, as shown in Figure A62.1.) You can now copy, move, or e-mail this folder, which is a lot smaller than the original file(s).

FIGURE A62.1
A compressed
folder containing
one or more files.

> **Tip**
>
> The compressed folder is actually a file with a .ZIP extension, so it can be used with other compression/decompression programs, such as WinZip.

Extracting Files

The process of decompressing a file is actually an *extraction* process. That's because you *extract* the original file(s) from the compressed folder.

In Windows XP, this process is eased by the use of the Extraction Wizard. Start by right-clicking the compressed folder; then, select Extract All from the pop-up menu. When the Extraction Wizard launches, click the Next button and select which folder you want to extract the files to. When you click Next again, the wizard extracts the files and displays the Extraction Complete page. Click the Finish button to view the files you've just extracted.

RENAME AND DELETE FILES

What You Need

- Basic computer system
- Windows XP

Goal

Rename selected files, delete files from your hard disk, and manage the Windows Recycle Bin.

Renaming Files

When you create a new file (or folder), it helps to give it a name that somehow describes its contents. Sometimes, however, you might need to change a file's name. Fortunately, Windows makes it relatively easy to rename an item.

Folder and filenames can include up to 255 characters—including many special characters. Some special characters, however, are "illegal," meaning that you ° use them in folder or filenames. Illegal characters include the following: \ / : * ? " < > |.

To rename a file (or folder), start by selecting the item you want to rename. Next, select Rename This File from the File Tasks list.

The filename is now highlighted. Type a new name for your folder (which overwrites the current name), and press Enter.

Deleting Files

Too many files eat up too much hard disk space—and disk space on your computer is limited. (Music and video files, in particular, can chew up big chunks of your hard drive.) Because you don't want to waste disk space, you should periodically delete those files (and folders) you no longer need.

The Easy Way to Delete

Deleting a file is as easy as selecting it and then selecting Delete This File from the File Tasks list. This sends the file to the Windows Recycle Bin, which is kind of a trash can for deleted files. (It's also a trash can that periodically needs to be dumped—as discussed later in this activity.)

You can also delete a file by dragging it from the folder window onto the Recycle Bin icon on the desktop or by highlighting it and pressing the Del key.

Restoring Deleted Files

Have you ever accidentally deleted the wrong file? If so, you're in luck. For a short period of time, Windows stores the files you delete in the Recycle Bin. The Recycle Bin is actually a special folder on your hard disk; if you've recently deleted a file, it should still be in the Recycle Bin folder.

To "undelete" a file from the Recycle Bin, start by opening the Recycle Bin folder. (Just double-click its icon on the Windows desktop, as shown in Figure A63.1.) Now select the file you want to restore, and then select Restore This Item from the Recycle Bin Tasks list.

FIGURE A63.1

The Recycle Bin, where all your deleted files end up.

This copies the deleted file back to its original location, ready for continued use.

Managing the Recycle Bin

Deleted files do not stay in the Recycle Bin indefinitely.

By default, the deleted files in the Recycle Bin can occupy 10% of your hard disk space. When you've deleted enough files to exceed this 10%, the oldest files in the Recycle Bin are automatically and permanently deleted from your hard disk.

If you'd rather dump the Recycle Bin manually (and thus free up some hard disk space), open the Recycle Bin folder and select Empty the Recycle Bin from the Recycle Bin Tasks list. When the Confirm File Delete dialog box appears, click Yes to completely erase the files, or click No to continue storing the files in the Recycle Bin.

SEND A FILE VIA E-MAIL

What You Need

- Outlook Express
- Internet connection
- Basic computer system

Goal

Attach a file to an Outlook Express e-mail message.

Sharing Files with Other Users

From time to time you'll want to share one of your files with another computer user. What kinds of files might you want to share? How about these:

- Graphics files, such as pictures of your kids and family

- Audio files, such as MP3 song files or audio clips from your favorite television programs

- Video clips, such as files captured from your videotaped home movies

- Documents, such as word processing files from Microsoft Word or spreadsheets from Microsoft Excel

There are several different ways to share files. You can copy a file to a floppy disk or writable CD and send the disk or CD to the other user. If you're both connected to the same computer network, you can use the Windows Copy command to copy the file from one computer to another. Or, if you're both connected to the Internet, you can send the file via e-mail.

Attaching a File to an E-mail Message

Attaching files to an e-mail message is a way to send files from user to user over the Internet—and it's easy to do, using the Outlook Express e-mail program.

To attach a file to an outgoing e-mail message, start with a new message and then click the Attach button in the message's toolbar. When the Insert Attachment dialog box appears, click the Browse button to locate the file you want to send; then, click Attach.

The attached file is now listed in a new Attach: field below the Subject: field in the message window. When you click the Send button, the e-mail message and its attached file are sent together to the Outbox.

Opening an E-mail Attachment

When you receive a message that contains a file attachment, you'll see a paper clip icon in the message header and a paper clip button in the preview pane header, as shown in Figure A64.1.

When you receive a message with an attachment, you can choose to view (open) the attached file or save it to your hard disk.

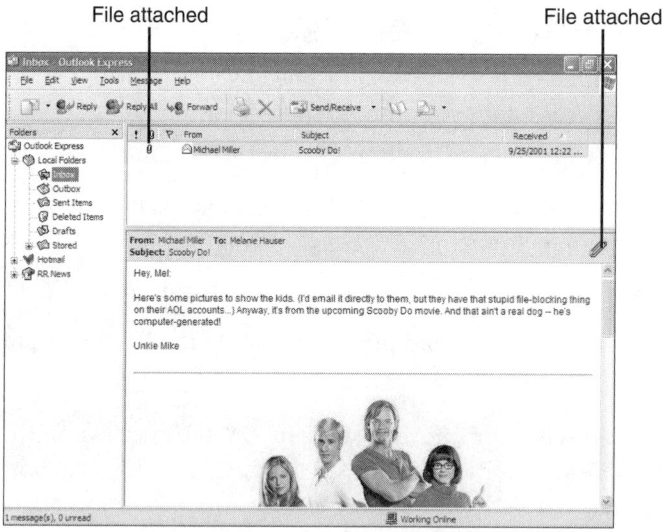

FIGURE A64.1

Receiving an e-mail message with an attachment in Outlook Express.

File attached   File attached

To view or open an attachment, click the paper clip button in the Preview pane header, and then click the attachment's filename. This opens the attachment in its associated application. (If you're asked whether you want to save or view the attachment, select View.)

To save an attachment to your hard disk, click the paper clip button in the preview pane header, and then select Save Attachments. When the Save Attachments dialog box appears, select a location for the file and click the Save button.

Watching Out for E-mail Viruses

Computer viruses are files that can attack your system and damage your programs and documents. One of the more popular ways of spreading viruses is through attachments to e-mail messages.

Note

Learn more about computer viruses in Activity 75, "Protect Your System from Viruses and Attacks."

Most e-mail viruses are spread when someone sends you an unexpected file attachment—and then you open the file. It's just too easy to receive an e-mail message with a file attached, click the file to open it, and then launch the virus file. Boom! Your computer is infected.

Viruses can be found in many types of files. The most common file types for viruses are .EXE, .VBS, .PIF, and .COM. Viruses can also be embedded in Word (.DOC) or Excel (.XLS) files. You *can't* catch a virus from a picture file, so viewing a .JPG, .GIF, .TIF, and .BMP file is completely safe.

The best way to avoid catching a virus via e-mail is to *not* open any .EXE, .VBS, .PIF, or .COM files attached to incoming e-mail messages—even if you know the sender. That's because some viruses are capable of taking over an e-mail program and sending copies of themselves to all the contacts in a user's address book. (Pretty tricky, eh?)

You can also configure Outlook Express to automatically reject files that might contain viruses. You do this by pulling down the Tools menu and selecting Options. When the Options dialog box appears, select the Security tab; then, check both the Warn Me When Other Applications Try to Send E-mail As Me and Do Not Allow Attachments to Be Saved or Opened That Could Potentially Be a Virus options. Click OK when done.

DOWNLOAD A FILE FROM THE INTERNET

What You Need

- Internet Explorer
- Internet connection
- Basic computer system

Goal

Find and download files from the Internet to your hard disk.

Finding Files Online

The Internet is a huge repository for computer files of all shapes and sizes, from utilities that help you better manage your disk drive to full-featured e-mail and newsgroup programs. There are hundreds of thousands of these programs available *somewhere* on the Internet; if you can find them, you can download them to your computer.

Interestingly, many of the program files you find online are available free of charge; these programs are called *freeware*. Other programs can be downloaded for no charge, but they require you to pay a token amount to receive full functionality or documentation; these programs are called *shareware*. (Both types of programs are in contrast to the software you buy in boxes at your local computer retailer, which is *commercial software*.)

Before you can use any of the programs available online, you first have to find them and then download them from their current locations to your PC. Fortunately, downloading files is a fairly easy process.

There are some variations to the procedure, but overall, it's pretty straightforward. In a nutshell, all you have to do is the following:

1. Create a special download directory on your computer's hard drive.
2. Find and download the file you want.
3. If the file was compressed (generally in a Zip file), decompress the file using Windows XP Extraction Wizard.
4. If the file you downloaded was a software program, you'll need to install the software. Installation instructions are usually included somewhere on the download information page or in a readme file included with the file download. In most cases, installation involves running a file named setup.exe or install.exe; after the setup program launches, follow the onscreen instructions to complete the installation.
5. Delete the compressed file you originally downloaded.

Downloading from a File Archive

Where do you find all these wonderful files to download? The best places to look are Web sites dedicated to file downloading. These sites are called *file archives*, and they typically store a huge variety of freeware and shareware programs and utilities.

We'll look at a few of the best and the biggest file archives, and show you how they work.

ZDNet Downloads

ZDNet Downloads (www.zdnet.com/downloads/) is a huge library of software provided by the ZDNet Web service. There are three ways to find files on this site. You can browse by category, browse by what ZDNet calls "special lists" (such as What's New, Most Popular, and so on), and search for specific files.

After you find the file you want to download, click its link to display a full-page description. To download the file, click the Download Now link and then follow the onscreen instructions.

Tucows

The second "big dog" in downloading sites is actually a big *cow*—Tucows (www.tucows.com). This is one of the oldest repositories of software on the Internet, serving up software downloads since 1993.

Like the ZDNet Software Library, you can either browse through Tucows or search for files. Tucows's browsing and searching are a little different, however, because they're operating-system–based. That is, instead of starting out by software category, you first click the operating system you're using. *Then* you can click through the different categories of software within the repository. Similarly, when you start a search, you have to select your operating system from a pull-down list and *then* click the Go button.

Tucows then directs you to one of its *mirror* sites, where the files are actually stored. Select the mirror closest to your current location; then, click the Download It Now button to start downloading.

CNET's Download.com

ZDNet Software Library and Tucows store copies of all their files on their huge servers. CNET's Download.com (download.cnet.com), on the other hand, doesn't store a single file on its site. Instead, it serves up links to and descriptions of some of the best software programs available for downloading. This is the site to go to if you're unsure about downloading because the Download.com team does the evaluation and categorization for you.

There are several ways to access the files listed on Download.com. You can browse by category, browse by "special lists," or search for files.

After you've found the file you want to download, read its description and download instructions and then click the Download Now link. This automatically starts the download via the best available download site.

Other File Repositories

If you can't find what you want at one of the big three download sites, you might want to try searching one of these other file repositories on the Web:

- FileMine (www.itprodownloads.com)

- Jumbo (www.jumbo.com)

- Shareware.com (shareware.cnet.com)

- Shareware Place (www.sharewareplace.com)

Downloading Files from Any Web Page

Most Web pages contain graphics files of one sort or another. If you see a pretty picture on a page, that picture is actually a graphics file; any background on a Web page is also a file. And any graphics file on a Web page can be downloaded to your PC.

To download a picture file from a Web page, right-click the picture and select Save Picture As from the pop-up menu. When prompted, select a location for the file; then, click Save. The graphics file will now be downloaded to the location you specified.

If a Web page contains a link to a file, you can download that file (of any type) without actually jumping to the file. Just right-click the link to the file and select Save Target as from the pop-up menu. When prompted, select a location for the file, and then click Save to start the download.

PART XVII

DO IT NOW: TAKING CARE OF YOUR PC

CHANGE YOUR DESKTOP BACKGROUND

What You Need

- Basic computer system
- Windows XP

Goal

Create a custom look for your computer desktop.

Personalizing Your Desktop

When you first turn on your new computer system, you see the Windows desktop as Microsoft set it up for you.

Fortunately, you don't have to keep it that way.

Windows presents a lot of different ways to personalize the look and feel of your desktop. In fact, one of the great things about Windows is how quickly you can make the desktop look like *your* desktop, different from anybody else's.

Changing the Desktop Size

You can configure your computer's display so that the desktop is larger or smaller than normal. A larger desktop lets you view more things onscreen at the same time—even though each item is smaller than before.

Changing the size of the desktop is accomplished by changing Windows's *screen resolution*. You do this by right-clicking anywhere on the desktop to display the Display Properties dialog box. Select the Settings tab; then, adjust the Screen Resolution slider. (The sample display changes to reflect your new settings.) While you're on this tab, you can also change the number of colors displayed. (More is better.) Just choose the desired setting from the Color Quality drop-down list, and then click OK when done.

To best use all the features of Windows XP, go for a 1024×768 resolution. If this setting makes things look too small (a problem if you have a smaller monitor), try the 800×600 resolution. As for color, 16-bit is my recommended minimum for Windows XP, but 32-bit looks a lot better.

Enabling ClearType

ClearType is a new display technology in Windows XP that effectively triples the horizontal resolution on LCD displays. (In other words, it makes things look sharper—and smoother.) If you have a flat-panel monitor or a portable PC, you definitely want to turn on ClearType.

To turn on ClearType, right-click the desktop to open the Display Properties dialog box; then, select the Appearance tab. Click the Effects button to display the Effects dialog box, check the Use the Following Method to Smooth Edges of Screen Fonts option, and select ClearType from the pull-down list. Click OK when done.

Changing Your Desktop Theme

Desktop *themes* are specific combinations of background wallpaper, colors, fonts, cursors, sounds, and screensavers—all arranged around a specific look or topic. When you choose a new theme, the look and feel of your entire desktop changes.

To change desktop themes, right-click the desktop to open the Display Properties dialog box. Select the Themes tab, and then select a new theme from the Theme pull-down list. Click OK when done.

Personalizing the Desktop Background

Although changing themes is the fastest way to change the look of all your desktop elements, you can also change each element separately.

For example, you can easily change your desktop's background pattern or wallpaper. You can choose from the many patterns and wallpapers included with Windows or select a graphic of your own choosing.

All you have to do is right-click the desktop to open the Display Properties dialog box and then select the Desktop tab. To choose one of Windows's built-in backgrounds, make a selection from the Background list. To select your own graphics file, click the Browse button and navigate to the file you want to use. Click the Open button to add this file to the Background list.

To determine how the image file is displayed on your desktop, select one of the options from the Position pull-down list: Center, Tile, or Stretch.

If you'd rather display a solid background color with no graphic, select None from the Background list and select a color from the Color list. Click OK to register your changes.

If you find a picture on the Web that you want to use as your desktop background, right-click the picture and select Set as Wallpaper from the pop-up menu.

Changing the Color Scheme

The default Windows XP desktop uses a predefined combination of colors and fonts. If you don't like this combination, you can choose from several other predefined schemes.

To change to a new color scheme, right-click the desktop to open the Display Properties dialog box. Select the Appearance tab, pull down the Color Scheme list, and select a new theme. Click OK when done.

Activating Special Effects

Windows XP includes all sorts of special effects, not all of which are turned on by default. These effects are applied to the way certain elements look or the way they pull down or pop up onscreen.

Some of these special effects are activated from the Display Properties dialog box. To change these special effects, select the Appearance tab and click the Effects button. When the Effects dialog box appears, make the appropriate choices; then, click OK. You can choose to add transition effects for menus, display drop shadows under menus, display large icons on the desktop, display the contents of windows when they're dragged, and hide the underlined letters on menu items.

Even more special effects are activated from the Systems Property dialog box. You access these effects by opening the Control Panel, selecting Printers and Other Hardware, and then clicking the System icon in the See Also panel. When the Systems Properties dialog box opens, select the Advanced tab and click the Settings button (in the Performance section).

When the Performance Options dialog box appears, click the Visual Effect tab and choose which effects you want to activate. Most of these effects are self-explanatory, although some are extremely subtle.

If you're not sure which effects to choose, select either the Adjust for Best Appearance or Adjust for Best Performance option. The first option turns on all the special effects, and the second option turns them all off. Even better is the Let Windows Choose What's Best for My Computer option, which activates a select group of effects that won't slow down your system's performance.

If your system is running sluggishly, click the Best Performance button to turn off all the resource-draining visual effects.

PERSONALIZE THE WAY WINDOWS WORKS

What You Need

- Basic computer system
- Windows XP

Goal

Make Windows work the way you want it to work.

Changing Your Click

How do you click? Do you like to double-click the icons on your desktop? Would you prefer to single-click your icons, the same way you click hyperlinks on a Web page? Should the names of your icons be plain text or underlined like a hyperlink?

Windows comes from the factory set up for traditional double-clicking. (This is where you single-click an item to select it and double-click to open it.) To change Windows's click mode, open the Control Panel, select Appearance and Themes, and then double-click the Folder Options icon. This opens the Folder Options dialog box.

If you want to use traditional double-clicking, check the Double-Click to Open an Item option. If you want to use Web-like single-clicking, check the Single-Click to Open an Item option. (In this mode, you select an item by hovering your cursor over it and open items with a single click.)

If you select single clicking, you can choose to underline the titles of all desktop icons or only underline titles when an item is hovered over. Click OK when done.

Changing the Way the Start Menu Works

Windows XP applies a handful of special effects to the Start menu. You can animate the Start menu when it opens, force submenus to open when you hover over them, and highlight new applications.

To change these special effects, right-click the Start button and select Properties from the pop-up menu. When the Taskbar and Start Menu Properties dialog box appears, select the Start Menu tab and click the Customize button. When the Customize Start Menu dialog box appears, select the Advanced tab.

To animate the Start menu, check the Animate Start Menu As It Opens option. To make submenus open when you point at them, check the Open Submenus on Hover option. To highlight the newest applications, check the Highlight Newly Installed Applications option. Click OK when done.

Displaying More—or Fewer—Programs on the Start Menu

By default, the Start menu displays the five most-recent applications you've run. You can reconfigure the Start menu to display more (up to nine) or fewer (as few as zero!) applications at a time.

To display more or fewer programs, right-click the Start button and select Properties from the pop-up menu. When the Taskbar and Start Menu Properties dialog box appears, select the Start Menu tab and click the Customize button. When the Customize Start Menu dialog box appears, select the General tab and select a new number from the Number of Programs on Start Menu list. Click OK when done.

Selecting Which Icons to Display on the Start Menu—and How

The default Start menu also displays icons for the Control Panel, My Computer, My Documents, My Pictures, My Music, Network Connections, Help and Support, and the Run command. You can configure Windows XP to not display any of these icons—or to display some of the icons as expandable menus.

Begin by right-clicking the Start button and selecting Properties from the pop-up menu. When the Taskbar and Start Menu Properties dialog box appears, select the Start Menu tab and click the Customize button. When the Customize Start Menu dialog box appears, select the General tab.

In the Show These Items on the Start Menu box, click As Link to display an icon as a link to the main item (in a separate window), As Menu to display a pop-up menu when an icon is clicked, or Never to not display an item. Make this selection for each of the items, and then click OK when done.

Adding a Program to the Start Menu— Permanently

If you're not totally comfortable with the way programs come and go from the Start menu, you can add any program to the Start menu—*permanently*. All you have to do is open the Start menu, click the All Programs button, navigate to a specific program, and then right-click that program. When the pop-up menu appears, select Pin to Start Menu.

The program you selected now appears on the Start menu, just below the browser and e-mail icons. To remove a program you've added to the Start menu, right-click its icon and select Unpin from Start Menu.

Using a Screensaver

Screensavers display moving designs on your computer screen when you haven't typed or moved the mouse for a while. This prevents static images from burning into your screen.

To activate one of the screensavers included with Windows XP, right-click the desktop to display the Display Properties dialog box; then, select the Screen Saver tab. Select a screensaver from the Screen Saver drop-down list, and click the Settings button to configure that screensaver's specific settings (if available).

Return to the Display Properties dialog box and select the number of minutes you want the screen to be idle before the screensaver activates. Click OK when done.

Changing System Sounds

Every operation in Windows can or does have a sound associated with it. When you take all the sounds together, you have a *sound scheme*—and Windows lets you change the entire sound scheme or individual sounds within the scheme.

Start by opening the Control Panel, selecting Sounds, Speech, and Audio Devices, and then double-clicking the Sounds and Audio Devices icon. When the Sounds and Audio Devices Properties dialog box opens, select the Sounds tab. To change sound schemes, pull down the Sound Scheme list and select a new scheme. To change an individual sound, select an item in the Program Events list and then select a new sound from the Sounds list. Click OK when done.

Resetting the Time and Date

The time and date for your system should be automatically set when you first turn on your computer. If you find that you need to change or reset the time or date settings, all you have to do is double-click the time display in the Windows Tray (at the bottom right of your screen).

When the Date and Time Properties utility opens, select the Date & Time tab. Select the correct month and year from the pull-down lists, click the correct day of the month on the calendar, and set the correct time on the clock.

Now select the Time Zone tab, and select the correct time zone from the pull-down list. For most states, you should also select Automatically Adjust Clock for Daylight Saving Changes.

To ensure that your system always has the most correct time, you can automatically synch your PC's internal clock with a time server on the Internet. Just select the Internet Time tab and check the Automatically Synchronize with an Internet Time Server option. Click OK when done.

PERFORM ROUTINE PC MAINTENANCE

What You Need

- The following Windows XP utilities:
  - Disk Cleanup
  - Disk Defragmenter
  - ScanDisk
  - Scheduled Tasks
  - Basic computer system

Goal

Keep your system running smoothly with simple maintenance activities.

Why Maintenance Is Important

"An ounce of prevention is worth a pound of cure."

That old adage might seem trite and cliched, but it's also true—especially when it comes to your computer system. Spending a few minutes a week on preventive maintenance can save you from costly computer problems in the future.

To make this chore a little easier, Windows XP includes several utilities to help you keep your system running smoothly. You should use these tools as part of your regular maintenance routine—or if you experience specific problems with your computer system.

Cleaning Up Unnecessary Files

Even with today's humongous hard disks, you can still end up with too many useless files taking up too much hard disk space. Fortunately, Windows XP includes a utility that identifies and deletes unused files on your hard disk—automatically.

Disk Cleanup is a great tool to use when you want to free up extra hard disk space for more frequently used files. To use Disk Cleanup, click the Start button and then select All Programs, Accessories, System Tools, Disk Cleanup. Disk Cleanup starts and automatically analyzes the contents of your hard disk drive. When it is finished analyzing, it presents its results in the Disk Cleanup dialog box.

When you select the Disk Cleanup tab, you have the option of permanently deleting various types of files: downloaded program files, temporary Internet files, deleted files in the Recycle Bin, setup log files, temporary files, WebClient/Publisher temporary files, and catalog files for the Content Indexer. You can safely choose to delete all these files *except* the setup log and Content Indexer files. Click OK to begin deleting.

Defragging Your Disk

If you think that your computer is taking longer than usual to open files or notice that your hard drive light stays on longer than usual, you might need to *defragment* your hard drive.

File fragmentation is sort of like taking the pieces of a jigsaw puzzle and storing them in different boxes along with pieces from other puzzles. The more dispersed the pieces are, the longer it takes to put the puzzle together. Spreading the bits and pieces of a file around your hard disk occurs whenever you install, delete, or run an application, or when you edit, move, copy, or delete a file.

If you notice your system takes longer and longer to open and close files or run applications, it's because these file fragments are spread all over the place. You fix the problem when you put all the pieces of the puzzle back in the right boxes—which you do by defragmenting your hard disk.

Windows XP's Disk Defragmenter utility not only defragments your hard drive, it also rearranges files on the drive according to how often you use them. In essence, Disk Defragmenter places those files you use most frequently together near the front of your hard drive, so they can be accessed more quickly.

To defragment your hard drive, click the Start button and select All Programs, Accessories, System Tools, Disk Defragmenter. When the Disk Defragmenter utility opens, select the drive you want to defragment (typically drive C:) and then click the Defragment button.

Defragmenting your drive can take awhile, especially if you have a large hard drive or your drive is really fragmented. So, you might want to start the utility and let it run while you are at lunch.

You should close all applications—including your screensaver—and stop working on your system while Disk Defragmenter is running.

Performing a Hard Disk Checkup with ScanDisk

Any time you run an application, move or delete a file, or accidentally turn the power off while the system is running, you run the risk of introducing errors to your hard disk. These errors can make it harder to open files, slow down your hard disk, or cause your system to freeze when you open or save a file or an application.

Fortunately, you can find and fix most of these errors directly from within Windows XP. All you have to do is run the built-in ScanDisk utility.

To find and fix errors on your hard drive, open My Computer and right-click the drive you want to work from. When the pop-up menu appears, select the Properties option, and then select the Tools tab.

Click the Check Now button and you'll see the Check Disk dialog box. Check both the options (Automatically Fix File System Errors and Scan for and Attempt Recovery of Bad Sectors); then, click Start. Windows will now scan your hard disk and try to fix any errors it encounters.

Scheduling Your Maintenance

If you can never seem to find time to run basic system maintenance, you're in luck—Windows XP includes a Scheduled Tasks utility that lets you automatically run essential system maintenance tasks while you're away from your computer.

To use this utility, click the Start button; then select All Programs, Accessories, System Tools, Scheduled Tasks. When the Scheduled Tasks window opens, you'll find that several maintenance-related tasks are already displayed. They're not activated, but they're displayed.

To turn on a scheduled task, click the icon to display the scheduling dialog box. Click the Schedule tab, and then select how often you want to run the task. If you're scheduling a disk cleanup, once a week is good. If you're scheduling disk defragmenting, once a month should be sufficient. Click OK to schedule the task.

For a scheduled task to run, your computer has to be turned on during the scheduled maintenance periods. Windows XP will *not* turn on your PC for you! If your PC is turned off when maintenance is scheduled, the Scheduled Task utility simply skips that scheduled activity.

BACK UP

IMPORTANT FILES

What You Need

- Microsoft Backup utility
- Some sort of backup media—floppy disks, tape drive, or CD-R/RW
- Basic computer system

Goal

Protect your valuable files by making backup copies to use in case of an emergency.

Why Backups Are Important

If your files are important to you—and they should be, or else why did you create them in the first place?—then you need to protect against any loss or damage to them. If, heaven forbid, your hard disk or system unit goes kablooey, do you want to completely lose all your data and documents—or do you want to be able to somehow recover from such a disaster?

The best way to protect yourself against catastrophic data loss is to make backup copies of all your important files. That means all your Word and Works documents, Money financial records, MP3 audio files, digital photographs, and so on—everything you have stored on your hard disk that you can't (or don't want to) create from scratch.

Once you get in the habit of doing it, it's relatively easy to make backup copies of these files. All you need is a file backup program (such as Microsoft Backup, included free with Windows) and some sort of backup media. This type of storage needs to be large (because you'll be backing up *lots* of files) and relatively inexpensive. Many users prefer removable tape cartridges, although Zip disks and rewritable CDs are also popular. (Floppy disks work as long as you're not backing up a lot of data; most users need to back up 100MB or more of data at a time, which would take a *lot* of 1.44MB floppy disks!)

How often you need to back up your files depends on how often the files change and how critical the changes are. For many users, once a month is often enough. If your system crashes, you'll lose some information, but nothing you can't reproduce with a little time and effort. If you store critical information that changes rapidly, however, you should consider backing up more regularly—even daily.

Backing Up Your Files

Windows providesa pretty good backup utility, called Microsoft Backup. You use Microsoft Backup to back up your personal files and settings. The entire operation is run from the Backup or Restore Wizard, which makes this somewhat dull task just a little easier.

Microsoft Backup lets you store your backup files on floppy disks, backup tapes, Zip disks, or CD-R/RW discs. If you ever happen to have a hard drive crash, you can also use Microsoft Backup to restore your backed-up files from your backup copies, and thus minimize your data loss.

You start the Backup or Restore Wizard by opening My Computer, right-clicking the drive you want to back up, and then selecting Properties from the pop-up menu. When the Properties dialog box appears, select the Tools tab and click the Backup Now button.

When the wizard launches, click the Next button, check the Back Up Files and Settings option, and click Next again. When the What to Back Up screen appears, as shown in Figure A69.1, select the files you want to back up: your personal documents and settings, everybody's documents and settings, all data on this computer, or specific files that you select (the Let Me Choose What to Back Up option). Most users back up either their own personal data or (if you've configured your system for multiple users) everyone's data.

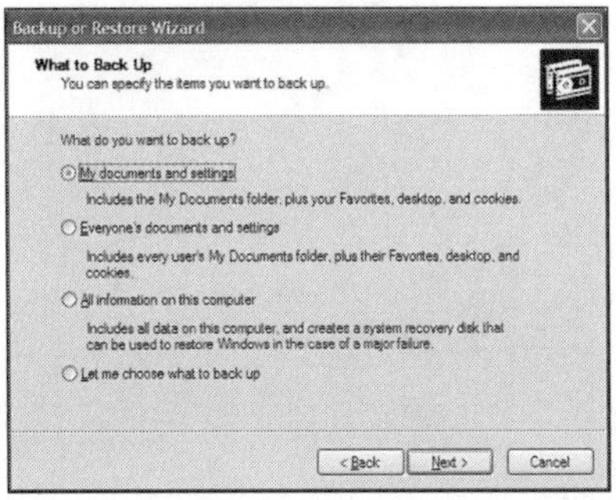

FIGURE A69.1

Use the Microsoft Backup utility to determine which files you back up from your hard drive.

If you choose the Let Me Choose What to Back Up option, the wizard will display an Items to Back Up screen. Use this screen to select specific drives, folders, and files to back up.

When you click Next, you get to choose where you want to send the backup files. Select the specific backup device, and then click Next. You'll now be prompted to insert the appropriate media; follow the balance of the onscreen instructions to complete the backup.

Make sure you keep your backup copies in a safe place—and, ideally, in a *different* place from your computer. This way, if your computer is damaged as part of a larger disaster (fire, flood, or something similarly dire), your backup data will still be safe.

Restoring Files from a Backup

If you ever need to restore files from a backup, you do it from the same Backup or Restore Wizard. In this instance, when you get to the second screen, select the Restore Files and Settings option.

The wizard will now display the What to Restore screen. Select which files and folders you want to restore, and then click the Next button. You'll be prompted to insert your backup copies; follow the onscreen instructions to copy your backup files back to their original locations.

The files you restore from a backup might not be the most recent versions of those files, especially if the original files were used anytime after your most recent backup. Still, recovering a slightly older version of a file is better than not having any version of that file at all.

SET UP A HOME NETWORK

What You Need

- Two or more personal computers, each equipped with a network interface card
- Home networking kit *or*
- Network hub and Ethernet cables
- Windows XP

Goal

Set up a network to share files, devices, and Internet connections between all your computers.

Planning Your Network

In Chapter 4, "Internet and Home Networking Basics," you learned why you might want to set up a network and the various types of networks you can set up. This activity shows you how to set up that network.

Setting up a network is as easy as installing a few pieces of equipment, connecting a few cables, and then running Windows XP's Network Setup Wizard. Windows is smart enough to recognize which devices are installed where and does almost all the configuration for you. You have to answer a question or two—and you still have to plug in all the cards and cables, of course—but that's about it.

Note
> The main computer on your network—the one connected directly to your Internet connection—is designated the *host* PC. The other computers on the network are called *clients*.

Choosing the Right Equipment

Begin by making a list of all the hardware and cables you'll need to purchase. Use Table A70.1 to determine what you'll need for each PC for your specific type of network.

Table A70.1   Equipment Needed for Each Type of Network

Type of Network	Host PC	Client PCs
Ethernet	Ethernet network cards (2) Ethernet network hub (1 for the entire network) Modem (dial-up or broadband)	Ethernet network card (1)
Wireless	Wireless network adapter (1) Ethernet network card (1) Modem (dial-up or broadband)	Wireless network adapter (1)
Phone line	HomePNA network adapter (1) Ethernet network card (1) Modem (dial-up or broadband)	HomePNA network adapter (1)

If you're connecting an Ethernet network, you'll also need one Ethernet cable to go from the hub to the host computer and additional cables to connect each of your other PCs to the hub. If you're connecting a phone-line network, you'll need telephone cables to connect each PC (including the host) to the nearest telephone jack. And, no matter which type of networking you're installing, if you're connecting a cable or DSL modem, you'll need an Ethernet cable to run from the modem to your host PC.

For simple two- or three-PC networks, you can probably find all the equipment you need in one of many available "home networking kits." These kits contain all the cards, cables, and hubs you'll need to set up a typical network—typically with step-by-step instructions and installation disks, and at a discounted price.

Setting Up the Network

After you've made the requisite trip to the computer store, it's time to install all that new hardware—including the network cards in each PC. This is normally as easy as turning off your PC, installing the card, and then turning your PC back on again. Windows should recognize the new card and install the appropriate drivers automatically.

Next, power down and turn off all your computers and printers. With the power off, run all the cables you need to run and connect them to each computer and hub in your network. After all the computers are connected, you can power them back on again—and run the Network Setup Wizard.

Running the Network Setup Wizard

After you've physically connected your computers together, Windows XP's Network Setup Wizard guides you through setting up your home network. This wizard must be run on each computer on your network.

Configuring the Host PC

You start by running the wizard on your host computer, by clicking the Windows Start button and then selecting All Programs, Accessories, Communications, Network Setup Wizard. When the wizard launches, proceed through the screens, reading all the onscreen information carefully and making the appropriate selections. When you come to the Select a Connection Method screen, be sure to select the first option, This Computer Connects Directly to the Internet—The Other Computers in My Home Network Connect to the Internet Through This Computer. Continue through the following screens to complete the host PC's configuration.

Configuring Client PCs

After you've run the Network Setup Wizard on your host PC, you have to run it on all the other PCs on your network. If a computer is running Windows XP, you can run the wizard as previously described. If a computer is running Windows 98, Windows Me, or Windows 2000, you need to run the wizard from the Windows XP installation CD. (Insert the CD and then, after the main screen appears, select Use Windows Support Tools; then, select Tools, Network Setup Wizard.)

When you run the wizard on a client PC, you should select the This Computer Connects to the Internet Through Another Computer in My Home Network option. Then, follow the onscreen instructions and let XP finish the network configuration for you.

After all your computers are configured, your network is now fully functional.

Sharing Files and Folders

To share files with other users on your network, you have to enable Windows XP's file sharing. You do this by using My Computer to navigate to the folder or file you want to share. Right-click the folder or file icon and select Sharing and Security from the pop-up menu. When the Properties dialog box appears, select the Sharing tab and check the Share This Folder on the Network option. Click OK when done—then repeat this procedure for every folder or file you want to share on every computer connected to your network.

PART XVIII

DO IT NOW: DEALING WITH PROBLEMS

HANDLE SOFTWARE AND SYSTEM FREEZES

What You Need

- Basic computer system
- Windows XP

Goal

Get your computer up and running again after a system freeze.

What to Do When Windows Freezes

For most computer users, their biggest fear is something going wrong with their PCs. And the unfortunate fact is that it's not uncommon for your computer to sometimes freeze up and act like something major is wrong.

If your system happens to freeze up, the good news is that there's probably nothing wrong with your computer hardware. The bad news is that there's probably something funky happening with your operating system.

Microsoft Windows can sometimes exhibit perplexing behavior—the most perplexing of which is simply freezing up. When Windows freezes up, the screen looks normal, but nothing works. You can't move the cursor, you can't type onscreen, you can't click any buttons. It's just frozen.

This doesn't mean your system is broken. It's just a glitch. And you can recover from glitches. Just remember not to panic and to approach the situation calmly and rationally.

What Causes Windows to Freeze?

What causes Windows to freeze? There can be many different causes of a Windows freeze, including the following:

- You might be running an application that isn't compatible with Windows XP. If so, upgrade the program.

- You might not have enough memory to run Windows effectively. Upgrade the amount of memory in your PC.

- A memory conflict might exist between applications or between an application and Windows itself. Try running fewer programs at once, or running problematic programs one at a time to avoid potential memory conflicts.

- You might not have enough free hard disk space for Windows to use for temporary files. Delete any unnecessary files from your hard drive.

- Your hard disk might be developing errors or bad sectors. Check your hard disk for errors.

If your system only freezes once and then starts working again, don't worry about it. Shut down your computer (you might have to press Ctrl+Alt+Del to do this) and start it up again. Chances are everything will be working just fine.

If your system crashes or freezes frequently, however, you should call in a pro. These kinds of problems can be tough to track down by yourself when you're dealing with Windows.

Dealing with Error Messages

Sometimes Windows displays an error message when it freezes up. These messages are just nice ways to say that something (who knows what) has bombed.

More often than not, it's just your current program that has frozen, and not all of Windows. In this case you get a Program Not Responding error message. Try pressing Ctrl+Alt+Del to bring up the Windows Task Manager; then, select the Applications tab, select the unresponsive program, and then click the End Task button.

The Blue Screen of Death

If the error message you get is displayed on a blue screen (known in the industry as the "blue screen of death"), follow the onscreen instructions to get rid of the blue screen. You might have to press Enter to close the program causing the error or press Ctrl+Alt+Del to reboot your computer. After you encounter the blue screen, your system typically gets unstable, so I recommend rebooting your entire system, even if you're able to close that particular program manually.

Blue screen messages are often caused when you start running out of space on your hard disk; you might need to delete some unused files to free up some disk space. These error messages can also be caused by errors on your hard disk. If you get a lot of these error messages, it wouldn't hurt to check for disk errors before proceeding.

Freezes Without Error Messages

Sometimes Windows freezes without displaying an error message. One of two things has happened: (1) Windows itself has locked up, or (2) Your current Windows application has locked up.

In either case, the solution is the same: Press Ctrl+Alt+Del.

If Windows itself has frozen, either nothing will happen or you'll start hearing a beep every time you press a key on your keyboard. If this happens, you'll need to press Ctrl+Alt+Del again to fully reboot, or you might have to turn off your PC at the On/Off button (or at the power source).

If, on the other hand, it's an errant program that freezes up, see "Dealing with Application Freezes," later in this activity.

If the Task Manager doesn't appear, or if you try to shut down a program but your system is still locked up, it's time to fully reboot by pressing Ctrl+Alt+Del twice in a row.

Windows Won't Wake Up

What do you do when Windows doesn't wake up from standby mode? Normally you "wake up" your computer by moving your mouse or pressing any key on your keyboard. If this doesn't wake up your system, you need to reboot your computer—*somehow*. Try the Ctrl+Alt+Del method first. However, if your system is in a really deep sleep, it might not recognize any keyboard input. So, you'll probably have to turn your system off at the main power switch/button, wait a few seconds, and then turn it back on again.

> If you're using a notebook computer and this happens, you might have to remove *all* of your power sources. This means unplugging the computer from the wall *and* removing the battery. Wait a few seconds, and then plug your notebook back in. That should do the trick!

It's also possible that your system woke up but your *monitor* stayed asleep. Yes, some monitors have their own sleep modes, and if they get stuck in that mode, you won't know whether your system is awake. It doesn't hurt to turn your monitor off and then back on (which definitely wakes it up!) just in case the sleep problem is the fault of your monitor, not your PC. (If this problem persists, of course, you might need to repair or replace your monitor.)

Dealing with Application Freezes

Everything works fine, but then—all of a sudden—your software freezes!

Fortunately, Windows XP is an exceptionally safe environment. When an individual application crashes or freezes, it seldom messes up your entire system. You can use the Windows Task Manager to close the problem application without affecting other Windows programs.

When a Windows application freezes or crashes, press Ctrl+Alt+Del. When the Windows Task manager opens, select the Applications tab, and then select the frozen application from the list. Now click the End Task button. After a few seconds, a Wait/Shutdown window appears; confirm that you want to shut down the selected application; then, click the End Task button.

This closes the offending application and lets you continue your work in Windows.

If you have multiple applications that crash on a regular basis, the situation probably can be attributed to insufficient memory. See your computer dealer about adding more RAM to your system.

RECOVER FROM SYSTEM CRASHES

What You Need

- Basic computer system
- Windows XP with System Restore utility
- Microsoft Backup utility and previously created backup files

Goal

Recover from the effects of a catastrophic system crash.

Dealing with a Major Crash

Perhaps the worst thing that can happen to your computer system is that it crashes—completely shuts down, without any warning. If this happens to you, start by not panicking. Stay calm, take a few deep breaths, and then get ready to get going again.

You should always wait about 60 seconds after a computer crash before you try to turn your system on again. This gives all the components time to settle down and—in some cases—reset themselves. Just sit back and count to 60 (slowly); then, press your system unit's "on" button.

Nine times out of ten, your system will boot up normally, as if nothing unusual has happened. If this is what happens for you, great! If, on the other hand, your system doesn't come back up normally, you'll need to start troubleshooting the underlying problem. Learn how to do this in Activity 73, "Troubleshoot Common Problems."

Even if your system comes back up as usual, the sudden crash might have done some damage. A system crash can sometimes damage any software program that was running at the time, as well as any documents that were open when the crash occurred. You might have to reinstall a damaged program or recover a damaged document from a backup file.

Undoing the Damage with System Restore

Perhaps the best course of action when your system crashes is to use Microsoft's System Restore utility. This Windows XP utility can automatically restore your system to the state it was in before the crash occurred—and save you the trouble of reinstalling any damaged software programs.

Think of System Restore as a safety net for your essential system files. It isn't a backup program per se because it doesn't make copies of your personal files. (You still need to use Microsoft Backup for that.) It simply keeps track of all the system-level changes that are made to your computer and (when activated) reverses those changes.

Setting System Restore Points

System Restore works by monitoring your system and noting any changes that are made when you install new applications. Each time it notes a change, it automatically creates what it calls a *restore point*. A restore point is basically a "snapshot" of key system files just before the new application is installed.

Just to be safe, System Restore also creates a new restore point after every 10 hours of system use. You can also choose to manually create a new restore point at any moment in time. It's a good idea to do this whenever you make any major change to your system, such as installing a new piece of hardware.

To set a manual restore point, click the Start menu and then select All Programs, Accessories, System Tools, System Restore. When the System Restore window opens, select Create a Restore Point and click Next. You'll be prompted to enter a description for this new restore point. Do this, and then click the Create button.

That's all you have to do. Windows notes the appropriate system settings and stores them in its System Restore database.

Restoring Your System

If something in your system goes bad, you can run System Restore to set things right. Pick a restore point before the problem occurred (such as right before a new installation), and System Restore will then undo any changes made to monitored files since the restore point was created. This restores your system to its preinstallation—that is, *working*—condition.

To restore your system from a restore point, all you have to do is click the Start button and then select All Programs, Accessories, System Tools, System Restore. When the System Restore window opens, check the Restore My Computer to an Earlier Time option; then, click Next.

When the Select a Restore Point screen appears, you'll see a calendar showing the current month, as shown in Figure A72.1; any date highlighted in bold contains a restore point. Select a restore point, and then click the Next button. When the confirmation screen appears, click Next.

FIGURE A72.1

Use the System Restore utility to restore damaged programs or system files.

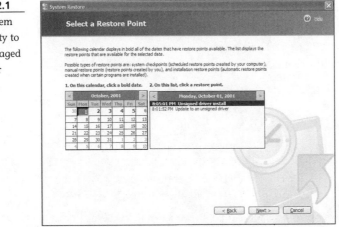

Windows now starts to restore your system. You should make sure that all open programs are closed because Windows will need to be restarted during this process.

When the process is complete, your system should be back in tip-top shape. Note, however, that it might take a half-hour or more to complete a system restore—so you'll have time to order a pizza and eat dinner before the operation is done!

Restoring Your Documents from a Backup File

System Restore will help you recover any damaged programs and system files, but it won't help you recover any damaged documents or data files.

If you made a backup of your data files (as described in Activity 69, "Back Up Important Files"), you can recover a damaged file by restoring its backup copy. You'll lose any work you did to the file since the backup, of course, but this option is probably preferable to starting completely from scratch.

For complete details on restoring files from a backup, turn to Activity 69.

TROUBLESHOOT COMMON PROBLEMS

What You Need

- Basic computer system
- Windows XP

Goal

Find and fix problems that might be plaguing your computer system.

How to Troubleshoot

No matter what kind of computer-related problem you're experiencing, there are seven basic steps you should take to track down the cause of the problem. Work through these steps calmly and deliberately, and you're likely to find what's causing the current problem—and then be in a good position to fix it yourself:

1. **Don't panic!**—Just because there's something wrong with your PC is no reason to fly off the handle. Chances are there's nothing seriously wrong. Besides, getting all panicky won't solve anything. Keep your wits about you and proceed logically, and you can probably find what's causing your problem and get it fixed. React irrationally, and you'll never figure out what's wrong—and you'll get a few gray hairs, in the bargain!

2. **Check for operator errors**—In other words, something *you* did wrong. Maybe you clicked the wrong button, or pressed the wrong key, or plugged something into the wrong jack or port. Retrace your steps and try to duplicate your problem. Chances are the problem won't recur if you don't make the same mistake twice.

3. **Check that everything is plugged into the proper place and that the system unit itself is getting power**—Take special care to ensure that all your cables are *securely* connected—loose connections can cause all sorts of strange results!

4. **Make sure you have the latest versions installed for all the software on your system**—While you're at it, make sure you have the latest versions of device drivers installed for all the peripherals on your system.

5. **Run the appropriate Windows diagnostic tools**—This is discussed later in this activity and in Activity 68, "Perform Routine PC Maintenance." If you have them, use third-party tools, as well, such as Norton Utilities (www.symantec.com) or McAfee Utilities (www.mcafee.com).

6. **Try to isolate the problem by *when* and *how* it occurs**—Walk through each step of the process to see if you can identify a particular program or driver that might be causing the problem.

7. **When all else fails, call in professional help**—If you think it's a Windows-related problem, contact Microsoft's technical support department. If you think it's a problem with a particular program, contact the tech support department of the program's manufacturer. If you think it's a hardware-related problem, contact the manufacturer of your PC or the dealer you bought it from. The pros are there for a reason—when you need technical support, go and get it!

Using Windows Troubleshooters

Windows XP includes several interactive utilities that can help you diagnose and fix common system problems. These utilities are called Troubleshooters, and they walk you step-by-step through a series of questions. All you have to do is answer the questions in the Troubleshooter, and you'll be led to the probable solution to your problem.

To run a Troubleshooter, click the Windows Start button and select Help and Support. When the Help and Support Center opens, click the Fixing a Problem link. When the next screen appears, click the link for the type of problem you're having, and then click the link to start a specific Troubleshooter. All you have to do now is follow the interactive directions to troubleshoot your particular hardware problem.

Troubleshooting in Safe Mode

If you're having trouble getting Windows to start, it's probably because some setting is set wrong or some driver is malfunctioning. The problem is, how do you get into Windows to fix what's wrong, when you can't even start Windows?

The solution is to hijack your computer before Windows gets hold of it and force it to start *without* whatever is causing the problem. You do this by watching the screen as your computer boots up and pressing the F8 key just before Windows starts to load. This displays the Windows startup menu, where you select Safe mode.

Safe mode is a special mode of operation that loads Windows in a very simple configuration. Once in Safe mode, you can look for device conflicts, restore incorrect or corrupted device drivers, troubleshoot your startup with the System Configuration Utility (discussed later in this activity), or restore your system to a prior working configuration (using the System Restore utility, discussed in Activity 72, "Recover from System Crashes").

 Depending on the severity of your system problem, Windows might start in Safe mode automatically.

Using Other Windows Tools

Windows includes a handful of technical tools you can use to troubleshoot system problems. You should use these tools if you feel technically competent to track down problems on your own.

 If you're less comfortable using these tools, that's okay, too. Turn your system over to a technical support specialist and let them use these tools to troubleshoot your PC's problems.

These tools include

- **System Information Utility**—Usedto track down conflicts between devices. To open this utility, click the Start button; then, select All Programs, Accessories, System Tools, System Information.

- **Device Manager**—Used to find device conflicts and update device drivers. To open this utility, open the Control Panel, select Printers and Other Hardware, and then click the System option in the See Also panel. When the System Properties utility opens, select the Hardware tab and click the Device Manager button.

- **System Configuration Utility**—Used to track down startup problems by simplifying your system's configuration. To open this utility, click the Windows Start button and select Help and Support. When the Help and Support Center opens, click the Use Tools option and select System Configuration Utility.

PROTECT YOUR FAMILY ONLINE

What You Need

- Internet Explorer
- Internet connection
- Basic computer system

Goal

Make sure your children and other family members aren't exposed to inappropriate content when they access the Internet.

Making the Web Safe for Kids

The Internet contains an almost limitless supply of information on its billion-plus Web pages. While most of these pages contain useful information, it's a sad fact that the content of some pages can be quite offensive to some people—and that there are some Internet users who prey on unsuspecting youths.

As a responsible parent, you want to protect your children from any of the bad stuff (and bad people) online, while still allowing access to all the good stuff. How do you do this?

While there are programs and services you can use to filter out inappropriate content (discussed later in this activity), the most important thing you can do, as a parent, is to create an environment that encourages *appropriate* use of the Internet. Nothing replaces traditional parental supervision, and, at the end of the day, you have to take responsibility for your children's online activities. Provide the guidance they need to make the Internet a fun and educational place to visit—and your entire family will be better for it.

That said, there are some guidelines you can follow to ensure a safer surfing experience for your family:

- Make sure your children know never to give out any identifying information (home address, school name, telephone number, and so on) or to send their photos to other users online.

- Provide each of your children with an online pseudonym so they don't have to use their real names online.

- Don't let your children arrange face-to-face meetings with other computer users without parental permission and supervision. If a meeting is arranged, make the first one in a public place and be sure to accompany your child.

- Teach your children that people online might not always be who they seem; just because someone says that she's a 10-year-old girl doesn't necessarily mean that she really is 10 years old, or a girl.

- Consider making Internet surfing an activity you do together with your younger children—or turn it into a family activity by putting your kids' PC in a public room (like a living room or den) rather than in a private bedroom.

- Set reasonable rules and guidelines for your kids' computer use. Consider limiting the number of minutes/hours they can spend online each day.

■ Monitor your children's Internet activities. Ask them to keep a log of all Web sites they visit; oversee any chat sessions they participate in; check out any files they download; even consider sharing an e-mail account (especially with younger children) so that you can oversee their messages.

■ Don't let your children respond to messages that are suggestive, obscene, belligerent, or threatening—or that make them feel uncomfortable in any way. Encourage your children to tell you if they receive any such messages, and then report the senders to your ISP.

■ Install content-filtering software on your PC, and set up one of the kid-safe search sites discussed in Activity 29, "Search for Homework Help," as your browser's start page.

■ Subscribe to America Online. AOL offers great filtering options for younger users; you can set up your kids' e-mail accounts so that they can't receive files or pictures in their messages. AOL's filtering options can also be configured to keep younger users away from chat rooms and other inappropriate content both on AOL and the Web.

Teach your children that Internet access is not a right; it should be a privilege earned by your children and kept only when their use of it matches your expectations.

Using Content Filtering Software

Another way to protect your family from inappropriate Web content is to install software on your computer that performs filtering functions for all your online sessions. These safe-search programs guard against either a preselected list of inappropriate sites or a preselected list of topics—and then block access to sites that meet the selected criteria.

The most popular filtering programs include

■ Cyber Patrol (www.surfcontrol.com/products/cyberpatrol_for_home/ product_overview/index.html)

■ Cyber Snoop (www.pearlsw.com/home/)

■ Cybersitter (www.cybersitter.com)

■ IamBigBrother (www.kidcontrol.com)

■ Net Nanny (www.netnanny.com)

Content Filtering with Internet Explorer

The Internet Explorer Web browser includes its own built-in content filtering via the Content Advisor, which can be used to block access to sites that meet specified criteria. Content Advisor enables you to set your own tolerance levels for various types of potentially offensive content and then blocks access to sites that don't pass muster.

To activate and configure Content Advisor, open Internet Explorer, pull down the Tools menu, and select Internet Options. When the Internet Options dialog box appears, select the Content tab.

To enable the Content Advisor, click the Enable button. When prompted for your Supervisor Password, enter your Windows password and click OK.

To adjust the tolerance level for different types of questionable content (such as language, nudity, sex, and violence), click the Settings button in the Content Advisor section. When the Content Advisor dialog box appears, click the Ratings tab and select a category. When a category is selected, a Rating slider appears. Adjust the slider to the right to increase the tolerance for this type of content; leaving the slider all the way to the left is the least tolerant level. Click OK when done.

Turning on Content Advisor (especially at the highest levels) is likely to block access to a lot of sites you're used to visiting on a normal basis. To disable Content Advisor, return to the Internet Options dialog box and click the Disable button.

Activity **75**

PROTECT YOUR SYSTEM FROM VIRUSES AND ATTACKS

What You Need

- Antivirus software
- Internet Connection Firewall (Windows XP) or other firewall software
- Internet Explorer
- Internet connection
- Basic computer system

Goal

Keep your system up and running by avoiding Internet-based hacker attacks and computer viruses.

How Computer Viruses Work

A computer *virus* is a computer program that places copies of itself in other programs on your system or somehow manipulates other files on your system, with the express purpose of causing mischief or damage. They're bad things and can do serious damage to your computer system.

Viruses can infect program files, the macro code found in some data files, or the HTML code used to create a Web page. Plain-text e-mail messages are not capable of being infected—although HTML e-mail and e-mail attachments *can* contain viruses.

How to Catch a Virus

Whenever you share data with another computer or computer user, you risk exposing your computer to potential viruses. There are many ways you can share data and many ways a virus can be transmitted.

You can catch a virus by sharing a floppy disk or sharing a file with someone else on your network. You can catch a virus by opening a file downloaded from the Internet or opening a file attached to an e-mail message. You can even catch a virus by reading an HTML-formatted e-mail message or viewing a Web page in Internet Explorer.

In other words, practically anything you do with your computer on a regular basis can be a means to transmit a virus.

Signs of Infection

How do you know whether your computer system has been infected with a virus?

In general, whenever your computer starts acting somehow different than normal, it's possible that you have a virus. You might see strange messages or graphics displayed on your computer screen or find that normally well-behaved programs are acting erratically. You might discover that certain files have gone missing from your hard disk or that your system is acting sluggish—or failing to start at all. You might even find that your friends are receiving e-mails from you (that you never sent) that have suspicious files attached.

If your computer exhibits one or more of these symptoms—especially if you've just downloaded a file or received a suspicious e-mail message—the prognosis is not good. Your computer is probably infected.

Practicing Safe Computing

Because you're not going to completely quit doing any of these activities, you'll never be 100% safe from the threat of computer viruses. There are, however, some steps you can take to reduce your risk:

- Share disks and files only with users you know and trust.

- Download files only from reliable Web sites.

- Don't open e-mail attachments from people you don't know—or even from people you *do* know, if you aren't expecting them.

- Don't execute programs you find in Usenet newsgroups.

- Use antivirus software.

These precautions—especially the last one—should provide good insurance against the threat of computer viruses.

Using an Antivirus Program

Antivirus software programs are capable of detecting known viruses and protecting your system against new, unknown viruses. These programs check your system for viruses each time your system is booted and can be configured to check any programs you download from the Internet.

The most popular antivirus programs include Dr. Solomon's Anti-Virus (`www.drsolomon.com`), McAfee VirusScan (`www.mcafee.com`), Norton AntiVirus (`www.symantec.com/securitycheck/`), and PC-cillan (`www.antivirus.com/pc-cillin/`). Whichever antivirus program you choose, you'll need to go online periodically to update the virus definition database the program uses to look for known virus files. As new viruses are created every week, this file of known viruses must be updated accordingly

Protecting Against Other Forms of Computer Attack

Connecting to the Internet is a two-way street—not only can your PC access other computers online, but other computers can also access *your* PC. Which means that, unless you take proper precautions, malicious hackers can read your private data, damage your system hardware and software, and even use your system (via remote control) to cause damage to other computers.

The risk of outside attack is even more pronounced if you have an always-on connection, like that offered with DSL and cable modems.

You protect your system against outside attack by blocking the path of attack with a *firewall*. A firewall is a software utility that forms a virtual barrier between your computer and the Internet. The firewall selectively filters the data that is passed between both ends of the connection and protects your system against outside attack.

If you're running Windows XP, you already have a firewall program installed on your system. You can make sure that Windows's Internet Connection Firewall is activated by clicking the Windows Start button and selecting Connecting, Show All Connections. When the Network Connections folder appears, right-click the connection you use for your ISP and select Properties from the pop-up menu. Select the Advanced tab and make sure that the Internet Connection Firewall option is checked.

There are also a number of third-party firewall programs available for purchase. The best of these programs include BlackICE Defender (www.networkice.com/products/ blackice_defender.html), McAfee Firewall (www.mcafee.com), Norton Personal Firewall (www.symantec.com/securitycheck/), and ZoneAlarm (www.zonelabs.com).

Index

H

X - Y - Z